Classic
Italian Jewish Cooking

Edda Servi Machlin

The recipes in this book were selected from the following books by Edda Servi Machlin: *The Classic Cuisine of the Italian Jews, I* (Croton-on-Hudson, NY: Giro Press, 1991), *The Classic Cuisine of the Italian Jews, II* (Croton-on-Hudson, NY: Giro Press, 1992), *The Classic Dolci of the Italian Jews* (Croton-on-Hudson, NY: Giro Press, 1999)

HarperCollins books may be purchased for educational, business, or sales promotional use. For information, please write: Special Markets Department, HarperCollins Publishers Inc., 10 East 53rd Street, New York, NY 10022.

FIRST EDITION

Designed by Cassandra J. Pappas
Illustrations by Laura Hartman Maestro

Library of Congress Cataloging-in-Publication Data

Machlin, Edda Servi, 1926–
   Classic Italian Jewish cooking: traditional recipes and menus / Edda Servi Machlin—1st ed.
      p.   cm.
   Includes index.
   ISBN 0-06-075802-3
   1. Cookery, Jewish. 2. Cookery, Italian. 3. Jews—Italy—Social life and customs. I. Title.
TX724.M271623   2005
641.5'676'0945 — dc22   2004057425

05 06 07 08 09 ❖/RRD 10 9 8 7 6 5 4 3 2 1

In memory of my parents and of my two brothers, Lello and Gino,
who were my teachers and mentors.

For my two daughters, Rona and Gia,
so that they may carry the torch of our beautiful heritage.

To my husband, Gene, who's everything to me.

Contents

A Note to the Reader

This new book encompasses the best of my original three books.

When *The Classic Cuisine of the Italian Jews* first saw the light, in 1981, it was received with great acclaim throughout the world. Not only did it make Americans and people from other countries aware of this delightful cuisine, but also of the existence and culture of the Jews of Italy, who have dwelled on the Italian soil since long before Christianity came into being.

Acknowledgments

My gratitude goes first to all the many friends and relatives, Jewish and Christian, in Italy and in America, who have assisted me in my endeavor.

Un grazie speciale to my brother Gino and his wife, Metella, who have not spared themselves in searching and procuring much vital information and documents; to my sister, Marcella Siegel, who inspired me and gave me the confidence much needed to undertake the writing of this book; to my brother Mario, who provided erudite advice and constant encouragement.

My tenderest feelings to my husband, Gene, who has lovingly nurtured this book throughout its creation. I wish to thank warmly Julia Serebrinsky for a great job in consolidating my original three books into a new beautiful one.

foreword

Before I ever met Edda Servi Machlin, I knew her through her cookbooks, which have become classics. In the delightful, two-volume *The Classic Cuisine of the Italian Jews*, Edda gathered recipes, culture, and history that without her careful research and recollection may well have been lost forever. Yet, in spite of the horrors and betrayal she witnessed during the Holocaust, Edda's books embrace the country and lifestyle that had been her family's for generations.

When I began writing my own book, *The Jewish Holiday Baker*, I asked Edda to be one of the cooks I planned to portray. At the time, I had only met her in passing, but still I knew that I had to have this amazing storyteller and cook in my book. Over the next fifteen years, I have had the chance to get to know Edda even better: cooking her exquisite *Carciofi alla Giudia*, Artichokes Jewish Style, on my television show, *Jewish Cooking in America with Joan Nathan*, and eating dinner at her home where she made for me *Tagliatelle all'Ebraica*, Tagliatelle Jewish Style, a savory noodle kugel with pine nuts and raisins like nothing I have ever tasted.

I am delighted that Ecco has decided to publish the best recipes from Edda's books: *The Classic Cuisine of the Italian Jews*, Volumes I and II, and *Classic Dolci of the Italian Jews*, a fabulous book full of sweets from throughout the country. Now, we have the full breadth of her knowledge and expertise in one volume with a major publisher.

A historian by trade and a humanitarian by nature, Edda is a living testament to the more than two thousand–year legacy of Italian Jewry. You have here a lifetime of recipes from a culture that was almost entirely wiped out. This book is a rare gift, to historians, to food lovers, to Jews—indeed, to the entire world.

—Joan Nathan

V esti da turco e mangia da ebreo is a well-known, ancient Italian adage, which advises one to "dress like a Turk and eat like a Jew." We are thus exhorted by the Italians—who created a cuisine that is the delight of gourmets the world over—to become acquainted with the cuisine of the Italian Jews if we really would like to eat well.

My own experience as an Italian Jew, born and brought up in Italy, confirms this. As I recall, during my childhood in Pitigliano, Tuscany—my native village—the buying of the choicest and freshest foods, together with the care and fuss in preparing and cooking them, was a matter of great importance, not only for my family but also for the other fifteen or twenty Jewish families then living in my village. The precise memory I have of those days in the early 1930s is that our little dresses might have been very simple and, more often than not, hand-me-downs, but our meals were always first-rate culinary treats.

Some form of Italian Jewish cuisine has existed for more than two thousand years—or for as long as there have been Jews in Italy. The complex Italian Jewish cuisine of today derives from many sources. Each wave of Jewish settlers brought foods from the country of origin (Near East, North Africa, and later on, Spain) and changed and enriched them to conform to local traditions and prevalence of products (see *Cuscussù*). Bound by dietary laws, Jews modified traditional Italian dishes to make them kosher, often creating delicate and delicious new ones (see *Lasagne Verdi*; made with tomato sauce instead of meat sauce, it becomes a dish of great delicacy). Foods such as fish with both fins and scales, eggs and dairy products, and fruits and vegetables, which were allowed to Jews, came to be prepared in many unusual ways (see *Pesce e Indivia* and *Testine di Spinaci*). And finally, symbolic foods, such as *Sfratti* and *Tagliolini colla Crocia*, were added to the existing ones.

While adapting the dishes of their host country to their kosher laws, the Jews in Italy, as in the rest of the world, enriched the local cuisine with their ancestral culinary customs. Obviously, then, many traditional Italian dishes have an unsuspected Jewish origin. It's hard to believe, for example, that eggplant and *finocchio* (fennel), the quintessence of Italian vegetables, were originally used only by Jews.

Ninety-five years ago, Pellegrino Artusi, in his famous cookbook, *La Scienza e L'Arte di Mangiar Bene* (Firenze, 1910, Salvatore Landi Editore), presented these vegetables to his readers with these words: "Forty years ago one could hardly see eggplant and fennel on the Florentine market; they were considered vile foods of the Jews; the latter offering evidence here, as in more important issues, of having, better than Christians, a flair for discovering good things."

Italian Jewish cuisine is, for all its goodness, simple, relying not on exotic ingredients or complicated procedures but on the right proportions of foods of the highest quality. The world-famous *Carciofi alla Giudia*, one of my mother's many wonderful specialities, consists of very fresh artichokes trimmed in the manner that was devised by the Roman Jews, seasoned with only salt and pepper, and pan-roasted in olive oil.

Many dishes that are traditionally and uniquely Italian Jewish are seldom, if ever, found in Italian cookbooks. When they are, no mention is made of their Jewish origin except for a very few such as *Polpette alla Giudia* (Meatballs Jewish Style) and *Carciofi alla Giudia* (Artichokes

Jewish Style), which was originally called *Carciofi Arrosto* by the Roman Jews and was changed to *alla Giudia* some seventy-five years ago. I have included as many as possible of these original Jewish recipes. They are the jewels of my collection. *Concia, Baccalà Mantecato, Maritucci* bread, and *Sfratti* come immediately to mind as examples.

Since the Italian Jews are either *Italkim* (from Italy) or *Sephardim* (from *Sepharad*, the Hebrew name for Spain), their dishes do not resemble the traditional Central and Eastern European (*Ashkenazic*) ones to which American Jews are accustomed. The names of the dishes, as well as their styles and tastes, will be different. For example, the popular *hamantashen* of Purim (triangular pastry pockets filled with prune butter or poppy seeds) were unknown to the Italian Jews who made, instead, *Orecchi di Aman*, Haman's Ears (twirls of fried sweet pastry), to celebrate the downfall of the Persian tyrant and the failure of his plan to destroy all the Jews. The Italian Jews never heard of gefilte fish, but used *Muggine in Bianco* (Jellied Striped Bass) for the High Holidays.

Other differences stem from the fact that some foods that are not considered kosher by the *Ashkenazim* are permitted by the *Italkim* or *Sephardim* and vice versa. For example, rice, which was a staple for us at Passover, is considered *chametz*, or leavened food, by the *Ashkenazim*, whereas chocolate, cheeses, and other milk products, so widely used by the American Jews during Passover, were absolutely forbidden for us, because we considered *them* to be *chametz*.

Besides the laws concerning Passover ("Seven days you shall eat unleavened bread . . . and no leaven shall be found, in all your territory," Exodus 13: 6–7), two basic laws make up *kashrut*, or the kosher laws:

1. The law that prohibits the mixing of milk and meat as stated repeatedly in the Bible: "You shall not boil a kid in its mother's milk" (Exodus 23:19 and 34:26; Deuteronomy 14:21). The reason for this law is highly ethical: one may kill in order to eat, but the callousness of mixing the flesh of the animal with the milk of its life-giver must be avoided.

2. The prohibition against eating certain animals as specified in great detail in Leviticus 11: 1–34. The acceptable animals, in order to be kosher, must be slaughtered by a *Shochèt* (an official Jewish slaughterer) with one stroke of a razor-sharp knife across the main veins. (My father was the official *Shochèt* in Pitigliano. The knives he used, in order to be kosher, had to be so sharp at all times that they would slice a very thin piece of paper in one cut. The tips, instead of being pointy, were squared off, and the blades were three times as long as the handles.) There are two ethical reasons for this ritual killing: one is that the animal loses consciousness immediately and does not suffer; the other is that the blood is drained out of the animal so that no one will "partake of any blood. . . . For the life of the flesh is in the blood" (Leviticus 17: 10–11).

The observance of *kashrut* varies according to the interpretation given by various Jewish denominations to the passages quoted above. We adhered to these laws almost to the letter, but we did not go to the extent of having two separate sets of dishes, pots and pans, utensils and silverware, and even separate sinks for dairy and meat meals as most observant *Ashkenazim* do. We ate the hind part of the animal (leg of lamb, veal rump roast, and so on) after removing the sciatic nerve, whereas the *Ashkenazim* do without these parts of the animal altogether. Also, we soaked chicken livers in many changes of cold water until no trace of blood was visible, but the *Ashkenazim* broil them. "Kosher kitchen" meant to us—besides the observance of the basic kosher laws—using first quality food and being extremely fussy about the preparation of our meals.

Only after I settled in America in 1958 did I find—because of all the modern kitchen appliances and aids available—that in order to prepare a good kosher meal it was not necessary to spend all my time and energy in the kitchen, excluding all other activities, as my mother and all the other Jewish women in Pitigliano did.

I have introduced gourmet cuisine into my everyday life and still have time for many other interests and activities. There are occasions when the preparation of a special dish does require extra attention and care, but I am happy to bother a little more when I know that the result is worth my trouble.

I have kept the American cook in mind in compiling this collection and have adapted the recipes to the products and foods that one can find in most American markets today. I remain convinced that the success of a dish begins with the quality of the ingredients, which should be the freshest, the finest, and those which are in season. With the availability of frozen vegetables, dried foods, and imported foods, however, one can still serve gourmet-quality meals all year round, some of which were once prepared only in a particular season or for some special holiday.

Sometimes, a few of the desired ingredients are simply not available, and I have included the tricks I have used in order to obviate this handicap. For example, in my opinion, nothing in the vegetable kingdom had a better taste and aroma than the *fungo porcino*, a wild mushroom of the bolete family. In America this precious item of fine cuisine is rather expensive. But by using a small amount of the dried porcino mushroom with the commercial white ones, I have obtained tastes and textures which, although they are not those of the fresh porcino, are still delicious.

When I first arrived in the United States, everybody found my Italian accent "charming," but I felt pressure from many friends and relatives to "Americanize" as quickly as possible. I don't deny the advantages of assimilation, but coming from a stock of people who resisted conformity for over two thousand years (according to historian Cecil Roth, my Servi ancestors were brought to Rome by Titus as slaves after the second destruction of the Temple of Jerusalem), and being satisfied with my own mores and habits, I wasn't eager to give them up. Food and its preparation was one of the ways in which my resistance showed itself. Giving in to fast foods would have been a betrayal of my heritage. No matter how busy or tired I was, I always managed to prepare a gourmet meal, either for company, or for my family, or even just for myself.

I was not, however, keeping up "the old ways" just for the sake of it, or for fear of venturing into the new and unknown. On the contrary, while retaining what was valid about the old traditions, I was ready to accept what was valid in my new life. I did not hesitate, for instance, to use kitchen aids and appliances that would save me time and energy without affecting the quality of the foods I prepared. Nothing can substitute for a good set of knives, but a blender and/or food processor and an electric mixer can work miracles and are as necessary, in a modern kitchen, as the knives.

I also learned quickly that sometimes frozen and canned foods retain at least some of the texture and nutritional value of fresh ones. I began to use, and still do when the fresh counterparts are not available, canned peeled tomatoes, frozen spinach, peas, string beans, and occasionally artichoke hearts.

To be sure, every form of fanaticism can prove limiting. This also applies to food. Good cooking is an art form and as such it requires freedom and imagination in order to be expressed fully. Everyone knows—or should know—that some of the most celebrated dishes were created by mistake, or by a daring combination of ingredients that were, up to that moment, never used together.

Although I work with original, ancient recipes the way one works with antique art objects (I restore them, using modern devices, but try not to change or modernize them), I have suggested, whenever possible, ways of preparing them that are more practical and less time consuming than the old ones.

With this approach in mind, I am confident that the adventurous cook, for whom this work is intended—whether inexperienced or already accomplished—will enjoy using my collection of recipes.

Every recipe in this book is kosher—with due consideration to the differences mentioned above—and can be used by those who observe the Jewish dietary laws. The book was intended for anyone who wants to enjoy a truly superb cuisine. The guests who have dined in my house range from orthodox Jews to non-Jews and all have reacted with enthusiasm to the dishes I have prepared.

I WAS URGED to write this book by my friends who have sampled the Italian Jewish cuisine in my house. But as I began to collect the recipes and test them, I realized that there is much more to my heritage than a cuisine that I would like to share with my readers. I have tried to reconstruct—through the recollections of my own experiences as described in the Pitigliano and Holiday sections—the life and character of a culture that is now practically extinct.

When possible I have included historical data to corroborate my recollections but, in the main, this work comes directly from the events in my own life and from the stories I heard during my happy childhood. Jewish life in Pitigliano no longer exists in anything like the rich and vibrant manner I knew it as a girl and as a young woman (only one Jew is now living there, but her daughter-in-law and grandchildren are all Catholic), but memories of those wonderful, joyous years are still fresh in my mind. I wish to share in the pages that follow the feasts of food and love that were my privilege and pleasure to have known.

PITIGLIANO, THE LITTLE JERUSALEM

Panoramic view of Pitigliano with the Catholic cathedral and the Jewish Center next to each other

itigliano, the medieval village in Tuscany where I was born and raised, was built on top of a titanic, boat-shaped, tufaceous rock, with constructions heaped one on top of the other as if they were an outgrowth of the rock itself. It is situated in a hilly zone, roughly 200 kilometers south of Florence, 150 kilometers northwest of Rome. Like many villages in that area, Pitigliano depended for its survival on small, private farming and did not differ from these other villages except for one important thing: it was the home of a large and culturally prominent Jewish community.

It is said that from the beginning of their settlement in the fourteenth century (there is some speculation that there were Jews in Pitigliano as early as 1100), the Jews in Pitigliano made up a large percentage of the population, with peaks that reached, at times, from 25 to 50 percent. What we know definitely is that during my father's childhood, in the 1880s, 10 percent of Pitigliano's entire population of three thousand was Jewish (a very high concentration, if we consider that in all of Italy the Jews comprised then, and still do, roughly only 0.1 percent of the population, or approximately fifty thousand). Among them there was a disproportionate number of highly educated people, who became professors, architects, astronomers, biophysicists; of statesmen, philosophers, psychiatrists, musicians, some of whom achieved national and even international fame. A few were landowners or dealers in grain and cheese. There were also shopkeepers, civil servants, dressmakers, shoemakers, bookbinders, photographers, and mechanics.

It is worth noting that in a preeminently agricultural village, where

Gate to the Temple

illiteracy was incredibly high, there was not one illiterate person among the Jews. But what was truly extraordinary was that all of them, from the richest and most cultured to the most humble, could read, speak, and write Hebrew. They all participated in the activities of their religious, ethical, and philanthropic institutions, such as a generous foundation that provided education and a dowry for every needy Jewish girl. The holidays and the traditions were respected by all, including the nonbelievers, and even those who had married outside Judaism. At the High Holidays, many who had tried their luck in the cities would come back to participate in the familiar services whose liturgy and splendid melodies, probably composed by the early settlers, were uniquely different from those of other Italian communities.

It was not unusual to see young men—and not-so-young men—spending their spare time copying ancient books, *meʒuʒòt* (parchment with a Hebrew prayer written on it, rolled into a case, and attached to doorposts), and psalms in beautiful Hebrew calligraphy. My father and his father were among such men. When my father came to the United States in the early 1960s for a brief visit, he was nearly eighty and his vision was quite weakened. But he presented many of our Jewish friends with *meʒuʒòt* written in his no longer perfect but still beautiful handwrit-

West view of the interior of Pitigliano's sanctuary

ing. During World War II, when we lost all of our possessions, and nearly lost our lives, we managed to save two of Pitigliano's Hebrew prayer books handwritten by my grandfather, Salomone Servi.

Men would also make *tzitziòt* (ritual fringes at the four corners of the tallit) for their *talitòt* (prayer shawls worn by male Jews; in some orthodox communities, women also wore them) while women sewed and patiently embroidered artistic scroll covers and *parochiòt* (curtains in front of the ark containing the Torah scrolls) in exotic, rich materials. No matter how busy, everyone found time in their crowded days for all sorts of *mitzvòt* (good deeds and prescribed religious precepts).

My father's mother, Debora Lattes, was a pious and dedicated woman. In addition to taking care of and educating her own fourteen children, she was a revered Hebrew teacher for all who wished to learn. Although I never met her, I did have the luck and honor to meet her cousin, Dante Lattes, a world-renowned philosopher of Judaism. There is an entry in the *Encyclopaedia Judaica* (Vol. X) that attests to the importance of this man.

The temple was open every day for three services. As one entered the beautiful sanctuary done in a superb blend of Renaissance and Baroque styles, one would see on the right wall an impressive mural tablet, written in block Hebrew letters on an embossed stucco relief ornately framed in gold leaf, which read: *"Imeshkachèch Yerushalàim, tishkàch yemini."* (If I should forget you, oh Jerusalem, may my right arm wither.) And every man, woman, and child tried to live up to this pledge.

My brother Gino, in an acclaimed series of lectures given in Florence, Milan, and Rome on the community of Pitigliano, calls this group of Jews who for over six hundred years have enriched their surroundings, "an élite rather than a minority . . . the Jews of Pitigliano constitute an exceptional and long page in the history of mankind . . . a society who lived its ethics in the reality of everyday life rather than in theories. . . . The word Jew, in Pitigliano, even now carries the meaning of superior human being, a concept which, I am sure, has no correspondence in any other part of the world."

My father—like his father and his grandfather before him—acted as Pitigliano's rabbi. During the High Holidays an ordained rabbi would be sent to Pitigliano from one of the larger communities, but his role was inevitably that of a helper rather than of a leader, since it was my father who had a greater knowledge of the traditions, needs, and ways of his congregation. He was also the *Morè* (the teacher of Hebrew and Hebrew culture who prepared all the children for their *Bat* or *Bar Mitzvà*, the coming of religious age, which is thirteen for boys and twelve for girls), the *Chazàn* (cantor), and the *Shochèt*. He was the last to carry on Pitigliano's rich Hebrew culture and heritage. Even long after the temple had closed down in the mid-1950s for lack of worshippers and because it had been severely damaged during the war, he would travel wherever he was needed to assist a dying person, or simply to conduct a Seder (literally "order"; it refers to the prayers over food at any festive meal, but it is especially important at Passover). He is cited in a manuscript entitled *Pitigliano*, written by Settimio Sorani, former secretary of the Jewish Community of Rome and chief executive of the Delasem, an ad hoc committee that saved the lives of thousands of Jews during the war and for which Sorani was tortured: "The last curator of the temple, of Pitigliano's Hebraism, and of the glories of the past has been Azeglio Servi. For nearly forty years he has been the conscientious spiritual head of Pitigliano's Jewish community with its Italian rites and its original liturgy."

So illustrious and widespread was his fame that a scholar of Judaism once came from Israel to Florence, where we had moved in the early 1950s, to interview him. My father was already seventy-three years old and finally retired. Nevertheless, he still had his warm and musical voice, and when asked by the Israeli, he did not hesitate to sing the entire liturgy of Pitigliano, with its beautiful original melodies, which was recorded in the studios of, and in collaboration with, R.A.I., the Italian broadcasting system, and the recording was then brought to Israel.

Pitigliano was a cradle of Hebrew culture that nurtured many scholars and dedicated people like my father. It is little wonder that it earned the nickname of *"Yerushalàim Shenì, "* the Little Jerusalem (literally, "the second Jerusalem").

LIKE ALL THE OTHER Jews of Pitigliano, I was proud of our glorious community, with its beautiful temple, two well-stocked libraries—one secular and one Hebrew—two *yeshivòt* (schools where the Torah is studied), the secular nursery, elementary and secondary schools, and the cemetery. A beautiful terraced piece of land on the outskirts of town, on a bright hill facing east and south, was reserved for the Jewish cemetery. Tall cypresses flanked the long shallow steps that led down to the various levels. The cemetery contained everything from primitive and simple

The Shamash of Pitigliano *kneading the dough for the* matzòt

tombstones dating from the fourteenth century to the most elaborate and artistic graves of more recent times.

But all these institutions would not have left me with such vivid memories of Jewish life in Pitigliano were it not for the fact that along with them we had our own kosher oven as well. And since traditional foods were so vital an aspect of our culture, the oven was one of our most important facilities.

Once I have indulged in the description of it, it will become apparent why it had such an impact on my life.

The oven was reminiscent of antiquity, or rather, of fairy tales, both in its structure and in its location. I suspect that the reason for this was that the oven was the first facility the *Marrano* (Jews forced by the Spanish Inquisition to convert to Catholicism, but who were then accused of continuing to practice Judaism) refugees provided themselves with long before they felt secure enough to reveal their true identity and begin to build the temple, the library, and so on. (Although my guess that it was the *Marranos* who conceived this hidden oven seems plausible, there is another theory that there were already Jews in Pitigliano during the Middle Ages. This would also explain the existence of so primitive a construction.)

The oven was situated in an underground vault, the accessibility to which was so nearly impenetrable that even merely going down to it was a dangerous, unforgettable adventure. From the upper western vault of the ghetto a steep lane, made of large, uneven stone steps, descended first eastward, then south, then sharply curved toward the north. At this point the stone steps ended and an underground passageway opened. No sooner had one advanced a few steps along this passageway than one would be enveloped by complete darkness. The steps were now carved directly into the porous, volcanic, eternally humid and viscid tufa, and one would gropingly make one's way down to the oven rooms (also carved into the natural rock), after innumerable slips and losses of balance. Since the whole

Classic Italian Jewish Cooking

Traditional Recipes and Menus

ecco

An Imprint of HarperCollins Publishers

village is built on top of this huge rock, even after descending for a considerable distance the oven was still, on its east side, well above the valley level. Through two big holes, chiseled into a wall of this cavern, opening on to the outside precipice, and framed with rudimentary windows, the inside was flooded with bright morning light, so that one's unaccustomed eyes would be blinded for a moment by the contrast.

At the time when I was growing up, the oven was not in operation all year round. But once a year, the opening of the oven just before Passover was a thrilling event for children and adults alike.

The place bustled with activity: spiderwebs were removed, walls carefully dusted, marble countertops scrubbed to a spotless shine, the small rolling pins washed in bleach, the combs (metal gadgets dented like saws with which the *matzòt* were pricked to prevent swelling during the baking process) were scrubbed and oiled. The gigantic copper mixer was also scrubbed and polished until it shone.

When the cleaning operations were over, the transportation of the raw material and equipment through that cryptic passageway kept everyone busy and excited. Everything that was needed, including water, firewood, sugar, eggs, oil, wine, spices, vessels, wire whisks, baking sheets and pans, had to be dragged down because the only things already there were the country oven, the kneading trough, the mixing tub stand, and three sarcophagus-like, crude cement worktables with white marble tops, one of which was used for the preparation of cakes and other sweets, and the other two to roll out bits of dough for each *matza* (plural: *matzòt*).

Finally, when all the necessary things were, with great difficulty—which included the constant risk of slipping and dropping a large basketful of eggs

Matza *hanging from a wall of the old* Yeshivà *in Pitigliano*

and even of breaking a leg—transported down to the oven rooms, all the Jews of the village would gather, a few families at a time, and prepare their own *matzòt,* and all the varieties of cookies, sweets, and cakes used during the eight days of the Passover celebration. Mountains of eggshells would pile up in a few seconds, as everyone went to work with precision and dexterity, knowing exactly what to do without the aid of a cookbook or reliable written recipes. For a few days a procession of enormous wicker baskets full of these goodies would make its way from the cave to various Jewish residences, leaving a delicious fragrance hovering over the narrow streets, a spectacle that always drew mobs of Christian children to the gateway of the ghetto.

For the young people the bakery was a happy hunting ground, a perfect place to gather to carry on flirtations and love affairs. Many a marriage was arranged while kneading the bits of dough, and perhaps even a few were wrecked during those vernal days.

I was too young to quite understand the allusions, the promises, and the reticences. Nevertheless, something very tender must have reached the very core of my being, because even today my heart is warmed by the sweet memory of those pre-Passover activities and of the laughter, songs, jokes, the tales exchanged during those memorable spring days.

Whether it was the *Marranos* or the earlier Jewish settlers, why did this extraordinary people choose to establish their new home in Pitigliano and remain there for over six hundred years? The geographical position of Pitigliano and politics were certainly important factors. Bordering both on Sovana, an ancient and onetime prosperous city, and on the Papal States where the Jews were brought in or expelled according to the whims and interests of the various Popes, Pitigliano, an independent county under the rule of the Orsini, and later of the Medici, offered a guarantee of freedom and peaceful cohabitation with the Gentiles.

During the Spanish Inquisition, many of those who were able to escape Torquemada's forced conversions, tortures, and crucibles sought refuge in the south of Italy where a great many Jews had lived since biblical times. But the Inquisition spread there also, compelling the Jews to migrate north. Some stopped at the first town they encountered in Tuscany—Pitigliano—where there may or may not already have been some Jewish families. In 1595 the Jews were also expelled from Florence, the capital of Tuscany, where some prosperous families had resided since the time of Dante and, apparently, they also found a safe haven in Pitigliano. Castro, a bordering town in the Papal States, had in the past hosted many Jews. Its complete destruction in 1649 by the troops of Pope Innocenzo X added still further to the Jewish population of Pitigliano.

These were stories I was told repeatedly as a child. Since then, I have not been able to discover much documentation. Time, wars, and other destruction have buried the real origins of Jewish Pitigliano. What we do know is that the temple was completed in the Hebrew year 5358 (1598). The date is written on the *Aaròn Hakòdesh,* the Ark where the Torah scrolls are kept. (We also know the dates of the two restorations of the Temple: 1756 and 1931.) However, the existence of a much older *Aaròn Hakòdesh*, preserved in the old *Yeshivà*, suggests that Jews lived in Pitigliano long before 1598 and they had built, probably on the same site, a house of worship before the present one was constructed.

The writing on three mural memorial tablets inside the temple mentions the visits of the Grand Dukes of Tuscany, Pietro Leopoldo in 1773, Ferdinando III in 1823, and Leopoldo II in 1829. These grand dukes of the Habsburg family, referred to in the *Encyclopædia Britannica* as the "enlightened tyrants," apparently protected and befriended the Jews of Pitigliano. As a child, I heard stories from the elderly, who heard them from their elders, of how our ancestors had reacted to, and prepared themselves for, the great event of the visits of such prominent personalities (see Sabbath).

Another good reason why these Jewish refugees, obviously scholarly and sensitive, may have chosen Pitigliano for their home instead of the surrounding villages, which were probably as friendly, is that *Lo Scoglio* (Pitigliano was lovingly nicknamed *Lo Scoglio*, The Rock, by its natives) is incredibly beautiful, surrounded by three small rivers with their magnificent valleys, and by a very picturesque countryside.

INEVITABLY, this nucleus of lively and intellectually active Jews influenced the cultural life of the entire village, but to what extent it is hard to assess now. The copious ancient records describing their noble deeds, jealously kept in the underground Jewish archives, were dispersed, lost, or destroyed during World War II, when the Jews were taken to the concentration camps. Some documentation is provided by Cecil Roth in his *History of the Jews of Italy* (1946). Without going into detail, he states that the Jews "in Pitigliano on the border of the Papal State, where a number of refugees from the rigors of Jewish life in Rome settled, had created a community out of all proportion to the natural importance of the town." This was still true at the time when I was growing up.

Pitigliano, unlike the neighboring villages, enjoyed a number of cultural and social institutions then usually available only in larger centers. The contribution of the Jews to their creation and perpetuation was a major one. The first school that Pitigliano ever had was created by the Jews for the education of their children, but many Gentiles attended our school before going away to the big city for higher education. My grandfather, Salomone Servi, had written a comprehensive textbook "for the pupils—boys and girls—of the second elementary grade," but the disciplines and concepts contained in it were so advanced that some are now taught in secondary schools in the United States.

There was an important printing house, *La Lente*, whose founder and publisher was a Jew; Pitigliano had an outstanding band that traveled throughout Europe, which had been organized and trained by my father's uncle; Pitigliano's small theater had been remodeled and enlarged by a Jewish architect and consequently was able to attract the most celebrated opera singers and theatrical performers of the time. The only secular library Pitigliano boasted was located within the gates of our temple. It was the legacy of two Jewish scholars, Giuseppe and Affortunata Consiglio, and was so important that not only Pitiglianesi Jews and Gentiles consulted it but also numerous people of learning who came from as far away as Grosseto, Florence, and Rome.

The Jewish influence was also visible at the popular level. For example, some Hebrew words that were part of our daily vocabulary were also included in the local colorful vernacular. No one knew that they had been borrowed from the Jews, and even I did not find out until I was much older. Here are a few examples: If a Jewish or Gentile child stole a piece of food before mealtime (such as a wing from a chicken, or a bite out of a pizza), his mother would reproach him by saying, "Why did you do *milà* on that?" She was probably not conscious of the fact that the word *milà* in Hebrew means circumcision. Or if a child left a bit of food on his dish at the end of a meal, his mother would say, "For whom did you leave that *peà*?" (Literally "corner" in Hebrew; it was the corner of the field that was not harvested and left for the poor. Today, the word means the side curl worn by orthodox Jews.) The populace was fond of swearing and one of their favorite exclamations was *B'Adonai*, "By God." *Zonà*, the Hebrew word for whore, was used by everyone. *Shofetessa*, the Italianization of the Hebrew *Shof'tà*, female prophet, was used as an epithet for pedantic women in the same manner as the English expression "know-it-all" is used. The verb *Shachtare* was also an Italianization of the Hebrew word *Sh'chità*, slaughter by cutting the jugular vein. But whereas the Jews used the word to mean killing the animals according to the ritual Jewish laws (slaughtering in the fastest and least painful way, draining all the blood out), the Christians used it to mean "to ruin something."

Once, as an old story goes, a Gentile Pitiglianese went to Rome to buy furnishings for his wedding. He entered a Jewish-owned store and asked for a length of material for a suit. The owner said to his shop assistant, "Bring down that piece of *shachor* (*shachorut* is more exact than *shachor*) from up there" (meaning that remnant that no one but this peasant would want to buy). But the "peasant" promptly replied, "I don't want any *shachorut*, but a piece that's *yafè melech*" (fit for a king).

Of course, there were learned Gentiles who knew Hebrew because they had studied it as part of their training. One such person was the bishop. When he and my father met in the street, they would ceremoniously bow to each other and exchange greetings, my father with the Latin *Pax Vobiscum* and the bishop with the Hebrew *Shalom Alecha*.

The Jews also influenced their Gentile neighbors in food and eating habits, and even in the superstitions that went along with them. One example of this is to be found in *Sfratti*, the honey and nut dessert in the form of sticks, representing the rods with which the Jews were evicted from their homes during the persecutions. The Christian Pitiglianesi adopted them. But whereas the Jews traditionally served them on Rosh Hashana to ward off the possibility of future evictions and as a wish for a good, sweet year, the Gentiles made them for weddings to ward off any marital battles.

Today, long after the Jews of Pitigliano have ceased to exist as a community, one of the public bakeries makes some of our exclusive Purim sweets and calls them *dolcetti dell'abbrei*, Pitigliano vernacular for "cookies of the Jews," and a sweet bread that is our *Bollo* of Yom Kippur.

SHOPPING FOR FOOD, when I was young, was quite different from what it is today. Most of the staples were home-delivered, but not from a supermarket in cans, boxes, and cartons. They were brought directly from the farm to our homes, usually by the farmers' wives. Milk, for example, was carried to town as soon as it had been milked from the cow, still warm, in large, hand-carried tin containers with a spout and a hook from which hung the three measuring mugs: the *quarto*, a little over a cup; the *mezzo litro*, a little more than a pint; the *litro*, just over a quart. The milkwoman would be the first to knock at the door in the morning, and she would pour the requested amount of milk directly into the milk boiler. Pasteurization and homogenization were unknown and the only means of sterilization was to boil the milk for twenty minutes. Occasionally, upon request, the milkwoman would also bring freshly churned butter, sheep's cheese, the fresh, sweet pecorino that resembles Muenster cheese, and ricotta, a creamy substance that comes to the surface upon heating the whey of the milk after the cheese (the casein part of milk) has been gathered.

Fruits and vegetables were also brought to our homes directly from the farming areas as soon as they were picked in the early morning, and were sold by the *masse*, or mounds, divided on a large, wooden tray by pieces of twigs. Fresh beans (cannellini, kidney beans, and so on) were either sold in their pods by the *masse*, or already shelled by the glassful. A short, cylindrical wineglass was used for this purpose.

Fish were caught in the nearby creeks and brought to the house still alive. The fisherwoman would come under our windows and sing the praises of her fish. My mother would have her come in, and I remember seeing the fish weighed on a hand balance while they were still jumping.

Bread was mostly made at home and baked in the public ovens for a small fee or for one of the baked loaves in payment. (Often people did not have the few pennies needed to pay the baker, so they gave her one of their loaves. She would then sell this bread to the few families of the foreign civil servants who didn't make bread at home.) The leavening was in the form of a hard piece of dried sourdough, which was then soaked in cold water for several hours. In the evening it was mixed with enough flour to make a batter and left overnight in an uncovered container, in the center of a big well of flour. At dawn the bakerwoman would call from the street to tell people to start making bread. (She would go around to call all those who had, the previous night, given notice of their intention to bake bread.) By this time the batter would have grown and overflowed out of the container onto the center of the flour well. According to the number of people in a family, enough warm water and flour were added, and from six to twelve loaves of bread of two kilos each (about four and a half pounds) were made at a time, since they would have to last for a couple of weeks. In our household the maid made the bread because my mother, a city girl from Rome, did not have the skill or the strength for so heavy a job. But by the time I was twelve, in 1938, all the Gentile maids had to stop serving in Jewish families because of the anti-Semitic laws. Being the oldest of the two girls by four years, I was assigned the task of making bread. It was quite an accomplishment for me. I had to stand on a footstool to knead that enormous quantity of dough with my little hands and delicate, thin arms but somehow I managed. What I never learned, though, was to carry the extremely heavy tray to the bakery and back, as any housewife did. So the baker herself would come to our house and balance the tray, weighing about thirty pounds, on her head as if it were a crown. She was so tall, so colorful in her Pitiglianese costume, and so erect in her posture, we used to call her "the Caryatid."

Balancing heavy loads on the head was something we were not even allowed to try, so this fascinating skill became something I was determined to learn. I felt envious of those who possessed it and secretly tried to learn it. But even after long practice I only succeeded in mastering the first part of it, which didn't involve the actual carrying of those weights, under which I was certain that I would be crushed. Using one hand, a rectangular rag was held by one corner and brandished in the air until it was all twisted like a rope. Then it was quickly rolled from the center outward in a spiral, forming a shape like a round cake, tucking the outer end under, and secured on the center of the head. On top of this cushion the women carried their heavy loads—from a jug full of water to a bundle of firewood, from a tubful of wet laundry to a tray containing all kinds of things. They walked long distances balancing any of these burdens on their heads.

Flour and cornmeal were not purchased already ground, but in grain form. Grinding was done at the local mills once every two weeks, or just before bread-making time or polenta time. Almost anything tastes better when eaten fresh, but you don't really know how delicious Polenta (page 170) can be unless you have eaten it made with freshly ground corn.

At Passover the mill was cleaned to produce kosher flour. The cleaning consisted of throwing away the first grinding of the wheat, which had been "watched" by my father from harvest to the mill and allotted for the making of the *matzòt*. This "watching" was to ensure that no water touched the wheat to cause fermentation. If that happened, the grain or flour would become *chametz*, or leavened, and thus unfit for Passover use.

Oil was something else that was not store-bought. Fresh, ripe olives were bought directly from the farmer and the oil was extracted, filtered, and bottled in demijohns before our eyes. In the fall, at oil-making time, I would go with my father to the oil mill to watch this fascinating process. Two gigantic stone wheels rotated on a horizontal axis in a frame that rotated on a vertical axis in the stone basin full of ripened, purplish olives. This double rotary motion hypnotized me, while I became drunk with the scent of freshly crushed olives. The pulp was then placed into hemp filters, which were piled up to be pressed. The moment of excitement came when the first drop of fluid swelling out of them would burst in a purple jet into a waiting receptacle. We waited a few minutes for the watery and heavy particles to settle at the bottom; then, with a special tin dish, one of the mill men would skim the golden-green oil and transfer it into another container. At this point we would cut the round loaf of bread we had brought along into eight wedges, roast each wedge carefully on the hot embers in the constantly burning caldron, rub them with cloves of garlic and dip them into the freshly gathered oil, still hot from the grinding. We would season this bread with pepper and coarse sea salt and take it home to feast on it with the rest of the family. Even today I would not exchange that *Pancrocino* for the best dish in the world. It was, I am sure, the precursor of the modern garlic bread, but with a more rustic texture and an infinitely more flavorful taste.

Wine was also made at home. Father would make enough not only for our family needs but also for shipment all over Italy to families who had emigrated from Pitigliano and still wanted to drink the genuine kosher wines made with our local grapes.

Pitigliano also had a few stores. One of the butchers carried the kosher meats that my father had slaughtered. Chickens, on the other hand, were sold alive and the Jews would come to our home to have my father perform the ritual slaughter. (His skill as a slaughterer did not make him one bit less gentle and peace loving.)

One lovely little store was a kind of fruit emporium, carrying all sorts of exotic and dried fruits and nuts, imported from the outside world. Once in a while it would also have fish from the Tyrrhenean coasts, but mostly eels (which the Jews are forbidden to eat because eels lack fins and scales) from the nearby laguna of Orbetello, squirming alive for days on end.

If it weren't for those appalling eels, this little store would have been my heaven on earth, since I am passionately fond of all dried fruits and nuts and especially so of anything made with chestnut flour, one of the products it carried. Eels notwithstanding, the owner, a Christian, was our next-door neighbor and good friend, and in deference to this friendship, during the Jewish High Holidays she would clean the store and refrain from stocking *tref* (that which is not kosher; ritually unfit for the Jews to eat) fish, ordering only the kosher kinds the Jews could use.

IN PITIGLIANO, Jews and Christians had a long history of peaceful cohabitation and true friendship. At Passover, for example, it was customary to present our Christian friends with *matzòt* and unleavened sweets, which they considered marvelous treats. When Passover was over, the Gentiles reciprocated our gesture of friendship by offering their Easter specialties. The exchanging of recipes was the main topic of conversation at the public ovens among cooks and housekeepers as they waited for the baked goods to be ready. A love of good food and dedication to the culinary arts were common ground upon which the Jews and Gentiles of Pitigliano met, mingled, and made friends.

But even the depth of these shared experiences could not undo the growing enmity engendered by the coming of the anti-Semitic propaganda campaign launched in the mid-1930s.

By this time Pitigliano's Jewry was already showing the first symptoms of its decline, due in part to the departure of young people in search of higher education, in part to the steady migration of entire families to larger cities or, less frequently, to *Eretz Israel* (the land of Israel), but mainly because the majority had almost completely assimilated into the mainstream of Christian life.

Until the lamentable day of Mussolini's alliance with Hitler, our life in Pitigliano had been integrated and as happy, or unhappy, as anyone else's. By the end of the 1920s the urge to conform was so prevalent among the Jews of Italy that our private schools had closed down to hasten assimilation. Jewish children now walked to public school with the other children, played and did homework with them, made "best friends" with Jews or Christians, depending only on affinities, common interests, and academic capabilities. The only notable difference was that, because the public schools were also open on Saturday and because Catholicism, the state religion, was taught to everyone as one of the subjects, the Jewish children, upon our parents' request, were excused from school on Saturday and during religious instruction. But this was accepted without question by the Gentiles, as was the fact that we had different holidays and worshipping practices.

After the Axis pact between Rome and Berlin, in 1936, things began to change, at first so imperceptibly that hardly anyone could really notice any difference, until the press started a subtle anti-Semitic campaign, which continued in a crescendo over the next two years, and reached its culmination in the promulgation of the first racial laws.

Toward the end of my sixth grade, on Shavuot 5698 (June 5, 1938), I celebrated my *Bat Mitzvà*, a sumptuous ceremony in which I performed the role of the rabbi. Roses of all kinds filled the temple and a carpet of rose petals covered its beautiful marble floor. The children's chorus sang *Baruch Abbà*, the song sung on festive occasions, while my father escorted me to the *Echal*, the steps in front of the Ark where the Torah scrolls are kept. All the Jews in the village, who had crowded into the temple, wept. Perhaps we were all consciously or subconsciously aware that the beautiful melody of *Baruch Abbà* was our "swan song."

Aside from my dressmaker—a good neighbor and friend who had made my dress in the style of Juliet Capulet—no Christian schoolmates or teachers were present. Tension by now had reached the point that an invitation to any Gentile would certainly have been refused, causing painful embarrassment to them and to us.

The school year ended, for the first time in our lives, without us receiving the usual honors. Even a gym award I earned during the public gymnastic meets was never given to me. During the next few months, the situation worsened. By the end of the summer of 1938, right before the reopening of the schools, the first law against the Jews was issued and enforced: all the Jewish children were banned from public schools and universities.

We heard the news one morning when my mother returned sad-faced from shopping, holding a newspaper. We reacted to the news the way most children would: with jumps and cheers of joy at the idea of no more regimentation. But our euphoria didn't last long. Immediately, all who had remained good friends up to that moment began to avoid us as if we were suddenly infected with a repulsive disease. When they met us in the street they would lower their eyes. In time they began to avoid us openly, turning their heads in the other direction, leaving us with a painful feeling of rejection and loneliness.

One anti-Semitic law followed the other and eventually all our civil rights were stripped from us. A few faithful friends remained secretly on our side and helped when they could. Two were openly friendly with us: one was a deputy to the Italian Parliament, a schoolmate of my father's who was too high up in the Fascist Party to be afraid of anything. He would tease my father with the provocative question, "Are you an Italian or a Jew?" To which my father would imperturbably answer, "First I am a Jew because I carry within me the faith and the heritage of my people, and this would be the same wherever I was born; but I am also Italian because Italy is the country where I was born and which I proudly served during the Great War."

My father was decorated during World War I, but during the more than twenty years of dictatorship, he never held a Fascist Party membership card, even though the lack of one meant that all opportunities for a job were closed to him. The small honorarium that the Jewish community gave him was not sufficient to support his wife and his five children, but rather than depend on jobs for which the membership card was indispensable, he survived by keeping account books for several farmers who paid him with half a dozen eggs, a small wheel of cheese, a chicken, and so forth.

The other person who was openly friendly with us was a young priest with a magnificent tenor voice in whose house we often gathered to sing operatic arias and engage in political discussions.

Isolated, rejected, despised, first we were banned from serving in public institutions, then also from private ones, until by the beginning of the war nothing was left to us as a means of livelihood except for commerce and manual skills. We no longer opened the temple every day, or even once a week. We gathered in the temple only once a year on the High Holidays. For Passover everyone came to our home, where my father officiated on a reduced scale before the Seder, which was held for everyone in our house. All of the Jews turned toward each other to help and to be helped. I was barely fourteen when I became a cook for a ninety-year-old Jewish lady until she found a more mature person, the sister of a rabbi.

Soon after the war started, the radio—the last of our contacts with the outside world—was forbidden to us and our sets were taken from our homes. Our lives had not, so far, been directly endangered, but September 8, 1943, the day on which Marshal Badoglio signed the armistice with the Allies, was a fatal day for the Jews of Italy. If up to that moment the Germans had chosen to ignore our existence, at this point they immediately made us the scapegoats for the treason of their Italian allies. With the help of the most loyal Fascists, they first confiscated all our property, then in a human hunt hard to imagine, they drove us from our homes and rounded us up to face the same fate as our European brothers and sisters in the extermination camps.

I WAS THEN SEVENTEEN and, along with two of my brothers and my younger sister, escaped in time and joined the partisans. My parents and a younger brother were taken to a transshipment concentration camp, but eventually, after a succession of fortuitous and fortunate circumstances, they came back alive.

For years we had been forced to abandon our beautiful traditions and now, for a period that seemed to last forever, we had to abandon our homes as well and run for our lives. We found safety in the ranks of the partisans and with those generous farmers who risked their own lives and the burning of their farms to shelter us.

When the war was over, the odyssey of the Jews that culminated with the Holocaust also came to an end. When we returned to Pitigliano, we began to count our missing relatives and friends, often with a sense of guilt for being among the living, but with a commitment to Judaism and to its traditions that was stronger than ever.

Our temple, the school, the yeshiva, the libraries, and the oven were severely damaged by the bombardments and declared unusable. Despite the risk, for several years my father continued to open the temple once a year for Yom Kippur, and the survivors among those Jews who had left Pitigliano for larger cities long before the war came back for the celebration. We had moved to Florence in September 1952, but my father still went back to Pitigliano for Yom Kippur and tried to get as many as he could of the former members of the community to come with him. It became increasingly difficult, however, to attract people since they risked their lives in the unsafe sanctuary. Attendance fell until once it even became necessary to use a child as the tenth man in order to make up the *minyan* (a quorum of ten; ten men, aged thirteen or over, are required for many communal religious services). After that, we no longer returned to Pitigliano. Eventually the temple collapsed and what we could save of it was sent to other Italian communities and to Israel.

The Jewish community of Florence, where we had temporarily resettled, had also been decimated, and the survivors were still mourning their losses. Jewish young people were looking for companionship, and intermarriages were becoming the rule rather than the exception. More and more often among our new female friends we heard the refrain, "I'd rather marry a Christian than end up a spinster."

For us—my younger sister and myself, that is—the alternative was either to marry within our faith someone who shared our heritage and experience, or remain single. There was a history in our family of mixed marriages that had ended in disasters, and there was a history of single people who had lived productive and dignified lives. In our view there was nothing shameful about remaining single, and marrying just for the sake of getting married was never even considered.

While we waited for the right Jewish man to come our way, we took advantage of the opportunities that the city offered and got ourselves the education that had been denied to us during our school-age years when all Jewish children had been banished from public schools. Nothing formal, of course, but we didn't let one day go by without our auditing a lecture at the university, visiting a museum or gallery, studying a foreign language, or taking an educational trip.

It was upon our return from one of these trips that we received a call from a Jewish young man just arrived from New York. A friend of a friend had given him our telephone number. He and my sister first met under the statue of David in Piazza Signoria. After a few months of correspondence, my sister followed her future husband to New York, got married within ten days of her arrival, and nine months later their son David was born.

By the time my sister was an expectant mother again, it had become apparent to me that my ideal man was nowhere in sight. I had to go and fetch him! Not without apprehension, I boarded a ship (the *Cristoforo Colombo*—what else?) and off I went to the land of opportunity.

I arrived in New York one chilly March morning when the Statue of Liberty was enveloped in a thick morning mist and the Hudson River was covered with floating slabs of ice. By the time the cab drove me to my sister's apartment on the Upper West Side, the sun had broken through the fog, I was dazzled and elated, and my love affair with America had begun.

Back then, the tastes of the natives were nowhere near what they are today. I recall that friends and relatives thought they were being nice to me by taking me out for dinner in Italian restaurants. I would not hurt their feelings by refusing, but their good intentions were indeed paving the road to my culinary hell! "Italian" food was, even in some of the better restaurants, mediocre, to put it mildly. I have eaten the most unpalatable ossobuchi and eggplant parmigiana in some of those restaurants. In inexpensive restaurants the keynote was spaghetti with meatballs, a dish I had never tasted or even heard of in all my life in Italy.

There is nothing wrong with inventing a new dish, especially if one had recently emigrated to the country of plenty where the cost of ground meat was next to nothing and one could convert the few crumbs of red meat which one could afford to put in a sauce in the old country into spheres the size of ping-pong balls!

Nothing wrong indeed. What was wrong was the way this dish was prepared and served. The meat was overly abundant and overseasoned; the tomato sauce overcooked and smothering; the spaghetti cooked until the texture resembled that of a thick glue.

Eventually I learned to decline the invitations and invited people to dine at my apartment instead. Since it is well known that a way to a man's heart is through his palate, my cooking might have swayed quite a few inveterate bachelors toward considering marriage. It took another two years for the magic to happen.

I began to cook more and more at home, using my memory of what my mother and father and aunts and friends prepared in Italy. People began to ask for doggy bags, and names of recipes. Whereas I was flattered by their asking for leftovers and happily complied, I was embarrassed to confess that my recipes had no names. Mamma was such a great cook that not only festive meals but every meal she prepared for the family twice a day every day, was a gourmet delight. Yet, when we children asked her, "What's this?" her reply would invariably be, "It's eatable stuff!"

The idea occurred to me to record and name my recipes. The insistence of my friends that I share with them my secret recipes inspired me to conduct a large scale research, which led to a considerable collection. Eventually, what I thought of as a legacy to my children and a few intimate friends caught the attention of a publisher and my "secret" recipes became public domain.

Do I regret it?

Yes, somewhat. I am a rather private individual and being in the public eye can be a disturbing intrusion at times. On the other hand, I am happy to see my prophecy fulfilled. When my first book saw the light, the cultural attaché of the Italian Consulate gave an elegant and delightful reception in my honor. To the question, "What do you predict the life of the book will be," I answered unhesitatingly, "It will be a great success, and from now on—America will eat better."

Everyone laughed.

SINCE THEN Americans, and especially New Yorkers, have indeed made tremendous strides in the matter of food taste. The diverse people that form our society have taught us to enjoy a large variety of cuisines. The world has become smaller, more and more people have traveled to all corners of the earth and have learned firsthand about, and indeed tasted, the specialties that various countries offer. The food industry has caught on quickly and has responded by importing all sorts of delicacies. Wonderfully exotic foods, once inaccessible to most people, are no longer reserved for the very privileged few. They have become known by and within reach of an increasingly larger number of people.

There is now a new breed of Americans who would raise a brow to an overcooked, overseasoned dish of spaghetti and meatballs. The new breed not only knows about sauces other than tomato, such as pesto sauce, but also the difference between a mediocre and a superb one. These new Americans have developed a taste for olive oil, and not just *any* olive oil, but the best tasting among the extra virgin olive oils, truffle-flavored olive oil, and so on. The children of those Americans who used *any* vinegar, now know and use balsamic vinegar and herb vinegar; and people who once only knew steamed frozen lima beans, have now learned to appreciate all varieties of beans and prepare them in many different ways. The list goes on and on.

It is my challenge and privilege to present my new collection of recipes to these new, most sophisticated Americans and to all those who can appreciate the legacy of this child of the ghetto.

THE SECRET OF GOOD CUISINE

il segreto della buona cucina

he secret of good cuisine, according to my mother, is no secret at all. She had a persuasive saying, "*Metti buono e cava buono*," which implies that if you use good ingredients you will end up with a good dish. This is true, but only to a point. It is true that the first rule of thumb for the attainment of a superb dish is to use ingredients that are the freshest and of the finest quality. On the other hand, this precaution in itself is no guaranty of a perfect result.

First, there is the question of quantities, of proportions. In olden times, when written recipes were a rarity, the cooks who would end up with a fabulous dish by putting in "a little bit of this and a little bit of that" were practically doing little else with their lives than cooking and had developed such dexterity and experience that seldom did they make a mistake. Today our lives and minds are cluttered with all kinds of responsibilities and demands, and cooking is only one of the many tasks we are called on to perform as if we were trained professionals in all of them. Sometimes even with the written recipe in front of us and the perfect ingredients ready to be measured we do make mistakes, as happened to me once, when I really wanted to make a good impression. I was baking my favorite cake, and since it preserves beautifully in the freezer, I decided to make two at the same time so I would have one ready for my next dinner. I diligently doubled every ingredient except—my mind must have wandered—the sugar. The result was a bland-tasting cake when it should have been an outstanding one. What's worse, I didn't realize it until I used it on my guests. They insisted that it was "delicious," but I knew Americans to be the most generous of peoples, and I knew that my favorite cake, my *pièce de résistance*, was a pitiful failure! What else would I have forgotten if I had to rely on my memory alone?

Then there is also the important question of the techniques and methods used in the preparation of certain foods. My mother, the advocate of "use good ingredients and the result will be good," was by instinct such a great cook that she had no notion of how much she knew. She took for granted that what she did know—with the exception of her ability to clean artichokes in her Roman Jewish way, which her Pitiglianesi sisters-in-law were ignorant of until she taught them—was common knowledge to all. With all the respect and admiration I have for my mother, I disagree also on the point that given the good ingredients and the right amounts, anyone would know what to do with them. She might have not known it, but even though no one had ever taught her how to do certain things, she had no doubt learned them by observation or even by osmosis from her elders, the way I learned from her, and my children from me. I have never given my children a lesson or a demonstration, and yet they are excellent cooks in their own right.

The point I am trying to make is clear. Not everyone has the good fortune to come from a household of skillful cooks; but even if this were the case, there are still ways of preparing foods that not everyone knows about, and it is to fill this gap that I am including a few pointers in methods and techniques.

TODAY THE EMPHASIS ON good eating is not so much in how good is what we eat as in how much we eat of a given food. The key word is moderation. There is nothing wrong with "moderation" as opposed to "excess." It would be nice if we were able to avoid all excesses. However, my emphasis is not in "how much" but precisely in "how good," how satisfying is what we eat. In fact, I have a theory that if what we eat is of the finest quality, if it satisfies our sense of smell and our taste buds, the likelihood is we won't eat it in excess. If the food is truly tasty, we want it to linger in our mouth so we can savor it longer. While we are enjoying the taste, our brains receive the message that we are satisfied and our voraciousness quiets down before we have a chance to ingest large quantities. Once in a while, we do eat more than usual or eat "bad" foods without feeling guilty or getting sick. For example, seldom, if ever, do we eat French fries or any other fried foods, except on the last night of Chanukah when we make a whole meal, from hors d'oeuvres to dessert, out of fried foods. We don't get sick when indulging on occasion, because I take the precautions of, say, interspersing the meal with cooked leafy vegetables, lots of salads and fresh fruits, skinning the chicken totally before I fry it, and substituting the used oil with fresh oil for each new batch of fried food I make.

SPEAKING OF OIL, I have a comment to make. Whenever I prepare a dish that requires oil, I use exclusively Italian olive oil. That should not be a surprise. I am Italian and I am used to certain tastes. But not all Italian oils satisfy me. I am picky about my oil and I favor only a few brands among the many I can choose from. Today there are so many olive oils on the market, one doesn't know which to use. These oils are imported not only from Italy but from other countries as well, and many are produced right here in America. To find the olive oil that best satisfies your palate, you might have to try a few. Start with one small bottle at a time. When you first open the bottle, sniff it. Not only does the smell tell you whether an oil is fresh or rancid but also if you think you might like it or not. Then pour a few drops of it onto the palm of your clean hand and taste it. Let it stay in your mouth for a few seconds before swallowing it. In addition to the flavor, this will give you the aftertaste and the degree of acidity. If you have doubts, repeat this tasting a few times until you are able to tell for sure whether this particular oil suits you.

Please note that I make a distinction between olive oil and extra virgin olive oil. The former has been refined and lends itself better for cooking, not imposing a strong flavor on your dish; the latter is best for salads and other dishes for which raw oil constitutes one of the distinct flavors and an enhancement to the overall taste of a dish. More on oils on page 40.

TO SUM IT UP, the secret of good cuisine *does* consist first and foremost in the use of the finest and freshest ingredients. However, it also consists in the skillful mastering of certain ways of preparing them, and in the wisdom of enhancing the quality of a dish with little touches, such as adding a tablespoon of just-chopped herbs and a generous sprinkle of fresh oil to a finished sauce, or rubbing garlic over the blade of the knife with which you slice tomatoes for a salad.

It is not necessary to read through the various techniques that follow right now (even though it never hurts to read helpful material before tackling any new recipe), because you will find a reference in each recipe that requires a particular or unusual technique.

To facilitate the task of finding them, the techniques are listed in alphabetic order using the names of the ingredients and sometimes also those of the techniques themselves.

Methods and Techniques
Metodi e Tecniche

AL DENTE. When directions call for pasta or rice cooked *al dente*, this means that they should not be overcooked but should instead remain slightly underdone and chewy. Not only do pasta and rice cooked al dente taste better but they are also more digestible. Starchy foods are mainly digested in the mouth, and if they are overcooked they are likely to be swallowed before the first and very important stage of digestion is accomplished.

ALMONDS AND OTHER NUTS. The flavor of most nuts is enhanced by toasting them. Very oily nuts such as walnuts and *pignoli*, however, taste better if left alone. When a recipe calls for toasted nuts, place them on a baking sheet in a single layer and place the sheet under the broiler for 4 to 5 minutes, shaking the sheet a couple of times. Or toast them in the microwave oven, using the same timing. Allow to cool at least 10 minutes before chopping in a blender or processor. Mixed with dried fruits, such as dates, unsulphured figs and apricots, apples, raisins, and currants, nuts make a healthful and delightful snack, appetizer, or dessert.

AROMATIC OLIVE OIL. To make your own aromatic olive oil, place 1 teaspoon, or one small branch, or a few pieces of your favorite spice or herb into a small pan with 4 tablespoons oil and a sprinkle of salt. Sauté for 1 minute. Cool to room temperature, then add to 1 pint oil in a glass jar and tightly close the lid. Leave at room temperature and use after not less than three weeks. After the first use, refrigerate. The oil will coagulate since it freezes at higher temperature than water. Leave the jar at room temperature until the oil resumes its liquid state before measuring and using, then refrigerate again. The herbs and flavors I generally use to make aromatic oil are: black peppercorns; red hot peppers; garlic; porcini mushrooms; truffles; rosemary branches; sage leaves; and fennel branches or seeds.

AROMATIC VINEGAR. Kosher aromatic vinegar can be purchased in America.

ARTICHOKES. For most dishes that use artichokes in this book, you need to buy small to medium ones, and to prepare them in such a way that when you eat you don't have to discard anything. The Roman Jews, who made great use of artichokes in their famous cuisine, devised an ingenious method for ridding the artichokes of their inedible parts. Here is how it works.

Keep the artichokes immersed in cold water for at least one hour before starting to trim them, so they are nice and crisp. Have at hand a bowl containing cold water, the juice of one lemon and the two squeezed halves. Take one artichoke at a time from its bath and pull and discard the smallest outer leaves. Hold the artichoke by the bottom in your left hand, and a small sharp knife firmly in your right hand, the sharp side of its blade facing you. Insert the tip of the blade behind one leaf where the tender part—the whitest—meets the tough, darker green part, and cut toward you, letting the latter fall off. With your left hand, rotate the artichoke a little in a clockwise motion. After rotating the artichoke, insert the blade in the next leaf and cut the tough part off. Continue to slowly turn and cut at the same time, in an upward spiral until all the inedible sections of the leaves are eliminated and you are left with the edible portion attached to the untrimmed bottom. Peel the green layer off the bottom and the stem; then drop the trimmed artichoke into the acidulated water until you are ready to cook. Preparing artichokes with the method described above requires some practice. You will know that you have mastered this skill when the artichoke thus cleaned looks like the one you started with, only rounder, smaller, and lighter in color. Fresh and tender artichokes do not have choke at all. If you find that the ones you bought do have choke, however, remove it before cooking, because you really want to be able to eat everything without actually choking.

These directions are for right-handed people. If you are left-handed, simply reverse the process.

BALSAMIC VINEGAR. See *vinegar*.

BEANS. Fresh beans in their shells or already shelled (*fagioli sgranati*) are a rarity in America. If you find them or grow them yourself, you will have a treat during their brief season. They cook in less time than the dried ones and they are more easily digested. However, since we cannot rely on them all year round, we turn to the dried beans, which have greater nutritive value. See *dried beans*.

BEATING EGG WHITE. The best method for beating egg white is the good old one of using an unlined copper bowl and a hand whisk. An electric beater, however, is a good enough substitute, provided all the white gets beaten. The purpose of beating egg white is to allow it to incorporate as much air as possible so that it makes whatever it is used for lighter.

BLACK PEPPER. See *pepper*.

BOILED EGGS. To make the perfect-looking hard-boiled eggs, have the eggs at room temperature; place them in a pot and add cold tap water to cover. Bring the water to a rapid boil, then turn the heat off and let the eggs cook gently as water and eggs return to room temperature. This will prevent the unsightly greenish-gray color and the undesirable hard, chewy texture of overcooked yolks which will, instead, remain friable and of a beautifully rich yellow. For soft-boiled eggs, let the eggs cook for one, two, or three minutes, according to the degree of softness desired. Then transfer to individual egg holders, to be eaten with a teaspoon, after cutting off the top of the shell with a fast slicing motion of a knife.

BREAD. Bread can be divided into two main categories: bread made with a baking powder, and yeast bread. We will not concern ourselves with the former. The latter represents probably one of the most ancient known branches of the culinary art. Yet, for all its seniority, yeast-bread baking is also one of the most difficult skills to master. Too many factors go into the baking of yeast bread, and it is rare that all of them are favorable at the same time. Relative humidity, atmospheric temperature, freshness of the yeast, consistency of the dough, leavening time, and oven temperature are only some of the things that can go wrong when one attempts to bake a yeast bread. However, this negative preamble is not intended to discourage anyone from trying, but to let the novices know that if they don't succeed at first, they are in good company. Few foodstuffs are so appetizing as a freshly baked homemade bread. So go ahead and try some of the yeast-bread recipes and the rewards, in spite of some inevitable frustrations, will be plentiful. To avoid some of the drawbacks, make sure that:

1. the place where you do your preparation is draft-free;

2. the ingredients are at room temperature, except for those that are supposed to be warm;

3. the yeast is fresh (for the commercial one, look at the date; for the homemade sourdough starter, see *Lievito Casalingo,* page 316);

4. the dough is stiff rather than soft, unless otherwise specified in the recipe;

5. you do not under- or over-leaven. (In winter use a warm oven [turned off]; in summer watch carefully. If the loaves look fully leavened, place them in a hot oven. If you are ready to bake and the loaves look slightly underleavened, place them in a cold oven and set the thermostat at the temperature required by the recipe. While the oven gets hot it gives the loaves a chance to leaven some more. For an electric oven, it is a good practice to place a small pan with cold water in the lower rack.)

At any rate, rarely is a home-baked bread so damaged that it cannot be eaten.

BREAD PAP. To make the bread pap that is generally used to soften ground-meat patties and loaves, place the stale bread in a saucepan with cold water to cover and let it soak until swollen and soft. Pour out any excess of water and cook the bread, stirring, until quite dry.

BROTH. Broth is a liquid soup made by boiling meats, fish, or vegetables in water. When the broth is made with meats, it ends up having a more or less thick stratum of fat at the surface. To remove this fat while the broth is hot, you may have to use an apposite vessel with a spout that starts low, where there is no fat, thus avoiding the fat at the surface when you transfer the strained broth to another pot. If you don't have such a vessel, place the broth in the refrigerator for several hours until the fat is coagulated, then proceed to remove it with a slotted spoon.

BUTTERFLYING MEAT. See *turkey breast*.

CHICKPEAS. See *dried beans*.

CHOCOLATE SHAVINGS. To make shavings, lightly and quickly pass a chunk of milk chocolate over a sharp slicer called a mandolin. Gather the shavings into a container as you make them and keep refrigerated until you are ready to use, so that they do not lose their beautiful, curly shape.

CHOCOLATE SYRUP. To make a dense chocolate syrup, milk chocolate is best. Place the pieces of chocolate in a glass or ceramic container and place the container in a 200°F oven until the pieces begin to melt. Remove from the oven, quickly add some boiling water, and stir vigorously. If you use the microwave oven, place the chocolate and boiling water in the container and microwave for 1 minute, then remove and stir vigorously. The proportions should be 3 tablespoons boiling water for each ½-pound chocolate.

COLD WATER STEAM. The tastiest pot roasts are first browned in abundant olive oil and then cooked with the help of some steam. When the meat is well browned on all sides, cooking of the inside must be done quickly to preserve tenderness. A sprinkle of water over the very hot oil generates the steam that will penetrate the inside of the piece. This is best achieved if you keep a bowl with cold water next to the range; when sprinkling is needed, dip your clenched fist inside the bowl of water, then force-fully open it over the roast. Be careful not to linger over the pot while doing this because steam can burn you more easily than boiling water.

DEFAT. To defat is a culinary term that means "to remove the fat." See *broth* for instructions.

DRIED BEANS. Most people are discouraged from cooking dried beans because they have been misled into believing that dried beans must be soaked for many hours or overnight before cooking them. Even though this preconception is very old and hard to die, nothing could be further from the truth. Beans—whether the soft lentils or the hard chickpeas—cook beautifully without any previous soaking. Follow my directions and you will find yourself cooking beans more often than ever.

Remove all stones and debris from the beans, then rinse them two or three times in warm water. Place in a large non-ferrous pot with warm water four to six times their volume (2 to 3 quarts water for each pound of beans). Add 1 tablespoon salt and bring to a rapid boil. Immediately reduce the heat to its lowest point and simmer, covered, for 10 to 20 minutes. Add 1 clove garlic with husk on and 2 sage leaves to the pot and simmer ½ to 1 hour longer. Cooking time depends on many factors, such as the freshness and size of beans, alkalinity of the water, and altitude at which cooking is performed. Keep in mind that lentils take the shortest time to cook (20 minutes at most), and chickpeas the longest (1 to 2 hours). If beans are to be used subsequently in another recipe that requires additional cooking, take them from the heat while they are still *al dente*.

EGGS. As a rule I use extra large eggs in my recipes. I make sure (and so should you) to always buy the freshest eggs. Even though eggs (the yolks only) contain cholesterol, they also contain lecithin, which counteracts cholesterol, and are one of the best sources of protein, iron, and some of the B complex vitamins. So, eggs have been and always will be part of my diet.

Make sure to run cold water over the vessel in which you have prepared, cooked, and eaten your eggs before cleaning it or putting it into the dishwasher to prevent a lingering, unpleasant odor subsequent to washing.

For hard-boiled and soft-boiled eggs, see *boiled eggs*.

EGG WHITE. See *beating egg white* and *folding egg white*.

FOLDING EGG WHITE. To incorporate beaten egg white into a mixture without losing much of the frothiness that makes the mixture soft and airy, mix ¼ of the beaten egg white with the mixture. Then place the remaining egg white on top of the mixture. Holding the bowl with one hand and a plastic or rubber spatula in the other hand, introduce the blade of the spatula perpendicularly into the mixture; with a swift motion of the hand, turn the spatula and pull it out. Turn the bowl slightly, so that each time you dip the spatula, it will be on a different spot. Continue to introduce and pull out the spatula while turning the bowl, until all the white has been incorporated.

FRITTATA. See *omelets*. Place the pan under the broiler until frittata swells up and looks well-cooked. (This is a better and easier way to obtain the same result as the one described under *omelets*.)

HARD-BOILED EGGS. See *boiled eggs*.

HOMEMADE PASTA. Fresh egg noodles can now be found in every supermarket. However, for the orthodox among us, homemade pasta, made only with fresh eggs and flour, is the only acceptable one. I used to make enormous sheets of pasta totally by hand with the aid of an

especially long and heavy rolling pin. Now I use the hand-operated machine with stainless steel rollers. The electric extrusion type gives an unsatisfactory result. Homemade pasta is easy to make and it is very versatile. Slightly beat the eggs. Add enough flour to make a stiff dough. Knead to smoothness and place in the refrigerator between two dishes for approximately 1 hour. To roll the pasta thin, use the old-fashioned heavy rolling pin, or the machine with rollers that give different thicknesses. Once the desired thickness is obtained, the pasta sheet can be cut into capellini, tagliolini, fettuccine, tagliatelle, and pappardelle, that is, from the thinnest to increasingly wider noodles; or left in the sheet form for lasagne, tortelli, tortellini, and so on. Egg noodles, unlike other pasta, should be always drained thoroughly after cooking.

KALE. See *spinach and other leafy vegetables.*

MUSHROOMS. See *porcini mushrooms.*

OLIVE OIL. See *aromatic olive oil*.

OMELETS. There are two types of omelet. French omelets are light and fluffy and folded over themselves without turning, while the other type is dense and in some cases needs to be turned. To turn the latter, use the help of a dish slightly smaller than the pan. When the bottom is firm, place the dish upside down over the omelet. Hold the handle of the pan in one hand and place the other hand over the dish. Firmly holding both, quickly turn the pan and dish so that the latter now rests on your hand and the omelet on the dish. (Do this over the sink to prevent any oil that escapes from dropping on the burner; also make sure that no oil spills on your hand when you turn the pan and dish.) Add a little fresh oil to the pan, then slide the omelet from the dish to the pan and cook the other side.

PAP. See *bread pap*.

PASSOVER FLOUR. Passover flour is the finest, purest (no bran, which would cause it to leaven quickly) wheat flour that has been expressly ground and carefully watched by a *mashgiach* for use on Passover. It is not available in supermarkets, but kosher stores on the Lower East Side of Manhattan carry it, and I suppose that it can be found in similar stores in other parts of the country.

PASTA. With the word "pasta," Americans designate all types of noodles that are cooked in salted water, drained and dressed with a sauce. How the pasta is drained determines very much the result of a dish. Therefore, the following instructions should be given attention. For store-bought hard pasta drain more or less dry, according to need. The degree of draining depends on the cut of pasta and on the density of the sauce to be used with the pasta. Cut pasta such as ziti and cannelloni is best drained with a pasta colander. For long pasta such as spaghetti and linguine, a two-tine long fork or a multi-pronged scoop are better suited than a colander. If the sauce is a dense one such as pesto or butter, you should drain the pasta very quickly so that it doesn't lose too much of its moisture. If the sauce is somewhat runny, such as a tomato-based sauce, take your time to drain the pasta thoroughly before dressing it. Fresh egg noodles should always be drained thoroughly.

PASTA FATTA IN CASA. See *homemade pasta.*

PEPPER. The two types of pepper we use most are: hot red, which comes either whole, crushed or ground; and black, available in either corns or coarsely and in a finely ground state. Once in a while white pepper is called for in a fish or dairy recipe. I prefer to buy peppercorns and grind them myself for that fresh and delightful aroma that is released in grinding. I often indicate the use of coarsely ground or crushed black pepper. If you don't own a peppermill that can be regulated to grind from fine powder to coarse particles, place a few peppercorns on your working surface, then place the blade of a large knife on them and with the palm of your hand push forcefully down until the corns are crushed. Use immediately and make fresh coarse pepper as you need it.

PEPPERS. By peppers we mean always sweet peppers, unless otherwise specified. Both green peppers, the bell-shaped and the so-called Italian peppers, are fine for most dishes. For colorful and delicious *Peperoni sott'Olio* red, yellow, and orange peppers are best. I favor, whenever possible, the imported ones, which are sweeter and brighter than their domestic counterparts. However, the latter are less expensive and quite acceptable.

PORCINI MUSHROOMS. Unless you are able to find fresh porcini on the American market, you must resort to the dehydrated ones. To restore dry porcini mushrooms to their soft state you must soak them in warm water for at least 10 minutes. Since porcini are not washed before being dried, you also have to remove and discard any parts on which dirt is still clinging. The water where you have soaked the porcini is too precious to be thrown away, but you must take great care not to include any dirt when you use it. The best way is to decant the liquid, after the mushrooms have been lifted with a fork, slowly into another container so that the heavier dirt remains at the bottom. You might have to repeat this step several times until no dirt at all remains at the bottom of the container. Even after the dehydrated porcini are restored to softness they don't compare with the fresh ones. When the texture of fresh mushrooms is desired, fresh shiitake mushrooms are, in my opinion, a good enough substitute, if used together with the restored porcini.

POT ROAST. See *cold water steam*.

RICOTTA. The word *ricotta* in Italian means "cooked twice." This name derives from the fact that ricotta is a by-product of cheese making. After the curdled milk is heated and the casein gathered to make pecorino (from *pecora*, sheep), the remaining liquid is brought to a boil and the white substance that surfaces, the ricotta, is gathered into wicker baskets to drain. The best tasting ricotta, in Italy, is made with sheep's milk. What we call "ricotta" here has nothing to do with what I just described and it does not bind with other ingredients in the same manner. In order to obtain something similar to the real ricotta, we must cook the one we buy again. Place ricotta into a heavy-bottomed saucepan and bring it to a boil, stirring frequently. Turn the heat down to a minimum and simmer, stirring occasionally, for 5 minutes. Allow the ricotta to cool before measuring it. To reduce the moisture from ricotta without cooking it, place it into a sieve and place the sieve over a bowl. Let it drain in the refrigerator at least overnight, but better for several days, before using it.

SALT. Sodium chloride, the common table salt, has been abused, over-used, and forced into the American diet through so-called junk and processed foods for so many years, that now that we have become more conscious of our diet, many of us have gone to the extreme of eliminating salt altogether. Unless we have a medical problem, and are specifically asked by our physician to avoid salt, we shouldn't deprive ourselves of the pleasure that salt provides in making food tastier. I know a young girl who stopped eating peas, a highly nutritious food she likes very much, because she has heard that they contain sodium. When I asked her if she had high blood pressure or any other problem for which sodium is forbidden, she answered that she had absolutely no physical problems, but *"sodium, sodium,"* she kept repeating as if she were talking about arsenic! Besides the fact that people can *die* from lack of sodium, certain foods are so enhanced by adding a little salt to them that we should feel sorry for those who are not allowed it, rather than mocking them by using their diet without having their problems.

SOFT-BOILED EGGS. See *boiled eggs.*

SOUP. See *broth.*

SPINACH AND OTHER LEAFY VEGETABLES. In order to retain most of their valuable nutrients, leafy vegetables should be cooked with no water other than the water they retain in washing. To drain cooked leafy vegetables, don't pour the whole potful into a colander, because no matter how many times you have rinsed them before cooking, there is always a chance that some dirt has been left behind. The best way is to lift the vegetables with a two-tine long fork so that any sand that might still be there remains at the bottom of the pot. When the directions call for thoroughly drained vegetables, wait until these are cool enough to be handled, then gather into balls and squeeze the liquid out with your hands. Or place in a piece of cheesecloth and then wring the liquid out.

SUGAR. Unless otherwise stated, by sugar I always mean the granulated white type. Once in a while you will find directions for vanilla-flavored sugar. In Italy one can buy *zucchero vanigliato*, a finely powdered sugar with a strong vanilla fragrance. Since I don't believe you can readily find it already prepared in the U.S. market, here is the way to make your own. Place 2 cups confectioners' sugar in a glass jar with 2 vanilla beans cut up into 1-inch sections. Close the jar tightly, and put it away for at least two weeks before sifting and using the quantity of sugar you need. Put the beans that might be in the sifter back into the jar. Replace the beans and replenish the sugar every 3 to 4 months.

SWISS CHARD. See *spinach and other leafy vegetables*.

THINNING SLICES OF MEAT. Use a meat mallet or the blade of a cleaver to pound the slices down to the thinness desired. For large chunks of meat, see *turkey breast*.

TOMATOES. To peel tomatoes, drop them into a pot with boiling water and let them boil for 1 minute. With a slotted spoon, transfer into a bowl with icy water. The peel will crack, and will be easily pulled away.

TOMATO ROSES. For perfect roses, use only firm tomatoes. With a very sharp knife, cut a thin film of peel in a spiral about 1 inch wide. Discard the tomato itself (or reserve it for a soup or salad) and use the peel. Roll the peel loosely around itself, place it on a flat surface standing, then flatten down the first, outer round; lightly open the rest and shape in the fashion of a rose. Use a metal spatula to transfer the rose to the desired spot on your plate.

TURKEY BREAST. Sometimes you need to shape a turkey breast—or any other piece of meat—into a large, thin sheet. If your butcher is not willing to butterfly it for you, you can do it yourself this way: place the piece of meat on a flat surface. With a very sharp long knife in your preferred hand and with the other hand pressing the piece of meat firmly down, slice the meat horizontally halfway down from the top, without cutting through. Open it like a book, and flatten it down with the blade of a cleaver or meat mallet. If the piece of meat is quite thick, you might want to thin it twice. After the first cut is done one-third down from the top, turn the meat upside down so that the cut side faces in the opposite direction and again cut one-third down, starting on the uncut side, still without cutting through, then open the "Z" and flatten down.

VANILLA-FLAVORED SUGAR. See *sugar*.

VEGETABLE BROTH. Make an excellent vegetable broth by boiling together a variety of vegetables (always including a potato, carrot, and an onion) with water to cover and salt to taste for ½ hour, then strain. The vegetables, seasoned with salt, pepper, olive oil, and vinegar, make a tasty side dish.

VINEGAR. Although kosher vinegar in its plain or aromatic forms can be easily found in the American marketplace, I have not been able, so far, to find kosher balsamic vinegar. So I use my own recipe, a mock balsamic vinegar. To make it mix 2 cups of an excellent red wine vinegar with ¼ cup red grape juice, ¼ cup prune juice, and 1 tablespoon raw sugar in a saucepan. Bring to a boil. Add ½ teaspoon rosemary leaves, ½ teaspoon fennel seeds, and after 1 minute turn the heat off. Let cool to room temperature, then filter and pour into a bottle.

WATER STEAM. See *cold water steam*.

INTRODUCTORY NOTES

On Cooking Utensils

 have often been asked what a good outfit of cooking utensils would be. I am reluctant to give specific rules, since cooks have their personal needs and styles. There is not much sense in cluttering the kitchen cabinets, for example, with a deep frying pan if fried foods never enter your menu. On the other hand, if you are fussy, let's say, about using absolutely fat-free ground meat, as we are in my family, a meat grinder seems an indispensable kitchen aid. There are, however, certain basic recommendations I can make for a minimum outfit of cooking utensils and tools that would make your work easier.

A good set of knives should be your first priority. The set should include the butcher cleaver; butcher knife; 10-inch chef; 2 slicers; at least 2 utility knives; 3-inch paring knife; carver; boning knife; fillet knife; bread knife with serrated edge; steel butcher sharpener. A heavy mezzaluna, poultry shears, and utility scissors should also be part of your cutlery collection.

Use pots and pans made of different materials for different uses. Good old heavy gauge aluminum is always satisfactory, but is not advisable for cooking foods with a high acid content. Enameled cast iron, stainless steel, the new glass compounds are all fine, but require more attention because they retain heat and easily burn at the bottom. A basic outfit of cooking utensils should include 8-quart, 6-quart, and 4-quart stockpots; 2-quart, 1½-quart, and 1-quart saucepans; 12-inch, 10-inch, 9-inch, 8-inch, 7-inch, and 6-inch skillets; 1 large, 1 medium, and 1 small iron frying pan, one 1½-quart double boiler; 1 large and 1 small fish poacher with handled racks to lift the fish; 1 stainless steel steaming rack; 1 couscoussier (which can double as a stockpot and steamer); several round, square, and rectangular baking pans of different sizes; 1 large turkey roaster; 2 baking sheets; 2 loaf pans; 3 sizes of springform cake pans; 1 tube sponge cake pan (10 × 4 inches); pie plates; 2 cooling racks. Rolling pins, cutting boards, sifters, strainers, slotted spoons, and long-handled forks are also indispensable. Finally, there is a host of small gadgets and electrical kitchen aids that can save you time and energy, which you will choose according to your needs and as you acquire experience. But beware of the impulse to buy everything new that comes on the market: it could be costly and cumbersome.

Herbs, Spices, and Flavorings
Gli Odori, Le Spezie, ed Altri Aromi

According to our ancestors, there are many reasons for adding spices and herbs to food. Spices, they used to say, add zest to otherwise dull foods; they stimulate the gastric juices, thus providing better digestion; they also (alas!) mask bad tastes and odors caused by spoilage. The latter problem was particularly true of meats. Without refrigeration meat spoiled very quickly and a common, accepted practice was to conceal its bad taste with a great number of herbs and spices. Unfortunately, even after the introduction of modern refrigeration, the habit of smothering the original flavor by the indiscriminate use of spices has not tapered off.

The Italian Jewish cuisine does not make use of many herbs or spices. Nevertheless, I wouldn't label it bland; on the contrary, it is a very tasty, savory cuisine. The secret lies in the quantity of the herbs or spices and the way they are used. For example, it makes a world of difference if a recipe calls for one or two sage leaves and a pinch of powdered or crushed leaves is used instead. The whole leaves let out a subtle flavor

and can then be easily discarded; the powdered or crushed leaves cannot be removed. As a result, not only do they exude more flavor than might be desirable but they must also remain part of the dish, thus distorting the result. In other words, just a suggestion of a strong herb might (and indeed does) enhance the tastiness of a dish; too much of it might detract from its *gusto*. *Odori,* as the name suggests, are used to add a pleasant smell, not smother a flavor.

I translated *odori* as herbs, but actually the term includes onion, fennel, celery, and carrots, which are normally considered vegetables. Here are some of the most commonly used herbs: garlic, parsley, rosemary, sage, savory, basil, anise seeds, fennel, carrots, celery, onion. Other herbs used much less frequently in Italian Jewish cuisine are thyme, bay leaves, oregano, marjoram, chives, and so on. Among the spices, prominence is given to black and white peppers, cinnamon, clove, saffron, nutmeg. Other flavorings include vanilla bean, lemon and orange peels, almond extract, and so on.

Among the herbs, garlic plays a very important role. But it is not used indiscriminately, or with the attitude that if a little is good, more is even better. The following on garlic is intended as a little parable, and also to give clues as to the optimum amounts and how to use them.

GARLIC *L'AGLIO* This strongly scented herb widely used in the cuisine of many cultures was considered by our ancestors a powerful remedy for many ailments. The survivors of the legendary Influenza Spagnola (the respiratory infection that according to Italian folklore killed more people in 1918 than did the four years of World War I) claimed that they owed their survival not to physical fitness or better medical care but to the fact that they habitually ate lots of garlic. Afterward, garlic fell into disuse among the aristocrats for many decades. Class-conscious people were able to recognize the common folk in a crowd not so much from their attire as from their smell of garlic. Nowadays garlic is enjoying a resurgence of popularity among health-conscious people (who attribute even greater curative powers to it than did our ancestors) and the sophisticated jet-set crowds. I am not sure that garlic's grandeur is here to stay, but I am sure of the fact that, properly used, it can add zest to many a meal.

The Italians use an entire vocabulary to specify the type and amount of garlic that should go into any given food. For example, if it is only the garlic greens that are used, the phrase is *code d'aglio* (tails of garlic). They are the green part that sprouts from the ground and looks like scallion greens. If a regular, medium clove of garlic is desired, they say *uno spicchio d'aglio*. When a stronger taste is necessary, it is *un grosso spicchio d'aglio*. For certain dishes such as roast chicken and boiled beans, the word *vestito* (with husk on) is added. Then there is *un dente d'aglio*, which means, literally, a tooth of a garlic, the thin, long cloves that cling around the central stem of the head, which indeed look like teeth. And finally, when even a *dente* is too much for a specific dish, *una puntina d'aglio* is all that's needed, a little tip of a small clove of garlic.

I have limited my directions to "small" and "large," saying nothing when it is average-sized. Also, it is always understood that a clove of garlic be peeled. In the rare cases when the peel should remain on the clove, I say specifically, "husk on."

Following is a brief description of the herbs I use most frequently:

PARSLEY *PREZZEMOLO* The type of parsley I prefer is the broad-leaved Italian parsley. One reason why is that it is the only parsley I ever saw before I came to this country, and is therefore the one that was used in the original recipes. Another reason, however, is its darker color and stronger flavor. My recipes always require fresh parsley because this is one herb that can be found fresh in American markets all year round.

ROSEMARY *RAMERINO* In Italy rosemary grows wild, especially in sunny, dry terrain. If you shop at the farmers' vegetable markets in Italy, you are likely to find big branches of *ramerino* in your bag when you go home, without having asked or having paid for it. In fact, rosemary is given to you with the assumption that sooner or later you will make a roast and will need it. If you buy *fagioli* you will automatically get your free garlic and sage; buy *funghi* and *nepitella* will go into the bag with them. The tradition for the precise use of aromatic herbs is so deeply rooted in Italy that farmers give them as *part* of the vegetable you buy. Rosemary is widely used for roasts, either fresh (the whole branch inside the cavity of poultry, for example) or dried, by the teaspoon. But, like sage, it is seldom used crushed or powdered.

SAGE *SALVIA* Sage, like rosemary, grows wild in Italy. It is strongly scented and the whole leaves, rather than crushed or powdered, are generally used.

SAVORY *NEPITELLA* *Nepitella* is mainly used for mushrooms and on liver.

ANISE SEEDS *ANACI* Anise seeds are believed to possess magical qualities to help the digestive system. For this reason, they are widely used in certain baked goods. They constitute the main ingredient in *Anisetta* and *Sambuca*, two liqueurs used at the end of a meal or to "correct" *caffè espresso*. Anise seeds are also used to give an aroma to dried figs. I heard a "guru" cook saying on TV that anise seeds and fennel seeds can be used interchangeably. Heresy!

FENNEL *FINOCCHIO* Two types of *finocchio* are commonly used in Italy. One is the sweet fennel, cultivated mainly for eating (the white part) and also as an herb in soups (the green part). The other is the wild fennel, which is a large, incredibly aromatic weed resembling dill. Its fragrance is so strong that it is used in small branches (for boiled chestnuts or inside some roasts) and then discarded. Here in America we can find only the sweet, cultivated variety whose seeds do not have as strong a scent as the Italian wild variety.

BASIL *BASILICO* There are many varieties of basil. The one most commonly used in Italy is the type with dark, small leaves. It is used with tomatoes and tomato sauces, and above all for *panzanella*, a delicious bread salad. The broad-leaved, curly type, which is more readily found in America, is also good, shredded, for those dishes. Basil is a must for many zucchini and other squash recipes and, of course, for pesto for which it is the main ingredient.

Basil is a highly perishable herb, and for this reason you will not find it in the market very often. However, it is one of the easiest plants to grow on a sunny windowsill and can be harvested throughout the year. When fresh basil is not available, dried, crushed basil may be used in its place, except for *panzanella* and *pesto*—to use dried basil for those is inconceivable.

APPETIZERS AND EGG DISHES

antipasti e uova

 have grouped all the recipes here that can be served as hors d'oeuvres and all those that were once called *tramezzi*. *Tramezzi* did not belong to any particular category, and were used between two main courses at formal dinners either to stimulate a second round of appetite or as a transition between a roast and a fricassee.

Nowadays, even at formal dinners, only one main course is served and the custom of the *tramezzo* has fallen out of favor. But *tramezzi* are still served as the main course for luncheons and suppers.

In America, where one can find a number of readymade kosher cold cuts, homemade ones are a luxury. They were a necessity for us and so we worked to perfect our skills in preparing them. My father was the expert at making Beef Sausage (*Salsicce di Manzo*); this dish was renowned and appreciated among the Jewish communities all over Italy. Only a couple of years ago, his fame in this regard was brought to the attention of my brother. He had gone to a concert in Italy and, when it was over, he went backstage to congratulate the young pianist, Vittoria Pontecorboli from Santiago, Chile, and introduced himself. When the young lady heard the name Servi, she exclaimed in excitement: "A certain Signor Servi used to send my grandfather, in Leghorn, packages of *carne secca* and kosher sausages that everybody liked very much. These homemade cold cuts were so good that I heard about them two generations later, in Chile where I was born and live. Was this Signor Servi a relative of yours?"

Of course, it was my father she was talking about.

Another specialty that came from our household was Pickled Beef

Tongue (*Lingua Salmistrata*), the aroma of which would "resuscitate the dead." My mother was the culinary artist who prepared it with meticulous care and skill. Often relatives or friends would beg her to make one expressly for them. Goose Salami (*Salame d'Oca*), on the other hand, was not our specialty. My mother's sister, who was also an experienced cook, would make it and send it to us all the way from Leghorn where she lived.

Undoubtedly, these specialties involve an investment of labor and some of them can be prepared only during the cold months. But I am confident that my readers will not mind the work required when they discover the rewards that await them.

All of these delicacies are not only excellent hors d'oeuvres, but they are also wonderful for Sabbath luncheons and weekday suppers. They are so superior to their commercial counterparts that any comparison is impossible.

I have also included in this chapter various ways of preparing eggs. Because of their versatility, they too belong on the list of foods that can be served as appetizers, and for lunches and suppers. (The classification of eggs, by the way, as "jumbo, extra large, large, and medium," is but one of the many euphemisms used by Madison Avenue to make a product more appealing. Since the "extra large" eggs are the average-sized eggs that were used in the old recipes, it is understood that eggs are always extra large unless otherwise stated.)

Eggs have always been the nutritious staple of mankind and are used by cooks the world over in every category of dishes from appetizers to desserts. For us they were not only a staple but also a universal remedy for most ailments, real or imaginary, much as vitamins are for many people today. In order to be fully effective, eggs had to be ingested raw and very fresh—in fact, warm, directly from the chicken nest. So, naturally, every family had a small poultry yard in their orchard. But we didn't own any land and had to rely on the generosity of our good neighbors for the daily fresh egg for the youngest in the family.

Another important aspect of this chapter is that here, more than in any other category, I have made use of leftovers to prepare new delicious dishes. The idea of using leftovers combined with a sauce and/or other ingredients to make a new dish is by no means peculiar to Italian Jewish cuisine. But as Jews we have had to be more inventive in order to create dishes that are tasty without combining ingredients that would make them unkosher.

Finally, the majority of recipes can (and in some cases must) be prepared ahead of time, and even frozen, giving the hosts the very advantageous possibility of serving an unusual and delectable meal without having to fuss and get overly tired on or around the day they entertain guests.

Garlic Bread

bruschetta

Bruschetta—so called in Rome, but also known as *fettunta* in Florence and *pancrocino* in Pitigliano—is a hearty garlic bread, which can be served as is or with any number of different toppings. It is always a favorite, whether it is served as an appetizer or as part of a buffet dinner. Here are a few examples, beyond which one's imagination is the only limit to the ways this delicacy can be prepared.

12 slices day-old Tuscan or four-grain bread

3 large cloves garlic

Coarse kosher salt

Coarsely crushed black pepper

Extra virgin olive oil

2 large ripe tomatoes

1 tablespoon shredded basil

1 small onion, chopped or one of the following:

Sweet Peppers in Olive Oil (page 76)

Marinated Eggplant (page 71)

Toast the bread under the broiler until nicely browned on both sides. Rub one side with garlic, then season with salt and pepper to taste, and an abundant sprinkle of extra virgin olive oil.

Serve as is or top with one of the garnishes. If you choose fresh, ripe tomatoes, dice them into a bowl; add the basil and onion, lightly season with salt, pepper, and oil and spoon over the bruschetta. If you prefer one of the other garnishes, just place a couple of strips of the peppers, or a slice or two of eggplant on each bruschetta and serve.

serves 6

Spicy Chicken Liver Toasts

crostini di fegatini piccanti

1 pound chicken livers

4 tablespoons olive oil

1 small onion, chopped fine

8 anchovy fillets

1 tablespoon tiny capers, drained

1 tablespoon freshly chopped Italian parsley

Salt

Freshly ground black pepper

36 diagonally cut thin slices one-day-old *fruste* bread (page 328)

1½ cups clear chicken broth

Discard the skins, fat, or any discolored parts from the chicken livers. Soak in cold water and rinse until the water is free from any trace of blood. Grind or chop the uncooked livers until they become like a paste.

Heat the oil in a skillet, add the onion, and sauté 1 minute. Add the chicken livers and sauté, stirring frequently, 3 more minutes. Add the anchovies and cook, stirring, 1 to 2 minutes longer. Add the capers and parsley and remove from the heat. Season with salt and pepper to taste and mix well.

Toast the bread slices until lightly browned on both sides. Dip each slice in the broth very quickly (toast should be moist but still crunchy). Spread the chicken liver mixture on each canapé and arrange on a serving plate. Serve immediately or at room temperature.

serves 8 to 12

Humus and Tahina

crema di ceci e sesamo

Humus is a chickpea puree you can make from scratch or from canned peas. Tahina, or tahini, is a sesame-seed butter that you can find canned in many supermarkets or in bulk in most health-food stores. Whether you are familiar with this dish or it is a new concept to you, try my version and your family and guests will fall in love with it.

1 large clove garlic

½ lemon with peel, cut up (optional)

2 cups cooked chickpeas with some of their liquid

¾ cup tahina

1 teaspoon salt

⅛ teaspoon ground red pepper

Oil-cured black olives

Marinated Squash Flowers (page 74)

Sweet Peppers in Olive Oil (page 76)

Other marinated vegetables

Place the garlic (and lemon if you opt for it) in a food processor and process for 5 seconds.

Add the cooked chickpeas and 2 tablespoons of their liquid and continue to process until smooth and fluffy.

Add the tahina, salt, and pepper and process to mix. Should the paste appear to be too thick, add a few drops of the remaining liquid at a time until you reach the desired consistency. Pour over a flat serving dish and garnish with oil-cured black olives, marinated squash flowers, peppers in olive oil, and other marinated vegetables, if desired.

NOTE: If you use lemon, make sure to finish the humus within a day or two since the lemon will cause it to perish quickly.

serves 6 to 12

Marinated Artichoke Hearts

carciofi marinati

> To prepare marinated artichoke hearts you don't have to be as picky as you must be for *Carciofini sott'Olio*. Small artichokes are generally better for any recipe; however, medium and large ones are fine for this. They can be cut in half or quartered without much damage to the quality of the dish.

12 medium to large
artichokes

2 lemons

2 cups white wine vinegar

Salt

1 cup water

2 cloves garlic, finely minced

1 tablespoon pickled red
pepper, chopped

2 tablespoons freshly
chopped Italian parsley

½ teaspoon freshly
ground black pepper

1 cup olive oil

Prepare the artichokes as described on page 40; slice each artichoke into 4 to 8 wedges and drop into a bowl of cold water with the juice of 1 lemon. Squeeze the second lemon and reserve the juice. Add the 4 halves of rind to the bowl of artichokes.

Bring the vinegar, 2 tablespoons salt, and water to a boil in a large pot. Add the artichoke wedges and boil, covered, 20 to 30 minutes, depending on the size and freshness of the artichokes. Drain and place in a large bowl. Add the reserved lemon juice, garlic, pickled red pepper, parsley, salt to taste, black pepper, and oil. Toss to combine the artichokes with all the other ingredients.

Store in the refrigerator for several hours before serving.

NOTE: Artichokes thus treated keep, if refrigerated, for several weeks. They are served as part of an antipasto plate, or with *carne secca, salame*, or *salsicce di manzo* for an unusually delicious lunch (see my suggestion for a combination with *Focaccia colla Cipolla* on page 327).

yields approximately 2 quarts marinated artichokes

Marinated Eggplant

concia di melanzane

E ggplant, which is considered in this country the Italian food par excellence, was not known in Italy until the Jews brought it from the Near East a little over a century ago. It is a staple in Jewish cooking, especially among those who practice vegetarianism.

3 medium eggplant

Olive oil

Salt

Freshly ground
black pepper

Garlic, minced

Fresh basil leaves,
shredded

Balsamic vinegar

Trim the eggplant and cut lengthwise into ½-inch slices. Spread over paper towels and let dry in a ventilated place overnight.

Heat about ½ cup oil in a large skillet; add only enough eggplant slices to fit in a single layer. Fry, turning occasionally, until the slices are browned on both sides and give out the oil they have absorbed during the first stage of frying. Transfer to a glass, porcelain, or plastic container and season each layer with salt, pepper, garlic, basil, and a sprinkle of vinegar. Repeat until you have used up the eggplant, adding fresh oil to the pan as necessary.

Cover the container and store in the refrigerator for at least a few hours before serving. Serve at room temperature as an appetizer or as a side dish.

NOTE: There are no proportions for the seasoning because marinated eggplant can be prepared more or less piquant according to taste. Remember, however, that with insufficient salt this dish will not keep for too long. Refrigerated, it will last a few days; tightly covered, it can be frozen for several months.

serves 12

Marinated Zucchini

concia

This is one of my staples. *Concia* is practically unknown in Italy except in the Roman ghetto where it was first created. In the old days *Concia* was used both by the rich as a side dish to a plate of mixed boiled meats (see *Bollito Misto*), and by the poor who made a meal out of it—with lots of bread. We used to love *Concia* between two slices of Tuscan bread as a *merenda* or midday snack. I now serve it as an appetizer as well.

Green zucchini
Olive oil for frying
Garlic, minced
Fresh basil leaves, shredded
Salt
Pepper
Wine vinegar

Trim off the ends of the zucchini; then cut each one in half; slice each half thinly lengthwise and place the slices on paper towels to dry for several hours or overnight. Fry in hot olive oil in a single layer until golden brown on both sides. Arrange in layers in a glass, plastic, or porcelain container and season each layer with small amounts of garlic, basil, salt, pepper, and a sprinkle of vinegar. Cover the container and store in the refrigerator at least several hours before using. The flavor will be enhanced if you turn the *Concia* as a block inside the container a couple of times while it is marinating to allow the juices to seep through.

NOTE: I gave no proportions because they are not important; *Concia* can be prepared to be more or less piquant, according to taste, by increasing or diminishing the quantity of herbs and spices used. It freezes beautifully in a tightly closed plastic container, but it must be used within a few days if stored in the refrigerator or after thawing, being a rather perishable food.

Squash Flowers

fiori di zucca

Long before the flowers that produce the fruits first appear, every squash plant, from zucchini to pumpkin, produces a great number of sterile or "male" flowers that continue to blossom throughout the life of the plant. These flowers are a true delicacy, but because they are short-lived if not picked promptly, and highly perishable even after they are picked, they are seldom found in American markets. There are, however, some stores that carry them, and more and more people are growing their own squash plants. Squash flowers, prepared in the ways described, will give great pleasure to those who can find them in stores, and even more to home growers. The best flowers are those picked early in the morning, before the corolla has completely opened. If left for later in the day, the heat turns the blossoms into wilted, pitiful rotting balls.

Squash flowers do not need much washing. After a rain, however, they might be splashed with some dirt. Also, a zucchini bug or two might be lingering around the pistils. To rid the delicate blossoms of both dirt and bugs, hold a few at a time by the stems and dip them, upside down, in cold water several times. Don't shake or squeeze; just tap them on paper towels.

Marinated Squash Flowers

concia di fiori di zucca

For every 12 squash flowers, you will need:

3 tablespoons olive oil

1 medium fresh basil leaf, shredded

1 small clove garlic, minced

⅛ teaspoon salt

2 dashes freshly ground black pepper

1 teaspoon wine vinegar

Wash the squash flowers a few at a time, holding them by the stems and letting cold water run over and inside them for a few seconds. Cut the stems down to about ½ inch.

Heat the oil in a frying pan, then add the flowers fanned out like the rays of a wheel, with the stems at the center. Place the pan over a small burner set at medium heat and fry until the flowers are wilted and golden on one side.

Turn the flowers one by one, keeping them in a wheel, and fry until golden on the other side.

Remove from the heat and arrange in layers in a glass, porcelain, or plastic container, seasoning each layer with small amounts of basil, garlic, salt, pepper, and a sprinkle of excellent vinegar. Repeat until you have used up the flowers. Cover the container and store in the refrigerator, where *Concia* will keep for about a week. For longer storage, freeze.

Serve at room temperature as an appetizer alone, with other antipasti, or to garnish Humus and Tahina (page 69).

Artichoke Hearts in Oil

carciofini sott'olio

For this recipe you will need artichokes that are no larger than large eggs. They are not easy to find in the market, but you should be able to find them in good Italian vegetable stores around Passover. It is also essential that they be fresh and snappy. Wilted artichokes are bitter, chewy, and develop a choke.

2 lemons
24 small, fresh artichokes
2 cups white wine vinegar
2 tablespoons salt
1 cup water
½ teaspoon whole peppercorns
1 pint olive oil

Fill a large bowl with cold water and the juice of 1 lemon. Squeeze the second lemon and reserve the juice. Add the 4 halves of rind to the bowl of water. Remove enough outer leaves from the artichokes to leave only the tender center part. Lop off the tips. Trim the stems and bottoms to make neat little pyramids. Put the vinegar, the reserved lemon juice, salt, and water in a large pot and bring to a boil. Drain the artichokes and drop into the boiling mixture. Boil, covered, for 20 minutes. Drain and, as soon as the artichoke hearts are cool enough to be handled, pick up one at a time and gently squeeze the liquid out. Cool thoroughly for several hours, then place snugly into a jar, dotting here and there with peppercorns. Add the olive oil to cover and store until ready to use.

NOTE: If artichoke hearts are properly handled (all liquid is squeezed out before storing in the jar, no air bubbles are left in the jar when the oil is poured over them, and oil totally covers them) refrigeration is not necessary to preserve them. My mother used to make hundreds of them at a time and, without refrigeration, she was able to keep them from spring to the holiday season, that is, from Passover to Rosh Hashanah. However, refrigeration will certainly not harm artichoke hearts. The oil might thicken, but a few minutes at room temperature will restore its liquid form.

yields 2 dozen artichoke hearts

Mushrooms in Olive Oil

funghi sott'olio

The smallest mushrooms you can find in the market are the best for preserving in oil. If you buy them in boxes that contain mixed sizes, reserve the larger ones for other uses. Mushrooms prepared this way, like artichoke hearts, make superb hors d'oeuvres when served with *salame*, *carne secca*, and other cold cuts.

1 pound small firm mushrooms

2 cups white wine vinegar

Juice of 1 lemon

2 tablespoons salt

1 clove garlic cut lengthwise into four pieces

½ teaspoon whole peppercorns

1 cup olive oil

Cut all the mushroom stems to be more or less the same length. Place the vinegar, lemon juice, and salt in a saucepan (not aluminum) and bring to a boil. Add the mushrooms and cook for 5 to 6 minutes. Drain and cool thoroughly for several hours. Add the garlic and peppercorns and toss lightly.

Place into glass jars and add the olive oil to cover. Store in the refrigerator, where they will keep a few weeks.

yields approximately 1½ pints

Sweet Peppers in Olive Oil

peperoni sott'olio

3 pounds sweet red and/or yellow peppers

½ cup red wine vinegar

Salt

Freshly ground black pepper

2 large cloves garlic, quartered

Olive oil

Wash the peppers and place them on a large baking sheet where they can fit in a single layer. Bake in a 550°F oven for 15 minutes or until the peel begins to burn and blister. Drop in a basin with cold water, then try to remove as much of the peel as possible. Remove and discard the stems, core, and seeds and cut the peppers into strips.

Bring the vinegar with 1 teaspoon salt to a boil in a nonmetallic saucepan. Add the pepper strips and cook 3 minutes, stirring frequently. Remove from the heat and let cool. Drain and season with salt and pepper to taste. Add the garlic and toss. Place in a glass jar with oil to cover. Let rest until all the bubbles of air have escaped through the top. Close the jar tightly and keep refrigerated if using within a week or freeze for longer storage. Because of their bright color and unique taste, *Peperoni sott'Olio* are an excellent complement and garnish to any antipasto platter.

yields approximately 2 pints

Jewish Caponata
caponata ebraica

3 pounds eggplant
1 tablespoon salt
¼ teaspoon pepper
¾ cup olive oil
2 stalks celery, diced
1 large onion, diced
3 peppers, green, yellow, and red, cored and diced
1 clove garlic, sliced
1 large carrot, peeled and diced
2 teaspoons flour
2 pounds ripe tomatoes, peeled and cut up
1 cup pitted green olives, coarsely chopped
2 tablespoons wine vinegar
1 teaspoon sugar
3 large basil leaves, shredded, or 1 teaspoon dried basil leaves
1 tablespoon chopped fresh Italian parsley
2 tablespoons tiny capers, drained

Peel and dice the eggplant. Season with salt and pepper and set aside in a colander to drain some of its liquid.

Heat the oil in a large skillet; add the celery, onion, peppers, garlic, and carrot and cook, uncovered, over moderately high heat, stirring occasionally, 10 to 12 minutes. Transfer the vegetables to a shallow baking dish, but retain the oil. Add the eggplant to the oil in a skillet and sprinkle with flour. Fry, stirring, over moderate heat, until lightly golden. Add to the baking dish with the vegetables. Add the tomatoes, green olives, vinegar, sugar, basil, and parsley and place in a 350°F oven for ½ hour.

Remove from the oven; mix well, taste for seasoning and add salt and pepper if necessary. Add the capers, stir, and place in the oven for a couple of minutes longer. Serve hot as a side dish or cold as an appetizer.

NOTE: To peel tomatoes, drop them first into boiling water for about 1 minute, and then in cool water, and the peel will come off easily.

serves 6 as a side dish, 12 as an appetizer

Spinach "Heads"

testine di spinaci

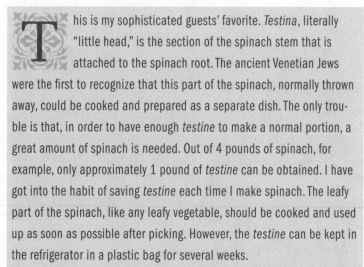

This is my sophisticated guests' favorite. *Testina*, literally "little head," is the section of the spinach stem that is attached to the spinach root. The ancient Venetian Jews were the first to recognize that this part of the spinach, normally thrown away, could be cooked and prepared as a separate dish. The only trouble is that, in order to have enough *testine* to make a normal portion, a great amount of spinach is needed. Out of 4 pounds of spinach, for example, only approximately 1 pound of *testine* can be obtained. I have got into the habit of saving *testine* each time I make spinach. The leafy part of the spinach, like any leafy vegetable, should be cooked and used up as soon as possible after picking. However, the *testine* can be kept in the refrigerator in a plastic bag for several weeks.

To free the *testine* of the sand that inevitably clusters in the interstices, soak them at least half an hour in fresh water, stirring frequently. The *testine* will float and the sand will sink to the bottom. Drain by lifting the *testine* with a slotted spoon and repeat the soaking and stirring until no sand is found at the bottom of the basin.

1½ pounds *testine*
4 tablespoons olive oil
1 cup water
1½ teaspoons salt
¼ teaspoon freshly ground black pepper
3 tablespoons red wine vinegar

Trim the *testine* and discard the roots and bruised stems. Soak ½ hour in cold water, stirring frequently, and rinsing often in fresh water, as described, until the *testine* are totally free of dirt or sand. Drain and place in a saucepan with the oil, water, salt, and pepper. Cook uncovered, over moderately high heat, until tender and all the water has evaporated, approximately 15 minutes. Add the vinegar and cook over high heat until all the moisture is gone and the *testine* turn quite red. Cool for a few minutes; place in the refrigerator for at least ½ hour before serving as an appetizer.

serves 6

Squash Flower Omelet

frittata di fiori di zucca

18 large squash flowers
Olive oil
1 medium onion, minced
Salt
Freshly ground black pepper
10 eggs, slightly beaten
1 tablespoon finely chopped Italian parsley

Wash the flowers, holding a few at a time by the stems and letting cold water run over and inside them for a few seconds. Pat dry.

In a large skillet, heat 4 tablespoons oil with the onion and sauté for about 1 minute. Shred the flowers directly into the skillet with the onion. Season with small amounts of salt and pepper and fry over moderately high heat, stirring occasionally, until the onion is soft and the flowers are wilted and lightly browned.

With a fork, transfer the sautéed onion and flowers to the bowl with the beaten eggs (reserve the oil). Add the parsley and salt and pepper to taste and stir to combine. Reheat the oil in the skillet and pour in the egg mixture. Reduce the heat and cook until the omelet is firm on one side. Place the pan under the broiler until the frittata raises and looks done. Carefully remove the hot pan from under the broiler and bring it to a trivet, and dish slices of it directly on individual dishes. Serve immediately.

Classic Artichoke Omelet

tortino di carciofi classico

 rtichokes are a staple with the Italian Jews, who invented a good many ways to prepare them, especially during Passover when these buds are tender and in season. The brilliant technique for trimming artichokes devised by the ancient Roman Jews is indispensable for the preparation of most artichoke dishes. (See instructions on pages 40-41.) *Tortino Classico* is a delightful main course for luncheons and suppers, and a desirable addition to any buffet dinner.

4 medium, tender artichokes, trimmed

1 lemon

Salt

Freshly ground black pepper

½ cup unbleached flour

Olive oil

6 eggs

Nutmeg

Cut each trimmed artichoke lengthwise into ¼-inch-thick slices and return to the lemon water. Drain and dry with paper towels. Lightly season with salt and pepper and dredge in the flour, shaking off the excess.

Place 4 tablespoons of oil in a large skillet over medium heat. Add the artichoke slices, possibly in a single layer, and brown on both sides.

Slightly beat the eggs with salt and pepper to taste and a dash of nutmeg. Pour over the browned artichokes and cook over very low heat, without turning, until the bottom is firm and the top still moist. Use a spatula to slide the omelet onto a warm dish.

serves 4

Eggs with Tomatoes
uova al pomodoro

Olive oil

1 clove garlic, minced

2 tablespoons freshly chopped Italian parsley

6 medium ripe peeled tomatoes or

2 cups canned peeled tomatoes

1 teaspoon salt

¼ teaspoon crushed red pepper

12 eggs

Peppercorns in a mill

In a very large skillet heat 4 tablespoons oil with the garlic and half the parsley. Sauté for 1 minute.

Cut the tomatoes into small strips and add, with their juice, to the skillet. Add the salt and red pepper and shake the skillet to mix. Cook uncovered, shaking frequently, for 5 minutes or until most of the liquid has evaporated.

With a small ladle make 12 depressions in the sauce and sprinkle the depressions with oil. Break the eggs and drop them directly into the little craters in the sauce. Cook over low heat, covered, for 5 to 7 minutes, or until the eggs are firm but not too hard. Spoon the eggs out into individual warmed dishes and place the cooked tomatoes around them. Top the eggs with the remaining parsley and with pepper from a few turns of the peppermill.

serves 6

Fried Mozzarella Sandwiches

mozzarella in carrozza

Mozzarella in Carrozza is prepared in Italy using mozzarella cheese made from buffalo milk, an extremely delicate and delicious cheese. However, even with the type of mozzarella one commonly finds here, the resulting dish is still delightful. The old method used for preparing *Mozzarella in Carrozza* was complicated (there were four steps of dipping—in milk, in flour, in egg, and in breadcrumbs), but the simpler method I use works just as well.

1 cup milk
1 cup unbleached flour
¾ teaspoon salt
2 dashes white pepper
4 eggs, slightly beaten
1 pound mozzarella cheese, cut into 12 thin slices
24 slices White Bread (page 310), crusts removed
1 cup fine breadcrumbs (page 311)
½ cup olive oil
½ cup unsalted butter

Combine the milk, flour, salt, and pepper; add the slightly beaten eggs and beat until you have a very smooth batter. Place 1 slice of cheese between 2 slices of bread. Wet the 4 edges of each sandwich with batter and dredge these edges in breadcrumbs. This will seal the sandwiches. Heat half the oil and half the butter in a small frying pan. Dip the whole sandwich in the batter and fry it in the hot mixture for 2 minutes, or until the bottom is browned. Turn once; cover the pan and fry another 2 minutes or until the other side is browned. Repeat until 6 sandwiches are done. Discard the old fat and wipe the pan clean with paper towels. Return the pan to the stove; heat the remaining butter and oil and fry the other 6 sandwiches.

NOTE: For a luncheon or supper, serve hot with Escarole Salad (page 296). However, if you plan to serve it as an appetizer, you can make it ahead of time. After all the sandwiches are done, let them cool thoroughly; cut into small diamonds and wrap in aluminum foil. Refrigerate or freeze. Just before serving, preheat the oven to 450°F and bake *Mozzarella in Carrozza* bits 5 minutes in a single layer.

serves 12

Chanukah Rice Pancakes

frittelle di riso per chanukà

 Although rice pancakes are traditionally made for Chanukah, I like to serve them throughout the year. They are a delightful alternative to plain rice as a side dish and they make a delicious breakfast, luncheon, or snack.

1 cup Italian rice

2½ cups water

1 teaspoon salt

1 cup dark, seedless raisins

½ cup *pignoli* (pine nuts) or slivered almonds

2 teaspoons freshly grated lemon rind

6 eggs, slightly beaten

1 cup olive or other vegetable oil for frying

Granulated sugar and cinnamon (optional)

Place the rice in a saucepan with the water and salt and bring to a boil. Lower the heat to simmer, cover, and cook, without stirring, for 30 minutes, or until the rice is well done and quite dry. Remove from the heat, add the raisins, nuts, and lemon rind and stir. Cool for at least ½ hour before adding the eggs; mix well.

Heat half the oil in a large frying pan. Drop the rice mixture into the hot oil by rounded tablespoonfuls. Fry 2 to 3 minutes, turn, and fry another 2 minutes or until the *frittelle* are golden brown on both sides. Transfer to a serving plate lined with paper towels. Place another piece of paper over them, and keep on stacking the *frittelle* with paper towels between layers. Add the remaining oil as necessary, until the mixture is used up. When you're through with frying, remove the paper towels and serve hot, plain, or rolled in sugar and cinnamon, if desired.

serves 6

Egg Pancakes Tripe Style

frittatine in trippa

During the first few months following the end of World War II, when our resources were very meager, this budget dish, prepared without such luxuries as black pepper, and with more breadcrumbs and water than eggs, was our staple. It remained, with slight variations, in our culinary repertory.

Salt

Water

2 tablespoons flour

1½ tablespoons
breadcrumbs

4 jumbo eggs

Olive oil

2 tablespoons tomato paste

1 large clove garlic, minced

2 tablespoons freshly
chopped Italian parsley

1 teaspoon chopped basil

½ teaspoon grated
lemon peel

Dash black pepper

Place ½ teaspoon salt, 3 tablespoons water, flour, and bread-crumbs in a bowl and mix to form a paste. Let rest for a few minutes, then add the eggs and beat until combined.

Heat 2 tablespoons oil in a large skillet. Add the batter by tablespoonfuls to form separate little pancakes. When firm on the bottom, turn and cook on low heat until firm on the other side. Continue to make pancakes, adding oil to the pan if it becomes necessary. When all the pancakes are done, cut them into strips.

Dilute the tomato paste in 2 cups water and place in a large skillet with 2 tablespoons oil, garlic, parsley, basil, lemon peel, ½ teaspoon salt, and pepper. Cook for 1 minute, then add the pancake strips, and allow to simmer 2 to 3 minutes before serving.

serves 4

Spinach and Ricotta Pancakes
frittelle di spinaci e ricotta

Two 10-ounce packages
frozen chopped spinach

Olive oil

1 tablespoon finely
chopped onion

¼ cup fine breadcrumbs

2 tablespoons grated
Parmesan cheese

2 cups ricotta,
moisture reduced

4 eggs, slightly beaten

Salt

Ground black pepper

Dash ground cloves

Let the frozen spinach stand at room temperature for a couple of hours before cooking. Cook according to directions with half the amount of water recommended.

In a medium skillet heat 2 tablespoons olive oil with the onion and cook, stirring, until the onion is soft, about 2 minutes. Drain the spinach, add to the skillet with the onion, and sauté, stirring frequently, until the moisture is substantially reduced.

Remove from the heat and after a while add the breadcrumbs, Parmesan cheese, ricotta, eggs, salt and pepper to taste, and clove. Mix well.

Drop by rounded tablespoonfuls in hot oil and fry until well browned on both sides. Serve immediately.

serves 4 to 6

Rice Cheese Croquettes

supplì al telefono

> I t is not easy to make *Supplì al Telefono*. Nevertheless, it pays to make the effort once in a while because this dish always makes family and guests happy. The name comes from the fact that a thread of cheese will spin between your mouth and the *supplì* while you are eating it, resembling the mouthpiece of an early model telephone from the time when this dish was first created. *Supplì* can be served as an appetizer, as a side dish in a dairy meal, or as a meal in itself for lunch or brunch.

2 cups short-grain rice

¼ cup finely minced onion

2 tablespoons olive oil

1 teaspoon salt

3½ cups hot water

1 cup peeled tomatoes (page 52)

2 eggs, slightly beaten

1 pound mozzarella cheese, cut into 24 ¼ × ¼ × 1-inch bits

1 cup fine breadcrumbs (page 311)

1 cup vegetable oil for frying

Place the rice, onion, and olive oil in a 2-quart saucepan and sauté 2 to 3 minutes, stirring frequently. Add the salt and hot water. Bring to a boil. Lower the heat to the minimum and cook, covered, without stirring, 15 minutes. Add the tomatoes and cook, uncovered, 5 minutes longer, stirring frequently. The rice should now be quite dry. Remove from the heat and cool for 15 to 20 minutes; add the eggs and mix well.

With damp hands, shape heaping tablespoons of the mixture into croquettes the size of a large egg; insert one piece of cheese in each croquette, making sure that the cheese is completely coated with rice. Roll in the breadcrumbs and fry a few at a time in the hot oil until golden on all sides.

NOTE: *Supplì* should be served piping hot. Tell your guests, who might never have had them before, that *supplì* should be eaten with the fingers.

serves 6

Pastry Dough for Turnovers

pasta per borricche e pasticcini

1 teaspoon salt
¾ cup lukewarm water
¼ cup vegetable oil
2½ cups unbleached flour
½ cup butter or chicken fat; or bone marrow, melted and cooled; or non-dairy margarine (pareve), soft

Combine the salt with the water and oil. Add enough flour to make a rather soft dough. Knead 2 to 3 minutes; wrap in wax paper and set aside to rest, at room temperature, for approximately ½ hour. Place on a well-floured board and roll to a ½-inch thickness, in a rectangular shape, with the long side three times the length of the short side. Brush the surface with fat, lightly sprinkle with flour, and fold into thirds. Wrap in wax paper and place in the freezer for 1½ minutes or in the refrigerator for 20 minutes. Return to the floured board and roll to a ¼-inch thickness, with one side three times the length of the other. Brush with fat and sprinkle with flour. Fold again into thirds and place in the freezer for 1½ minutes. Repeat the rolling, brushing with fat, and so on, three more times or until you have used all the fat. For the last rolling, follow the directions on each *borricche* and *pasticcini* recipe.

this much pastry will make turnovers for 6

Spinach Turnovers

pasticcini di spinaci

1 pound small-leaved bulk
spinach
1¼ teaspoons salt
½ cup shredded provolone
or sharp Cheddar cheese
1 egg, slightly beaten
2 egg yolks
2½ cups unbleached flour
¾ cup lukewarm water
¼ cup vegetable oil
½ cup butter, melted
Water, milk, or egg white
Sesame seeds

Remove the stems and roots from the spinach and save for later use (see *Testine*). Rinse the leaves in cold water many times until any trace of sand is removed. Place in a large pot with no water other than the water the spinach retains from washing. Add ¼ teaspoon salt and cook over moderately high heat until of desired tenderness. Lift with a fork and transfer to a colander to drain and cool. Squeeze out all liquid. Chop finely and combine with the cheese, egg, and 1 egg yolk; set aside.

With the flour, lukewarm water, 1 teaspoon salt, oil, and butter, prepare the dough as described on page 85. At the last rolling, roll to less than an ⅛-inch thickness. With a very sharp knife cut into twelve 3-inch squares. Place one heaping tablespoon of filling in the center of each piece of pastry; wet all around the edges with water, milk, or egg white and fold over in half, forming triangles or rectangles. Press gently to seal the sides.

Beat the remaining egg yolk with 2 teaspoons water and brush the tops of the turnovers with it. Sprinkle with sesame seeds. Transfer to an ungreased baking sheet and bake in a 400°F oven for 20 to 25 minutes, or until the tops are golden. Serve hot or cold.

serves 6

Festive Pasta Rolls with Parmesan and Cinnamon

masconod

This ancient Italian Jewish pasta specialty was traditionally served during Sukkot in my village. In other parts of Italy, *Masconod* are a practically ever-present addition to festive family meals and during the High Holiday season.

4 eggs

2½ cups unbleached flour

1 teaspoon salt

4 quarts salted, boiling water

½ cup sugar

1 teaspoon ground cinnamon

3 cups freshly grated imported Parmesan cheese

½ cup butter, melted

Make a dough with the eggs, flour, and salt. (For a detailed description, see my section on homemade pasta, page 138.) Roll it very thin; cut into 5-inch squares (you should get approximately 30 pieces). Cook in the salted, boiling water, 6 pieces at a time, for 3 minutes. Drain, drop into a basin of cold water, and drain again. Line up on a clean, slightly damp towel (I use an old linen tablecloth large enough to hold all the squares in a single layer).

In a medium bowl, combine the sugar, cinnamon, and cheese. Brush each square with butter; spread 2 tablespoons of the sugar-cinnamon-cheese mixture on each buttered square. Roll like a cigar and arrange in one layer in a buttered 9-inch baking dish. Brush the rolls with butter and sprinkle with the sugar mixture. Make another layer in the opposite direction, repeating the dressing and the layers until you have used up all the pieces of dough. Top with the remaining butter and sugar-cinnamon-cheese mixture. Bake in a 350°F oven for 20 minutes or until the tops are brown.

NOTE: Sugar and Parmesan cheese are not everyone's favorite combination. You can substitute 1 teaspoon black pepper for the sugar and cinnamon.

serves 6

Passover Fish Balls

polpette di pesce per pesach

Gefilte fish is traditionally served on Passover and other festivities in the home of the Ashkenazim. In Italy we had never heard of gefilte fish, even though fish was very much part of our festive meals. The following recipe is as close as we got to gefilte fish for the Passover Seder.

1 pound boneless raw fish
½ cup cold water
1 clove garlic
6 sprigs Italian parsley
2 tablespoons olive oil
Salt
White pepper
Dash or two nutmeg
2 tablespoons *pignoli* (pine nuts)
2 tablespoons non-dairy margarine
3 tablespoons Passover flour
1 egg, slightly beaten
½ cup matza meal
Oil for frying

Cook the fish for 6 minutes with water, garlic, parsley stems (reserve the leaves and chop them fine), olive oil, and salt and pepper to taste. Discard the parsley stems and garlic, drain well (reserve the liquid and keep it hot), and place in a bowl with the chopped parsley, nutmeg, and *pignoli*. In a small skillet heat the margarine and flour and cook, stirring, for a minute or two. Add the reserved hot liquid from the fish all at once and stir vigorously with a wire whisk. Cook 3 minutes, then add to the fish bowl. Stir to cool a little, then add the egg and mix well.

Spread the matza meal on a piece of wax paper. Form small balls with the fish mixture and roll in the matza meal. Fry in hot oil until golden brown.

yields 3 to 4 dozen

Fish and Olives Antipasto Platter

antipasto di pesce e olive

1 small onion, minced fine

⅓ cup black caviar

3 hard-boiled eggs, separated

½ pound smoked herring fillets

½ pound sliced smoked salmon

Two 6-ounce cans anchovy fillets, flat or rolled around capers

1 pound oil-cured black olives

½ lemon, sliced lengthwise very thin

1 cup green olives

1 cup Sweet Peppers in Olive Oil (page 76)

Coarsely ground black pepper

Extra virgin olive oil

Sourdough Crackers (page 330)

At the center of a serving plate, pack a medallion of minced onion and spread caviar over it. Pass the yolks through a vegetable mill with its large-hole sieve attached and arrange in a ring around the onion. Pass the white through the same mill and make a ring around the yolks.

Cut the herring fillets into ½-inch pieces and the salmon slices into small strips, and arrange with the anchovy fillets around the center.

Mix the black olives and lemon slices and arrange around the fish, alternating with green olives and marinated red or yellow peppers.

Sprinkle with pepper and abundant extra virgin olive oil. Serve with sourdough crackers.

serves 12 to 20

Fish-Filled Pastry

pasticcini di pesce

1½ cups boneless cooked fish

¼ cup slivered blanched almonds, toasted

1 tablespoon freshly chopped Italian parsley

¼ pound butter

Unbleached flour

½ cup hot milk

2 egg yolks

Dash or two nutmeg

Salt

White pepper

2 tablespoons brandy

¼ cup cold water

Oil for frying

Place the fish, almonds, and parsley into a bowl. In a small skillet heat 2 tablespoons butter with 2 tablespoons flour and sauté until the flour begins to attain a light brown color. Add the hot milk all at once and stir vigorously with a wire whisk. Cook, stirring occasionally, 3 minutes, then add to the fish bowl. Let cool for a while, then add 1 egg yolk, nutmeg, and salt and pepper to taste. Mix well and set aside.

In a small bowl combine 1½ cups flour, 6 tablespoons butter, 1 egg yolk, 1 teaspoon salt, brandy, and enough water, a few drops at a time, to keep everything together. Do not manipulate too much. Pour onto a floured working surface and roll down to approximately a ¹⁄₁₆-inch thickness. Cut into 2½-inch disks, fill each disk with a rounded teaspoonful of the fish mixture, moisten the edge, and fold over in half. With the prongs of a fork press the semicircular edge to seal it, then poke a few holes on the top. Fry in hot oil, drain, and serve.

serves 6

Non-Dairy Fish-Filled Pastry

pasticcini di pesce senza latte

1½ cups boneless cooked fish or ¾ pound boneless raw fish

¾ cup cold water

1 clove garlic

4 sprigs Italian parsley

1 tablespoon olive oil

Salt

White pepper

¼ pound non-dairy margarine

Unbleached flour

2 egg yolks

Dash or two nutmeg

2 tablespoons brandy

¼ cup cold water

Oil for frying

If you don't have leftover fish, place the raw fish in a saucepan with ½ cup water, garlic, parsley stems (reserve and finely chop the leaves), olive oil, and small amounts of salt and pepper, and cook for 6 minutes. Discard the garlic and parsley stems, drain the fish and shred it into a bowl (reserve ½ cup of the liquid and keep it hot).

In a small skillet heat 2 tablespoons margarine with 2 tablespoons flour and sauté until the mixture is lightly browned. Add the fish liquid all at once and stir vigorously with a wire whisk. Cook 3 more minutes, stirring occasionally, then add to the fish bowl. Let cool for a while before adding the chopped parsley leaves, 1 egg yolk, nutmeg, and salt and pepper to taste. Mix well and set aside.

In a small bowl combine 1½ cups flour, 6 tablespoons margarine, 1 egg yolk, 1 teaspoon salt, brandy, and enough water, a tablespoon at a time, to keep everything together. Do not manipulate too much. Pour onto a floured surface and roll down to approximately a ¹⁄₁₆-inch thickness. Cut into 2½-inch disks, fill each with a rounded teaspoonful of fish mixture, moisten the edge, and fold in half. With the prongs of a fork, press the semicircular edge to seal it, then poke a few holes on the top. Fry in hot oil, drain, and serve.

serves 6

Meat-Filled Pastry

pasticcini di carne

 My Aunt Delia, the wife of the late *chazàn* of Pisa who was in office during the period that included the two World Wars, was a famed cook of budget Jewish specialties. A few years before she died, Aunt Delia revealed her secret to me. "When you have meat or fish leftovers," she said, "save them to make these delicious *pasticcini* and everyone will praise you."

¼ ounce imported dry porcini mushrooms

¾ cup warm water

1½ cups leftover meat or chicken, chopped fine

¼ cup walnut meats, coarsely chopped

1 tablespoon freshly chopped Italian parsley

¼ pound non-dairy margarine

Unbleached flour

2 egg yolks

Dash or two nutmeg

Salt

Black pepper

2 tablespoons brandy

¼ cup cold water

Oil for frying

Soak the mushrooms in the warm water for 10 minutes. Lift from their bath with a fork, discard any parts with dirt still attached, and chop fine. Pour the mushroom water into a small pan, taking great care to leave any sand at the bottom of the cup, and keep warm.

Place the meat in a bowl with the mushrooms, walnuts, and parsley. In a small pan heat 2 tablespoons margarine with 2 tablespoons flour and sauté until the flour turns lightly brown. Add the warm water from the soaked mushrooms all at once and stir vigorously with a wire whisk. Cook 3 minutes, stirring occasionally, then add to the meat bowl. Add 1 egg yolk, nutmeg, salt and pepper to taste, mix well, and set aside.

In a small bowl, make a pastry with 1½ cups flour, 6 tablespoons margarine, 1 egg yolk, 1 teaspoon salt, the brandy, and add enough cold water, a few drops at a time, to keep everything together. Do not manipulate too much. Pour onto a floured working surface and roll down to approximately a 1/16-inch thickness.

Cut into 3-inch disks (if you don't have a cookie cutter of this diameter use a glass or cup), place 1 level tablespoon of the mixture on each disk, moisten the edge, and fold over in half. With the prongs of a fork press the semicircular edge to seal it, then poke a few holes on the top. Fry in hot oil until golden on both sides. Drain and serve.

serves 6

Goose Salami

salame d'oca

This and the following recipe for Goose "Ham" (*Prosciutto d'Oca*) should be planned at the same time since, in a sense, they complement each other. For *salame* you will use the breast and all you can scrape from the wings and back of the goose, whereas the two thighs and legs are best for an incredibly delicate *prosciutto*.

1 goose
1 clove garlic
Salt
Freshly ground black pepper

Cut the skin of the neck very low, below the wings, to obtain a good-sized *salame*. Turn it inside out and scrape all the fat off it. Crush the garlic with the bottom of a glass or with the blade of a large knife and rub it all over the skin. Sew one end of the skin to make a sac. Grind all the meat, except for the legs and thighs, which you will save for the *Prosciutto*, and weigh. Add 2 teaspoons salt and ½ teaspoon freshly ground pepper for each pound of ground meat. Mix very well. Fill the skin sac with the seasoned ground meat and sew the other end closed. With a large needle, prick the skin all over to force the air bubbles out.

Hang the *salame* in a cool, ventilated place for 4 to 6 weeks, when it will be ready for slicing and eating.

Goose "Ham"

prosciutto d'oca

2 goose legs, with thighs attached
Coarse, unrefined salt
Fine table salt
Freshly ground black pepper

Carefully remove the bones and tendons from each connected leg and thigh without tearing the skin. Match the two units in mirror image, skin sides out. With needle and thread, sew the skins together all around so that the sewn pieces look like a stuffed sock. Place in a small bowl and add enough coarse salt to cover the meat and to fill the spaces between it and the sides of the bowl. Cover with an inverted dish smaller in diameter than the bowl so that it touches the meat, and place a weight on it. Keep the bowl in a cool place (the warmest part of the refrigerator will do) for 5 days. After the second or third day, turn the "ham," drain the liquid that may have gathered around it, and add some salt, if necessary, to keep the meat covered with salt. On the fifth day remove the "ham" from the bowl, wash it thoroughly under cold running water, dry it carefully, and sprinkle all over with table salt and pepper in equal amounts.

Hang in a cool, ventilated place for 4 weeks.

Slice paper thin before serving as an appetizer, as part of a lunch, or for snacks.

Beef Sausage
salsicce di manzo

 n some parts of Italy these sausages are made—like the kosher salami found in this country—with meat and fat ground together. But my father, who was a connoisseur, would make them without any fat at all or with a few little cubes of fat here and there used only as an aesthetic contrast to the darkness of the dried sausages. Since these sausages are served in very thin slices, the little squares of fat can be discarded if desired. His *Salsicce*, like his *carne secca, salame*, and wines, were acclaimed and requested all over Italy.

3 pounds very lean
ground beef
2½ tablespoons salt
2 teaspoons freshly ground
black pepper
½ pound white fat, diced
2½ yards beef casing,
soaked in salted water,
and drained
Butcher string

Have your butcher grind or grind a very lean piece of meat yourself, after removing any skin or gristle. Since ground meat is highly perishable if not treated promptly, season with salt and pepper as soon as possible and mix well. The most efficient way of distributing the seasoning evenly is to knead the ground meat with your clean hands and squeeze it through your fingers several times. Add the fat and mix well again.

To fill the casing quickly and efficiently, you will need a meat grinder with a special attachment, which looks like an enlarged funnel. Place the mouth of the attachment inside one open end of the casing and push as much of the casing as you can over the attachment; tie the other end of the casing closed. Place the ground meat inside the grinder and force the meat inside the casing, stuffing it very tightly. Tie the casing closed at this end, too. Prick the casing all over with a pin or needle to force all air bubbles out. Tie at 4-inch intervals and hang in a cool, ventilated place, preferably in front of a slightly open window.

After 3 to 4 weeks, the sausages will be ready for eating.

Pickled Beef Tongue
lingua salmistrata

One 4- to 5-pound fresh beef tongue
Salt
Freshly ground black pepper
3 large cloves garlic
10 to 12 fillets of anchovies
2 tablespoons dry capers
2 bay leaves

Have your butcher remove all the fatty parts from the tongue or do it yourself. Wash thoroughly; place in an oval dish and rub it all over with salt and pepper, being careful to coat all parts as evenly as you can. Cover with an inverted dish and refrigerate for 24 hours. Repeat this operation—from washing to seasoning—every day for 6 to 8 days, depending on the size of the tongue.

On the last day, wash thoroughly and transfer to a clean dish. Finely chop together the garlic, anchovies, and capers and spread over the tongue. Cover with aluminum foil or plastic wrap and refrigerate overnight.

Place in a large kettle with all the marinade, bay leaves, and cold water to cover. Bring to a boil, then reduce the heat and cook, covered, for at least 2 hours, until fork tender.

Lift from the kettle, peel, place in a bowl, cover with an inverted dish, and refrigerate thoroughly before slicing.

SOUPS, RICE, PASTA, POLENTA, COUSCOUS, AND GNOCCHI

minestre

nder the heading of *Minestre*, in Italy, we include pasta dishes, rice dishes, crêpes, gnocchi, and, of course, all varieties of soups. Although the English translation of *minestra* is simply "soup," *minestra* in Italy is also designated as *primo*, or first course, which can be any of the foods mentioned above. *Primo* follows the antipasto (literally, "before the meal") and it is followed by the main dish, or *secondo*, generally consisting of a small amount of meat, fish, or other protein dish, accompanied by *contorni*, generally two or three cooked vegetables and/or raw salads.

Occasionally, a main course for one person might be a single mushroom cap—*cappella di fungo porcino*. *Funghi porcini* do not resemble in any way the cultivated mushrooms we can buy in supermarkets and vegetable stores. Porcini grow wild and derive their name from *porco*, the Italian word for pig. The aroma of this fungus attracts the pigs, which were used by mushroom hunters to find this precious species. In English it is called "Cep" or "Squirrel's Bread." It belongs to the bolete family, and it is found in late summer and in fall in many different kinds of wooded areas. Large caps (8 to 9 inches in diameter) are not unusual and one mushroom may weigh well over a pound. In ancient Rome, *fungo porcino* was enjoyed by the wealthy and the aristocrats who called it *Cibus Deorum*, or "food of the gods." Today, only sophisticated restaurants in Italy list *cappella di fungo* (mushroom cap) among their main courses during its short season. It is served broiled, seasoned with olive oil, salt, pepper, *nepitella* (savory), with cloves of garlic inserted here and there. In spite of the fact that its price is closer to that of gold than of meat and fish, some Italians manage to afford it once in a while, because when it comes to good food, Italians can become very extravagant.

The variety of *minestre*—precisely because they encompass such an apparently dissimilar profusion of dishes—is almost infinite in Italy. *Minestra* is the simple consommé, and *minestra* is also the complex couscous.

Actually, consommé was not so simple when I was growing up. It was made out of fat-free bits of red meat cooked in a double boiler without any water; the few tablespoons of liquid that were squeezed out of the meat were so precious that they were used only to help speed up the recovery of a convalescent. Today consommé means any clear broth made by boiling meat in a relatively small amount of water. But couscous, or, as the Jews in Leghorn called it, *cuscussù*, is the epitome of a complicated dish. It contains several kinds of meat, a variety of vegetables, and a starch—the coarse semolina—which is its base. Its preparation is so involved and time-consuming if done according to orthodox rules that it became proverbial among Italian Jewish mothers, when any of their children were finicky and wouldn't eat anything, to exclaim in impatient irony, "Do you want me to make you *cuscussù?*"

Jews have contributed enormously in enriching the list of *minestre* with their exotic additions and holiday specialties. *Cuscussù* is an example of the former; *Hammin di Pesach* and *Tagliolini colla Crocia* are examples of the latter. These three dishes are so rich and complete that each one is usually served as a whole meal.

Soups

minestre chiare, minestroni e zuppe

Broth

il brodo

2½ quarts cold water

2 pounds beef

1 pound spongy bones from veal leg joints

1 large carrot, peeled and sliced

1 small onion, quartered

1 stalk celery with leaves

1 large sprig Italian parsley

1 tablespoon salt

3 whole peppercorns

2 medium potatoes, peeled

3 or 4 very ripe cherry tomatoes

In Italy, the cure-all for a number of minor ailments was *caffè ristretto*, something resembling espresso. But Jews are Jews wherever they may be, and for us it was *il brodino*—an unspiced, clear chicken soup—that was supposed to perform miracles against a cold and other disorders, or after a trip, after a fast, and so on. My father used to say that a bit of hot broth, taken before and after a big meal, would "adjust" his stomach. There were several types of broths. One was the consommé, which was made expressly for convalescents. There was the *Brodino* for small children and sick people; the *Brodo delle Feste* made with three or four different types of meat; the *Brodo Vegetale*; and the plain, everyday *Brodo*. One difference between the festive broth and the everyday broth was that the former was made without tomatoes. There was no refrigeration and broth made with the addition of tomatoes would turn acid from one day to the next—and for holidays almost everything *had* to be made ahead of time.

The following recipe is the ordinary broth for our everyday meals.

In a large kettle containing the cold water, place the meat, bones, and vegetables, except the potatoes and tomatoes. Bring to a boil; remove the scum and add salt and pepper. Lower the heat and simmer, covered, for 2 to 2½ hours. Add the potatoes and tomatoes; cook, covered, another ½ hour or until the potatoes are tender. Strain and refrigerate several hours. Remove coagulated fat before using broth.

serves 6

Clear Chicken Soup

il brodino

The difference between *Brodino* and any ordinary chicken soup is that the latter is generally made with the addition of vegetables, herbs, and spices. If the chicken used to make this broth is fresh, as it should be, no other flavors are necessary in order to have a very tasty broth. The very best broth, when I was growing up, was made with an old chicken, since as the proverb went, *gallina vecchia fa buon brodo*, old chicken makes a good broth. However, the young fowl I find here is good enough.

It is said that chicken soup contains a substance that inhibits the common cold. Just to be on the safe side, I make *Brodino* whenever the symptoms of an incipient cold are present, and often the development of the annoying ailment is averted.

1 fresh fowl
3 quarts water
Salt

Remove and discard as much fat as you possibly can from the cavities of the fowl. Wash thoroughly and place in a stockpot with cold water to cover. Add 1 tablespoon salt and bring to a boil. Lower the heat and simmer very gently, covered, for 2½ hours without uncovering or turning. Thereafter, begin to test with a fork the tenderness of the meat every 15 minutes.

Transfer the fowl to a plate. Strain the broth. Defat with the apposite vessel, or refrigerate for several hours, then completely remove the coagulated fat. Serve clear or with pastina, capellini, fine egg noodles, or Meat Tortellini (page 145) cooked in it.

yields approximately 2½ quarts

Holiday Broth

brodo delle feste

The recipe for this outstanding holiday broth is essentially the same as the one for *Il Brodo*, except for the quality and quantity of the meats used. This makes a world of difference. The meats themselves were sometimes served as part of a holiday meal, but generally they were used at a later time, since it is impossible to have good boiled meats and a good broth at the same time. The rule of thumb is this: if broth is more important than the boiled meats, the meats are placed in cold water all at the same time and cooked very slowly. If, on the other hand, the meats are more important than the broth, the technique is quite different (see *Bollito Misto*).

1 small fowl (about
3 pounds) or 2 pounds
turkey legs and wings
1 pound brisket of beef
1 pound breast of veal
1 pound spongy beef bones
½ medium onion
1 small carrot, peeled
1 small stalk celery
3 to 4 sprigs Italian parsley
4 quarts cold water
1½ tablespoons salt
3 whole peppercorns

Carefully remove all the breast from the fowl and save it for *Polpette di Petto di Pollo* or *Polpette di Pollo e Matza*. Place the remainder of the chicken or turkey legs and wings in a large stockpot with the other meats, the bones, and all the vegetables. Add 4 quarts cold water and bring to a boil. Remove the scum and add salt and pepper. Lower the heat and simmer, covered, for 2 to 2½ hours. Strain and refrigerate several hours. Remove and discard all the coagulated fat before using the broth.

serves 12

Vegetable Broth
brodo vegetale

2 medium leeks

2 quarts cold water

2 large carrots, peeled and diced

2 medium turnips, peeled and sliced

1 medium onion, sliced

2 large stalks celery, cut into 2-inch pieces

3 large sprigs Italian parsley

2 medium parsnips, peeled and cut up

2 medium sweet potatoes, peeled and quartered

2 bay leaves

2 large basil leaves or 1 teaspoon dried basil

½ teaspoon whole peppercorns

2 green zucchini, trimmed and cut up

¼ pound green beans, trimmed and cut up

1 tablespoon salt

Remove the roots from the leeks and trim off the tough darker leaves. Cut the leeks lengthwise in half, and each half again lengthwise. Cut into 3-inch pieces and drop into a large basin with plenty of cold water. Wash thoroughly, spreading the leaves apart to remove the dirt. Place in a large stockpot with 2 quarts cold water and all the other ingredients. Bring to a boil, lower the heat, and simmer, covered, for approximately ½ hour. Strain through a fine strainer.

NOTE: The vegetables used to make the broth can be served as a side dish. Season them with 2 tablespoons wine vinegar, 2 tablespoons olive oil, and salt and pepper to taste.

serves 6

Fish Broth

brodo di pesce

For this tasty soup all you need is the heads and bones of any fine fish such as striped bass or red snapper. You can save these scraps in your freezer each time you have some fish filleted for you, or obtain them simply by asking the people at a fish store to save them for you. Generally the bones, the scraps, and the heads are thrown away, but if you tell the person who serves you that you are willing to pay for them, he will remember to save some for you. Make sure that the heads are cleaned of the gills.

Olive oil

1 medium onion, chopped

One 6-inch celery stalk, chopped

1 medium carrot, peeled and sliced

1 large ripe tomato, cut up

1 teaspoon salt

¼ teaspoon crushed red pepper

1 tablespoon coarsely chopped Italian parsley

¼ cup dry white wine

2 pounds or more fish heads and bones

8 cups cold water

Bread croutons or 4 ounces fresh tagliolini

Place 2 tablespoons oil, onion, celery, and carrot in a 4-quart pot and sauté, stirring occasionally, 2 minutes. Add the tomato, salt, pepper, and parsley, and cook 5 minutes over moderately high heat, stirring occasionally. Add the wine and raise the heat to let the alcohol evaporate. Add the fish scraps and water, and simmer, covered, 30 to 45 minutes.

Strain and discard the fish scraps and vegetables. Serve with fried bread croutons or with tagliolini cooked in it.

serves 6

Chicken–Matza Balls (opposite)

Thin Noodle Soup

tagliolini in brodo

Homemade pasta made
with 2 eggs and 1½ cups
flour (page 138)

2 quarts broth

Roll the pasta as thin as you can. If you roll it by hand, place the sheet on a tablecloth to dry for 1 to 2 minutes, but be sure that it doesn't become too dry and brittle. Make a roll as described in the recipe for *Quadrucci in Brodo*. With a very sharp knife, cut the roll into ¹⁄₁₆-inch slices. Toss the slices to unravel the *tagliolini* and spread over the tablecloth to dry completely. If you use the pasta machine, repeat the last thinning twice (see page 139) and cut with the smaller cutters.

Bring the broth to a boil. Add the *tagliolini* and cook 1 minute, uncovered.

serves 6

Chicken–Matza Balls

polpette di pollo e matza

 his is my own original recipe. It is a cross between Italian Passover soup (*Minestra di Riso per Pesach*) and the traditional Ashkenazic matza balls. As often happens, the hybrid offspring is better than either parent.

1 boned chicken breast
(2 halves)

3 eggs, slightly beaten

8 cups chicken broth

3 tablespoons olive oil

1 teaspoon salt

Dash white pepper

Dash nutmeg

¾ cup matza meal

Grind or finely chop the chicken breast. Combine the eggs, ¼ cup broth, oil, salt, pepper, and nutmeg. Add the matza meal and ground chicken and mix well. Set aside in the refrigerator for at least 1 hour.

Bring the broth to a boil. Shape the chicken mixture into 12 balls and drop directly into the boiling soup. When it comes to the second boil, lower the heat, cover the pot, and simmer 20 minutes without removing the lid. Serve immediately.

serves 6

Passover Sfoglietti Soup

minestra di sfoglietti per pesach

foglietti is a homemade pasta for Passover. There is a basic difference between this and an ordinary pasta. As soon as it is rolled thin, this pasta is quickly baked in the oven to prevent leavening. This treatment also changes the texture of the pasta, and provides a delightful gourmet experience.

3 eggs, slightly beaten

2½ to 3 cups Passover flour (Passover flour, a wheat flour, is available at kosher stores on New York's Lower East Side.)

2 quarts chicken broth

1 cup hot cooked peas

Mix the eggs with enough flour to make a rather stiff dough. Divide into 12 pieces. With a rolling pin or pasta machine, roll each piece of dough very thin and immediately bake on an ungreased baking sheet in a 550°F oven for 2 minutes. Turn over and bake 1 minute longer. *Sfoglietti* should be completely dried, but not browned. Remove from the oven, let cool, and break into uneven pieces.

Bring the broth to a boil; add the *sfoglietti* and cook for 4 to 5 minutes. Mix in the peas and serve.

NOTE: You can make *sfoglietti* ahead of time and store them in a plastic bag after they are thoroughly cooled and broken. They will keep well for the eight days of Passover and even longer.

serves 6 to 8

Passover Chicken Soup with Rice

minestra di riso per pesach

I did not learn of the traditional matza ball soup served during the first two nights of Passover until I came to this country. Our classic Seder soup was a chicken soup with rice to which were added balls of chicken breast and whole immature eggs (which are still at the stage where the outer shell and the white have not yet formed; they are perfectly round and vary from 1 inch to less than 1 millimeter in diameter). It was a beautiful soup to look at, with the white rice, the golden meatballs, and the orange eggs (from chickens raised on private farms, which have a much richer color than those from commercially raised chickens), and was delicious and nutritious, too. Here in America I could never find immature eggs, so I replace them with hard-boiled egg yolks.

1 boned chicken breast (2 halves)
1 egg, slightly beaten
¼ cup matza meal
2 tablespoons water or broth
½ teaspoon salt
Dash nutmeg or cinnamon
2½ quarts chicken broth
½ cup uncooked rice
8 small hard-boiled eggs

Grind or finely chop the chicken breast. In a bowl, combine the beaten egg with the matza meal and the water or broth. Mix well; add the ground chicken, salt, and spice, and mix well again. Set aside to rest in the refrigerator for at least 15 minutes.

Shape the mixture into tiny balls, no larger than egg yolks. Bring the broth to a boil; add the rice and chicken balls and cook, covered, for 15 to 20 minutes. Peel the eggs; discard the whites, and place one hard-boiled egg yolk in each of eight bowls. Pour the soup over the egg yolks and serve immediately.

serves 8

Soup with Tiny Pasta Squares

quadrucci in brodo

Quadrucci can be cooked a day ahead of time and reheated at the last minute without becoming soggy. This is why this soup was served on Yom Kippur, when everything had to be cooked the previous day.

Homemade pasta made with 2 eggs and 1½ cups flour (page 138)

2 quarts broth

Roll the pasta thin and place over a tablecloth to dry for a minute or two. Make sure that it does not become too dry and brittle. Starting from one side, begin to fold the sheet, making each fold 2½ to 3 inches wide; continue to fold as for a jelly roll. With a very sharp knife cut this roll into slices about ⅙-inch wide. Take 10 or 12 slices at a time and turn them, all together, 90 degrees. Cut again into ⅙-inch slices and this time you will obtain many little squares. Spread these squares over the tablecloth and continue cutting a few slices at a time until all the pasta is cut. Let the *quadrucci* dry thoroughly before cooking in boiling broth for 4 to 5 minutes, uncovered.

NOTE: If the *quadrucci* are not to be cooked immediately, they should be left to dry for several hours before storing in a plastic bag or in a glass jar, which should not be tightly closed. They keep several weeks without refrigeration.

serves 6

Garlic Bread Soup

pappa con aglio e olio

When dentistry was not as advanced as it is today, and oral hygiene was practiced only by the upper classes, it was not unusual to see young people with only a few teeth left in their mouths. *Pappa*, a pap made of cooked, soaked bread, and *farinata*, a cream soup base, was conceived to replace solid foods. Cheese or egg was added for protein. Of course, many people who had few problems with their teeth developed a taste for *pappa*. My uncle Aldo, my father's older brother, had all his teeth, but every morning before starting his busy workday as a successful architect, he would spend a couple of hours in his garden; then, for breakfast, he would eat a big dish of *Pappa con Aglio e Olio*.

½ pound Tuscan bread or, in place of it, any homestyle bread, stale

4 cups cold water

1 teaspoon salt if Tuscan bread is used; ½ teaspoon for other bread

3 large cloves garlic, lightly crushed

4 tablespoons olive oil

6 heaping tablespoons grated pecorino cheese

In a 2-quart enameled saucepan, soak the bread in the cold water for 10 minutes or until the bread is soft and swollen. Add the salt and garlic; place over high heat and bring to a boil. Cook rapidly for 3 to 4 minutes, uncovered. Discard the garlic and spoon out any water not absorbed. Add the oil, mix well, and serve topped with cheese.

NOTE: Omit the cheese if you wish to serve *pappa* with a meat meal.

serves 6

Tomato Bread Soup Peasant Style

pappa col pomodoro alla paesana

This is the original *Pappa col Pomodoro* made in Pitigliano (and, I believe, throughout all of Tuscany) when Tuscan bread was the only bread available. Later on, when other kinds of bread appeared, *Pappa* evolved into a more delicate dish. It is now fashionable among sophisticated people to favor rustic foods, and this soup has been revived and is very much in vogue.

4 tablespoons olive oil

3 cloves garlic, sliced

6 large ripe tomatoes, peeled and cut up

1 tablespoon freshly chopped Italian parsley

3 teaspoons salt

¼ teaspoon freshly ground black pepper

4½ cups cold water

Two 2 × 4 × 5-inch slices Tuscan bread, stale

6 heaping tablespoons grated Romano cheese

Place the oil and garlic in a large saucepan and heat until the garlic begins to discolor. Add the tomatoes and parsley and cook over high heat for 5 to 6 minutes. Remove from the heat; add the salt and pepper and stir. Set aside to cool for at least 1 hour. (Up to this point, the soup can be prepared in advance and kept in the refrigerator for 1 day, or in the freezer for several months.) Add the cold water; break the bread into large pieces and add to the tomato and water mixture. Soak the bread for 10 minutes or until it is soft all the way through. Return the saucepan to the heat; bring to a rapid boil and cook, covered, for 5 to 6 minutes. Remove from the heat, stir in the cheese, and serve immediately.

NOTE: To serve this soup with a meat meal, omit the cheese.

serves 6

Cauliflower and Bread Soup

il crostino

his is one of the soups I learned from the peasants who gave us shelter during World War II. I make it to remember and honor them, but also because I like it very much.

1 large white cauliflower
3 cups cold water
Salt
Extra virgin olive oil
Juice of 1 large lemon
Coarsely ground black pepper
Six ¾-inch-thick slices Tuscan bread
1 large clove garlic
2 tablespoons balsamic vinegar

With a sharp knife separate the florets from the main core of the cauliflower. Divide the large florets into 4 sections and the rest in half. Place in a saucepan with the cold water and 1 teaspoon salt; bring to a boil and cook 8 to 10 minutes. Drain, transfer to a warm bowl (reserve the water), and season with oil, lemon juice, and salt and pepper to taste.

Toast the bread slices until brown on both sides, then lightly rub the garlic all over them. Dip in the reserved cauliflower water until thoroughly soaked and arrange in a tureen. Season the toast with oil, vinegar, and salt and pepper to taste. Top with cauliflower and its seasoning and serve.

serves 6

Bean and Bread Soup

zuppa di fagioli

*Z*uppe are best in summer when a large variety of vegetables are in season and one can mix a number of different flavors; however, *zuppe* made with dried beans, cauliflower, and other winter vegetables are delicious as well and can be enjoyed all year round.

1½ cups dried red kidney beans

2 quarts hot water

Salt

1 large clove garlic, husk on

1 teaspoon dried sage leaves

Olive oil

1 medium onion, sliced very thin

2 stalks celery, diced

1 large carrot, peeled and diced

1 cup canned peeled tomatoes

Crushed red pepper

½ pound day-old Tuscan bread

Remove any stones or debris from the beans and rinse twice in warm water. Place in a large pot with the hot water and 2 teaspoons salt. Bring to a rapid boil; reduce the heat and simmer, covered, for 1 hour. Add the garlic and sage and cook ½ hour longer or until the beans are tender and some have popped open.

Meanwhile, heat 4 tablespoons oil in a medium skillet; add the onion, celery, and carrot and cook over moderate heat approximately 10 minutes, stirring occasionally. Add the tomatoes and small amounts of salt and pepper, and cook 5 more minutes.

Remove and discard the garlic and sage from the pot with the beans. Add the contents of the skillet and simmer, covered, 10 to 15 minutes to bring the flavors together. Taste for salt and correct if necessary.

Into a large tureen, slice the bread paper thin. Pour the soup over it; cover with a clean kitchen towel and let steep 5 to 10 minutes before serving.

serves 6

Vegetable and Bread Soup

zuppa di verdura

With *Zuppa di Verdura* you can use your imagination to the fullest as regards the variety of vegetables you use. This recipe is just an example of a typical summer *zuppa*, when all the vegetables and herbs are fresh and in season.

1 pound fresh cranberry beans in their shell, or 1 cup dried great Northern beans, or any dried beans

1½ quarts hot water

1 clove garlic with husk on

2 large fresh or 1 teaspoon dried sage leaves

Salt

3 scallions, cut up

4 tablespoons olive oil

2 small zucchini, diced

2 small potatoes, peeled and diced

½ cup diced celery

1 medium carrot, peeled and diced

¼ pound Swiss chard, washed and shredded

¼ small head cabbage, shredded

2 artichokes, trimmed (page 40) and sliced

1 sprig Italian parsley, coarsely chopped

3 large basil leaves, chopped

3 ripe plum tomatoes, sliced

Freshly ground black pepper

¼ pound stale Tuscan bread

Shell the beans and cook them in the hot water, with the garlic, sage, and 1½ teaspoons salt for approximately 20 minutes. (If you use dried beans, follow the directions on page 45.)

Place the scallions and oil in a large pot and cook over moderate heat, stirring frequently. Add all the other vegetables and herbs and cook, stirring, another 2 minutes. Add small amounts of salt and pepper; lower the heat and cook, covered, 15 to 20 minutes, stirring occasionally.

Remove and discard the garlic and sage; then add the beans and their water to the pot with the vegetables. Bring to a boil and cook 2 to 3 minutes. Turn the heat off.

Slice the bread paper thin directly into a large tureen. Pour the vegetable soup over it; cover with a clean kitchen towel and let soak 5 to 10 minutes. Delicious hot or cold.

serves 6

Vegetable Cream Soup

passato di verdura

The vegetables that go into this soup vary according to season and taste, but two ingredients, in addition to the onion and herbs, remain constant. These are potatoes and beans, which give the soup body and that wonderful, creamy texture. In summer you might find fresh beans in their shell, such as cranberry or lima beans, which you would add with all the other vegetables. At other times you will use cooked dried beans, which are added separately.

¼ cup olive oil

2 cloves garlic, crushed

1 medium onion

2 pounds of a variety of vegetables, such as green beans, zucchini, yellow squash, carrots, celery, turnip, potatoes, leek, spinach, green peas, all trimmed and coarsely chopped

2 cups cooked dried beans (page 45) or 2 cups shelled fresh beans

2 large sprigs Italian parsley

2 tablespoons shredded fresh or 1½ teaspoons dried basil leaves

1 tablespoon salt

¼ teaspoon crushed red pepper

5 cups cold water

2 cups fried or toasted Croutons (page 309)

In a large pot, heat the oil and lightly brown the garlic in it. Discard the garlic and add the onion. Lightly brown the onion; add all the remaining vegetables and herbs. (If you use cooked dried beans, don't add them at the time you add all the raw vegetables; add them with the cold water.) Add the salt and red pepper and cook, stirring, 5 to 6 minutes, to allow all the seasonings to blend with the vegetables. Add the cold water and bring to a boil. Lower the heat and simmer, covered, 45 minutes to 1 hour.

Strain through a sieve or blend in a blender or processor. Taste and correct the salt. Serve hot or cold according to season, with fried or toasted croutons.

serves 6

Cream of Spinach Soup

vellutina di spinaci

One 10-ounce package chopped frozen spinach

2 cups hot chicken broth

2 tablespoons non-dairy margarine

2 tablespoons unbleached flour

2 tablespoons olive oil

½ cup chopped onion

1 cup chopped fresh mushrooms

1 clove garlic, minced

1 tablespoon chopped Italian parsley

1 cup cold chicken broth

Salt

Freshly ground black pepper

Cook the spinach in 1 cup hot chicken broth (for cooking time, follow the manufacturer's directions). Let cool a little, then pour the spinach and its liquid into a blender. Place the margarine in a skillet, add the flour, and sauté 2 minutes, stirring. Add the remaining cup hot broth all at once, stirring vigorously with a wire whisk. Cook 5 minutes, then add to the blender.

Heat the oil in a small saucepan. Add the onion, mushrooms, garlic, and parsley, and sauté 5 minutes, stirring frequently. Add to the blender with 1 cup cold broth and blend until velvety and creamy. Taste for salt and pepper and correct if necessary. Blend another few seconds.

serves 4 to 6

Cream of Spinach Soup–Dairy

vellutina di spinaci alla crema

One 10-ounce package
frozen spinach

3 cups Vegetable Broth
(page 103)

4 tablespoons butter

2 tablespoons
unbleached flour

2 cups hot light dairy cream

½ cup chopped onion

1 clove garlic, minced

1 cup chopped mushrooms

1 tablespoon chopped
Italian parsley

Salt

Freshly ground white
pepper

Sour cream

1 tablespoon freshly
chopped chives

Cook the spinach in 1 cup broth following the manufacturer's directions and set aside. In a small skillet place 2 tablespoons butter with the flour and cook 2 minutes, stirring. Add 1 cup hot cream all at once and stir vigorously with a wire whisk. Cook 3 more minutes.

In a small saucepan place the remaining butter, onion, garlic, mushrooms, and parsley, and sauté for 5 minutes, stirring frequently. Place the spinach and its liquid, white sauce, mushroom mixture, and the remaining broth in a blender or processor and blend until velvety and creamy. Pour into a tureen. Add the remaining cream and salt and pepper to taste, and stir to combine.

Serve hot or at room temperature garnished with a dollop of sour cream and a sprinkle of chopped chives.

serves 4 to 6

Potato Soup

minestra di patate

 In spite of its pedestrian name, this is an elegant soup one should not hesitate to include in a formal dinner menu. We often served it on Erev Shabbat.

1¼ pounds potatoes
4 eggs, slightly beaten
3 tablespoons fine breadcrumbs
3 tablespoons flour
Salt
White pepper
2 dashes cinnamon
1 tablespoon finely chopped Italian parsley
4 cups boiling water
8 cups chicken broth

Steam the potatoes until tender. Peel, mash, and after cooling a little, combine with the eggs, breadcrumbs, flour, salt and pepper to taste, cinnamon, and parsley. Gather the mixture over a piece of cheesecloth, wrap the cheesecloth around it, and tie the two ends with a string. Flatten down.

Bring 4 cups water with 1 tablespoon salt to a boil in a large skillet, gently add the potato loaf and simmer, covered, for 20 minutes. Transfer to a tray, cover with an inverted flat dish, and place a weight over it (a tightly closed jar filled with water will do). Cool thoroughly.

Remove and discard the cheesecloth wrap and cut the potato loaf, using a sharp knife, into small cubes. Bring the broth to a gentle boil, drop the potato cubes into it, and heat through. Avoid overboiling or the cubes will fall apart.

serves 6

Lombard Soup

zuppa lombarda

I first learned to enjoy this soup from one of our maids at the time when most of the foods we ate didn't have a name. Recently I was baffled to discover that in Tuscany this soup is called *Lombarda* even though it is a true Tuscan dish practically unknown in Lombardy. I have liked this peasant soup ever since I was a child and I still like it, its fancy name notwithstanding.

1 pound dried white beans

3 quarts hot water

Salt

3 large cloves garlic

3 sage leaves

Eight 3½ × 5 × ½-inch slices Tuscan bread

Extra virgin olive oil

Coarsely ground black pepper

Balsamic vinegar (optional)

Remove all the stones and debris from the beans and rinse twice in warm water. Place in a large pot with the hot water, add 1 teaspoon salt, and bring to a boil. Lower the heat and gently simmer, covered, for half an hour; add 1 clove garlic with husk on and the sage and cook another half hour or until the beans are tender but not mushy.

Toast the slices of bread until brown on both sides, then lightly rub the remaining cloves of garlic all over them. Place a toast on each of 8 individual soup dishes, then ladle the cooked beans and some of their liquid over the toast. Season with abundant oil, salt and pepper to taste and, if desired, a sprinkle of vinegar.

serves 8

Lentil Soup
minestra di lenticchie

2 cups lentils

2½ quarts warm water

2 sage leaves

1 clove garlic, husk on

Salt

¼ cup olive oil

2 tablespoons minced onion

1 clove garlic, minced

1 tablespoon chopped
Italian parsley

¼ teaspoon crushed
red pepper

2 tablespoons tomato paste
diluted in 2 cups water

1 cup tubettini pasta

Pick any stones or debris from the lentils and rinse twice in warm water. Place in a large pot with 2 quarts warm water, sage leaves, 1 whole garlic clove, and 1 teaspoon salt. Bring to a boil, then lower the heat to a minimum, and simmer for 10 minutes.

In a small skillet, heat the oil with the onion and sauté for 2 minutes; add the minced garlic, parsley, red pepper, and 2 teaspoons salt and sauté, stirring, 1 more minute. Add the diluted tomato paste, stir to combine, then pour the contents of the skillet into the pot with the lentils. As soon as boiling resumes, add the tubettini and cook 10 minutes or until the pasta is tender.

NOTE: Lentils, unlike other legumes, cook very quickly. Overcooking will result in a mushy, pureed product.

serves 6

Lentil and Ground Beef Soup

la minestra di esaù

Most people are familiar with the biblical story of Esau who gave up his birthright in exchange for a plate of lentils, but no one knows with certainty how that plate of lentils was prepared. The ancient Italian Jews believed that it must have been very good indeed to be worth all the privileges which at that time were granted to the firstborn. So they devised this soup, which has always been a success with both my family and guests.

1 pound lean ground beef

2 teaspoons salt

¼ teaspoon black pepper

4 tablespoons olive oil

1 large carrot, peeled and diced

1 stalk celery, diced

2 cups chopped onion

1 cup tomato sauce (page 152) or one 8-ounce can tomato sauce

5 cups warm water

¾ pound lentils, well washed

1 clove garlic, chopped very fine or squeezed through a garlic press

1 tablespoon chopped Italian parsley

Combine the ground meat with 1 teaspoon salt and the pepper; mix very well. Roll into many tiny balls measuring less than ½ inch in diameter.

Heat the oil in a large pot; add the meatballs and all the vegetables. Brown over high heat for approximately 15 minutes, shaking the pot at first to allow the balls to become firm, and then stirring occasionally with a wooden spoon. Add the tomato sauce and simmer for 5 minutes. Add the warm water and 1 teaspoon salt. Bring to a boil, then stir in the washed lentils. When boiling resumes, lower the heat and simmer, covered, ½ hour to 45 minutes.

Remove from the heat and add the garlic and parsley. Taste for salt and tenderness of lentils, and return to the stove if they are not cooked enough, but bear in mind that this dish looks and tastes better when it is not mushy.

serves 6

Rice Minestrone

minestrone di riso

½ cup dried great Northern beans

1½ quarts hot water

Salt

1 clove garlic, with husk on

2 sage leaves

1 medium onion, thinly sliced

4 tablespoons olive oil

1 stalk celery, chopped

1 medium artichoke, trimmed and sliced or 2 small zucchini, trimmed and diced

1 potato, peeled and diced

1 medium carrot, peeled and sliced

½ cup broccoli florets

Crushed red pepper

1 cup Italian rice

1 tablespoon coarsely chopped Italian parsley

Pick all the stones and debris from the beans and rinse twice in warm water. Place in a pot with the hot water and 1 teaspoon salt. Bring to a rapid boil, decrease the heat to very low and gently simmer, covered, for ½ hour. Add the garlic and sage and simmer another ½ hour, or until the beans are tender but not mushy.

Meanwhile, place the onion and oil in a large pot and cook over moderately high heat 2 minutes, stirring frequently. Add all the other vegetables and cook, stirring, another 5 minutes. Add the rice and small amounts of salt and pepper and sauté 5 minutes, stirring occasionally.

Remove and discard the garlic and sage from the beans and add the beans and their liquid to the pot with the vegetables and rice. Cook, stirring frequently, for about 15 minutes, or until the rice is done *al dente*. Remove from the heat, add the parsley, and correct the salt and pepper if necessary. Stir and let stand 5 minutes before serving. This is excellent also at room temperature.

serves 8

Meat Minestrone

minestrone grasso

2 pounds beef shank

2 quarts cold water

Salt

1½ medium onions

2 whole cloves

2 peppercorns

1½ medium carrots, peeled

3 small stalks celery

Olive oil

1 medium potato, diced

2 small zucchini, diced

1 small wedge of savoy cabbage, shredded

½ cup shelled peas

½ cup canned or fresh peeled tomatoes, drained

1 cup cooked spinach or Swiss chard

Ground red pepper

1 cup broken-up fresh egg noodles

Place the shank in a pot with the water, 2 teaspoons salt, and half an onion studded with cloves and peppercorns. Add half a carrot and 1 celery stalk and bring to a boil. Cook until the meat feels tender and easily parts from the bones. Strain, discard the bones, dice the meat, and set it aside. Defat the broth.

Dice the remaining onions, carrots, and celery stalks, and place in a large pot with 3 tablespoons oil and the rest of the vegetables. Add small amounts of salt and red pepper and sauté, stirring, approximately 10 minutes. Add the meat and sauté 5 more minutes to bring the flavors together. Add the broth (you should have 4 to 6 cups), bring to a boil, and cook the pasta in it for 15 minutes.

serves 6

Rice

riso

taly is one of the greatest rice producers of the world, and Italian Jewish cuisine abounds in rice dishes of many varieties.

When Italian rice was a rarity and its cost accessible only to a lucky few here in America, my directions for *risotti* and some of the other rice recipes might have called alternatively for short-grain rice, which is inexpensive and resembles Italian rice somewhat. Because of the emphasis advertisers have put on long-grain rice, whose grains remain separate, it is now difficult to find the good old short-grain rice whose grains clump together. This characteristic, which short-grain rice shares with most Italian rices, is desirable not only for *risotti* but also for most rice desserts, such as *frittelle* or puddings, in which the rice grains are supposed to stick together.

The kind of Italian rice one chooses to buy depends on the use one wants to make of it. Most Italian rices have on their packages the description of what they are best suited for. However, Arborio seems to meet most needs.

When recipes call for rice without any specifications, this means that the type of rice one uses does not really matter and depends only on individual tastes.

According to some Italian culinary authorities, the difference between *risotti* and other first courses made with rice is that *risotti* should be thick enough to be eaten with a fork. The preparation of most *risotti* starts with the technique used for *Risotto Semplice* and then the condiment is added along with the broth or water, halfway through the cooking. This way, it is believed, the rice absorbs the seasoning and becomes more flavorful. I find that this method dulls rather than enhances the flavor of both the rice and the condiment. I prefer to cook the rice separately in just enough salted water so that it becomes thick and sticky; I cook the condiment with fat and spices until a concentrated and savory sauce forms; then I combine the two. This way the flavor of both the rice and the condiment is actually intensified.

Rice for desserts should be cooked until quite soft. However, *risotti*, like *paste asciutte*, taste better and are more easily digested *al dente*.

Simple Risotto
risotto semplice

isotto Semplice is not usually used as *primo* or in place of a soup, as most *risotti* are. It is more commonly used as a side dish.

¼ cup Oil from a Roast (see following recipe) or 2 tablespoons bone marrow and 2 tablespoons olive oil

1 small onion, finely chopped

1½ cups long-grain rice

3 cups hot broth

Salt

Pepper

Heat the oil in a 2-quart saucepan, add the onion, and cook over low heat until the onion is soft but not browned. Add the rice and stir with a wooden spoon until the rice begins to make a dry, sharp noise, approximately 3 minutes. Add the broth all at once; lower the heat and cook, covered, for about 15 minutes without disturbing it. When the rice is done, add salt and pepper to taste and stir.

NOTE: This is a very versatile *risotto*. Try it as a side dish with *Spinaci Saltati*, or *Carciofi Trifolati*, to accompany *Scaloppine al Madera* or any type of roast or chicken.

serves 6

Oil from a Roast

olio di arrosto

For want of a better name, I have translated *Olio di Arrosto* literally. But "oil from a roast" can be misleading, since one might associate it with the fatty drippings from an oven roast. Nothing could be further from the truth. "Oil from a roast" is the oil that is used to pan roast very lean meats such as veal, lamb loaf, and so on. These pan-roasted meats must be so lean when they go into the pan that when they are cooked the remaining oil is as clear as it was when you started. The cooking is done almost solely with oil (a few drops of water or wine are added to produce steam, but oil is the main medium). When the roasts are served, some of the tasty gravy that forms during the cooking process is served with them. But most of it and the remaining oil are what's called "oil from a roast." Store this oil in a little jar in the refrigerator and before you know it you will find a good use for it.

Sometimes, however, you may find that a recipe you want to make lists *Olio di Arrosto*, but you don't have any on hand. In that case, rather than giving up trying your recipe until you make a pan roast, prepare the following substitute, which works very well.

½ cup olive oil

1 large clove garlic, lightly crushed

One 4-inch branch rosemary or 1 teaspoon dried rosemary leaves

2 or 3 fresh or 1 teaspoon dried sage leaves

2 teaspoons salt

¼ teaspoon freshly ground black pepper

Heat the oil with all the other ingredients and cook, stirring, for 4 to 5 minutes or until the garlic is quite brown. Add a few drops of water or white wine to produce the steam, which will bind the flavors to the oil.

Remove from the heat and let cool. Discard the garlic and fresh herbs by simply lifting them with a fork. If you use dried herbs, strain the oil, but be sure that the salt and pepper are not removed.

NOTE: You may add a shank bone or any other bone for a more authentic flavor.

yields ½ cup

Green Risotto

risotto verde

1 pound small-leaved
bulk spinach

¼ cup olive oil

2 scallions, including
greens, chopped fine

One 6-inch stalk celery
with leaves, chopped fine

1½ teaspoons salt

⅛ teaspoon white pepper

Hot water

1½ cups Italian rice

1 tablespoon freshly
chopped Italian parsley

Remove all the stems and use only the leaves of the spinach. Rinse thoroughly in many changes of water until any trace of sand is gone. Drain, then chop very fine. Reserve the liquid that forms in chopping.

Heat the oil in a 2-quart saucepan. Add the scallions, celery, salt, and pepper and cook 2 minutes, stirring. Add the chopped spinach and cook, on moderately high heat, 6 to 7 minutes, stirring frequently.

Add enough hot water to the reserved liquid from the chopped spinach to make 2 cups. Add the rice and liquid to the saucepan and bring to a boil. Reduce the heat, cover the pan, and cook 15 minutes, without stirring. Add a few tablespoons hot water if the rice becomes too dry. Just before serving, add the parsley and mix well.

NOTE: For an elegant presentation of this rice, and for a complete protein dish, I spoon it out around the edge of a large serving platter forming a ring of green rice "eggs." Then I fill the center with *Ceci Conditi*.

serves 4 to 6

Risotto with Artichokes

risotto coi carciofi

 he preparation of this *risotto* is relatively simple, yet it is one of the most delicious *risotti* you can serve either as a first course or as a side dish. In Pitigliano it was traditionally served during Passover, when artichokes are in season and tender.

6 medium artichokes
or 4 large artichokes
½ cup olive oil
3 teaspoons salt
Freshly ground black
pepper
3 cups cold water
1½ cups short-grain rice

Trim the artichokes as described on page 40; remove any choke and slice very thin. Heat the oil thoroughly in a large skillet and add the artichoke slices. Season with 2 teaspoons salt and pepper to taste. Cook over high heat, stirring frequently, for approximately 5 minutes. Lower the heat to medium and cook, stirring frequently, another 10 minutes.

Bring the water with 1 teaspoon salt to a boil. Add the rice and stir until boiling resumes. Lower the heat to a minimum and cook, covered, for 12 to 13 minutes. Add to the skillet with the artichokes and stir to combine.

serves 6

Rice with Raisins

riso coll'uvetta

 iso coll'Uvetta is an ancient Venetian dish prepared mainly during Chanukah. It has an interesting taste, but is not for every palate.

4 tablespoons olive oil
1 small clove garlic, finely
minced
1 tablespoon freshly
chopped Italian parsley

Heat the oil in a large skillet. Add the garlic, parsley, and rice. Cook over high heat, stirring with a wooden spoon, until the garlic begins to discolor. Add the raisins and salt. Add the hot broth or water, ¼ cup at a time, and continue to cook, uncovered, over high heat until the rice is done, about 15 minutes in

1½ cups short-grain rice
½ cup dark, seedless raisins
½ teaspoon salt
3 cups hot broth or water
Black pepper

all. Taste for salt and pepper and add if necessary. Serve hot or at room temperature.

serves 6

Sabbath Saffron Rice

riso del sabato

Saffron, used in Italy in some dishes, is said to have been brought there from Asia Minor by the Jews for their Sabbath rice. In Ferrara, the saffron Sabbath rice was called *risi gialli* because of its intense yellow color, and was regarded as the Jewish food par excellence. But a fable provides another explanation: One day a poor Jewish boy left his native Ferrara in search of greater opportunities. He came back a rich man. His return to the family was such a big event that his old mother treated it as Shabbat, the holiest of the holy days. She said to him, "I am so happy you came back that I'm going to make *risi gialli*." To which he replied, "What's *risi gialli*?" From that moment on, a new meaning was added to those words: a person who is trying to forget his past and his heritage—such as a *nouveau riche* or a renegade—is called *risi gialli*.

1½ cups long-grain rice
6 tablespoons Oil from a Roast (page 126)
3 cups hot broth
1 small envelope (¹⁄₁₆ teaspoon) dried saffron
Salt
Freshly ground black pepper

Place the rice in a saucepan with the oil and cook, stirring with a wooden spoon, until the rice begins to make a sharp, dry noise, approximately 3 minutes. Add 1 cup hot broth and cook, covered, over high heat for 5 minutes, or until almost all the liquid has evaporated. Add a second cup of broth and continue to cook on high heat until the rice is almost dry again. Add the saffron and the last cup of broth and cook another 5 minutes. Add the salt and pepper to taste. Mix well. Remove from the heat and spread over a large flat dish to cool as quickly as possible. Serve at room temperature.

serves 6

Rice with Beets

riso rosso

When we depended exclusively on fresh seasonal vegetables, red rice was made only around Rosh Hashanah, when beets are in season. Now that we are able to find beets throughout the year, either from other regions or in cans, it is possible to prepare this delightful rice at any time of the year. Served hot, it can accompany a plate of boiled meats or fish; served cold, it adds an exotic note to any summer salad.

4 tablespoons olive oil
1 small onion, chopped fine
1½ cups long-grain rice
½ teaspoon grated lemon rind
1 teaspoon salt
1 cup juice from boiled beets
2 cups warm water
1 cup cooked beets, diced
1 tablespoon red wine vinegar

In a 2-quart saucepan, heat the oil; add the onion and cook over low heat until the onion is soft but not browned. Add the rice and cook, stirring with a wooden spoon, until the rice begins to make a sharp, dry noise, approximately 3 minutes. Add the lemon rind, salt, beet juice, and water; cook, covered, over low heat, about 15 minutes. Remove from the heat, add the diced beets and vinegar, and mix well. Serve immediately.

NOTE: For a cold-rice main dish, spread on a platter in order to cool it quickly. Then mound at the center of a green salad, surrounded by hard-boiled egg slices, black olives, fillets of anchovies, and so on. Top with sour cream for a striking visual contrast.

serves 6

Rice with Tomatoes

riso e pomodori

This is one of my family's favorite rice dishes. It is simple to prepare, goes well with any kind of meal, and is good both hot and cold. The recipe is intended for summer, when tomatoes are ripe and cheap and all the herbs are fresh. But in winter you can use dried herbs and canned tomatoes and still have a very flavorful dish.

1½ cups short-grain rice

6 large ripe tomatoes, peeled

1 clove garlic, finely minced

1 tablespoon salt

½ teaspoon black pepper

1 teaspoon dried oregano

1 tablespoon freshly shredded basil leaves, or 1 teaspoon dried

1 tablespoon freshly chopped Italian parsley

½ cup olive oil

Place the rice in an ovenproof baking dish large enough to contain the rice and tomatoes. Cut the peeled tomatoes in half and squeeze the juice and seeds onto the rice. Cut up the squeezed halves and place in a bowl. Season the rice and tomatoes separately, sharing the seasoning ingredients, including the oil. Mix each well. Spread the tomatoes on top of the rice and place in a 375°F oven for 45 minutes.

serves 6

Rice with Turnips

rape e riso

To be really good, turnips should be small, firm, and very fresh. Turnips that have become soft and porous lose their lovely bittersweet flavor and are hard to digest.

1 pound small fresh turnips

1 medium onion, thinly sliced

5 tablespoons olive oil

1½ teaspoons salt

¼ teaspoon freshly ground black pepper

3 cups hot water

1½ cups rice

Peel the turnips and slice thin. Place in a 2-quart saucepan with the onion, oil, salt, and pepper. Cook 3 to 4 minutes over moderate heat, stirring occasionally. Add the hot water and cook, covered, another 10 minutes. Add the rice; stir once and cook, covered, for 9 to 10 minutes. Taste for salt and correct if necessary. Stir and cook 5 minutes longer, or until the rice is *al dente*.

serves 4 to 6

Rice with Eggplant

melanzane e riso

1 pound eggplant	Trim the eggplant and peel only if you are not sure of its fresh-
1 large clove garlic, minced	ness. Dice and place in a 2-quart saucepan with the garlic, oil,
5 tablespoons olive oil	salt, pepper, and basil. Cook for 5 minutes over moderately

1 pound eggplant

1 large clove garlic, minced

5 tablespoons olive oil

1½ teaspoons salt

2 dashes ground black pepper

1 tablespoon shredded basil leaves

1½ cups rice

3 cups hot water

Trim the eggplant and peel only if you are not sure of its fresh-ness. Dice and place in a 2-quart saucepan with the garlic, oil, salt, pepper, and basil. Cook for 5 minutes over moderately high heat, stirring frequently. Add the rice and sauté, stirring, 5 minutes. Add the hot water, lower the heat, and cook, covered and without stirring, another 10 minutes. Taste for salt and correct if necessary; stir and cook just until the rice is *al dente*.

serves 4 to 6

Rice with Peas

riso coi piselli

3½ cups water

6 tablespoons olive oil

1 tablespoon dehydrated minced onion

1½ teaspoons salt

2 dashes freshly ground black pepper

1 tablespoon freshly chopped Italian parsley

2 cups shelled fresh peas or one 10-ounce package frozen June (tiny) peas

1½ cups rice

Place ½ cup water, oil, onion, ½ teaspoon salt, pepper, and pars-ley in a small saucepan. Bring to a boil and cook for 3 minutes. Add the peas and cook, over moderately high heat, uncovered, 5 minutes.

Bring 3 cups water with 1 teaspoon salt to a boil. Add the rice and stir a little. As soon as boiling resumes, reduce the heat and cook, covered, 10 minutes. Add the peas with all their juice and cook an additional 5 minutes. Mix well and serve.

NOTE: Dehydrated onion is preferred for cooking peas because it adds sweetness to the naturally sweet peas.

serves 4 to 6

Gino's Vegetable Risotto

risotto con le verdure di gino

Olive oil

1 medium onion, diced

2 cloves garlic, sliced

3 stalks celery,
coarsely chopped

2 large carrots, peeled
and diced

½ pound spinach or Swiss
chard, thoroughly washed
and coarsely chopped

1 small bunch Italian
parsley, coarsely chopped

Salt

Crushed red pepper

1½ cups Italian rice

Hot water

1 tablespoon shredded
basil leaves

In a medium pot place 2 tablespoons oil with the onion and sauté for 1 minute. Add the garlic, celery, carrots, and spinach or Swiss chard and sauté, stirring frequently, 6 to 7 minutes. Add half the parsley, 1 teaspoon salt, ⅛ teaspoon red pepper, 2 tablespoons oil, and the rice and stir. After 1 minute add ½ cup of boiling water and lower the heat. Cook gently, stirring occasionally, and keep on adding water, ½ cup at a time, until the rice is halfway done, about 10 minutes. Taste for salt and pepper and correct if necessary. Add the basil and remaining parsley, and finish cooking, keeping the rice *al dente* and moist.

Serve hot or, in summer, at room temperature.

serves 4 to 6

Gia's Rice and Cheese Omelet

bomba di riso gia

1¼ cups short-grain rice

1½ cups cold water

1 cup milk

1 teaspoon salt

½ cup dark, seedless raisins

1 teaspoon grated lemon rind

4 eggs, slightly beaten

3 tablespoons vegetable oil

½ pound shredded mozzarella cheese

Place the rice in a saucepan with the cold water, milk, and salt. Bring to a boil over moderate heat; reduce the heat and simmer, covered, for 15 minutes. Remove from the heat and add the raisins and lemon rind. Stir for a couple of minutes to cool. Add the beaten eggs and mix well. In a large frying pan, heat 2 tablespoons oil; pour in half the rice mixture and immediately reduce the heat to its lowest point. Spread all the cheese over the rice and cover with the remaining rice mixture. Cook over low heat until a golden crust is formed at the bottom, shaking the pan occasionally to make sure that the mixture is not sticking to the pan. The whole process of browning the bottom should take 10 to 12 minutes. Turn the *bomba* by placing an inverted dish over the pan. With one hand holding the handle of the pan and the other hand over the inverted dish, turn the pan and dish at the same time. Heat the remaining oil in the pan and carefully slide the *bomba* into it. Cook over low heat for 5 minutes or until the other side is golden brown. Serve hot.

NOTE: The method described above for turning a large omelet is actually very simple, but for an inexperienced cook it may take a bit of practice.

serves 6

Pasta

he word pasta in Italian has different meanings. The term can be used for dough, paste, a single piece of pastry (such as an eclair or a napoleon), cake, and macaroni, among other things. When the Italians talk about pasta in the sense that this term has come to mean here in America—any variety of macaroni from egg noodles to penne, cooked in salted water, drained, and dressed with a sauce—they say *pasta asciutta,* dry pasta (to distinguish it from pasta in a soup).

Pasta asciutta is divided into two main types: *pasta fatta in casa o pasta all'uovo,* which is homemade pasta or fresh egg noodles, and *pasta comprata,* or store-bought hard pasta. The latter can be *lunga,* such as spaghetti and linguine, or *tagliata,* cut pasta, such as ziti and cannelloni.

I learned how to make homemade pasta when I was still a child. In time I developed a skill in rolling enormous sheets, measuring up to 40 inches in diameter, without making any tear in them. Part of the merit was due to the rolling pin. It was about 40 inches long and 2½ inches in diameter and was carved out of heavy fruitwood so that, even though the rolling back and forth was done gently and in small, even strokes, the weight of the pin itself did most of the thinning. But the skill was mainly in the motion of the hands toward and away from the center of the pin as they rolled the sheet of dough around it, and in the flapping of one side of the sheet at a time on the pasta board (see description on page 138).

Today, rolling pins are not custom-made by the cabinetmaker as they once were. Even in Italy, the commercial ones are much shorter and lighter than the ones we used. More often, the pasta machine takes the place of the rolling pin and, I must say, it is a good investment. Some

Italians still resist this kitchen aid on the ground that pasta made with a metal machine acquires some of the taste and texture of the metal. This is an unproven claim and I cannot subscribe to it. What is true, however, is that the dough to be thinned by the machine must be much harder than the dough to be thinned by hand. A soft dough will stick and jam the rollers of the machine; therefore, the ratio of egg to flour must be changed. Also, when rolling by hand one can never produce a dough as even a thinness as that produced by a machine; consequently, the texture is also different.

In spite of these drawbacks, I use the pasta machine very often, at least whenever I have to make pasta for more than my family of four. In this way I can afford the time to make pasta more often than I would were I to make it by hand. One way to make machine-made noodles resemble handmade ones more closely is to oil the rollers constantly while the machine is in use, so you'll need less flour. At least the taste, if not the texture, will be like handmade noodles. (But using this method, you cannot use the pasta around a stuffing because the oil would prevent the sealing of the pasta.)

A whole world of delicious meals is yours when you are willing to make pasta at home. And, I might add, no one in my family is overweight despite the many delicious pasta dishes we habitually eat, from *Tagliolini colla Crocia* to Lasagna, from ravioli to *Manicotti di Purim*, and dozens of others.

Even though in Italy 1 egg is the traditional amount recommended per serving for *pasta asciutta* (macaroni, lasagna, and so on) and half an egg per serving for liquid soups, I find these amounts excessive and definitely recommend no more than 1 egg for every 1½ to 2 servings for *pasta asciutta* and 1 egg for every 3 to 4 servings for liquid soups.

Some use water and salt in making noodles. In my mother's household adding water or anything else to the two basic ingredients—eggs and flour—was blasphemous, and I never dared to tempt fate! One practical advantage of this method is that cooked pasta made without water and salt will not be soggy the next day—and many Jewish recipes call for pasta to be cooked ahead of time.

The cooking technique is quite simple. One good rule is to use 1 quart water and ½ tablespoon salt for each serving of pasta, although one should bear in mind that there is nothing ironclad about these measurements. Pasta should be added to rapidly boiling water at the same time that salt is added. Salt will prevent the boiling process from slowing down when the pasta is added, which is what causes some of the noodles to stick together. Incidentally, this method of cooking is valid for any kind of pasta, be it homemade or store-bought, including spaghetti, macaroni, and so on. But homemade pasta or cut, store-bought pasta such as *mostaccioli* and *rigatoni* must be drained thoroughly in a colander before dressing with sauce, whereas spaghetti is lifted from the cooking water with a long-handled, two-tined kitchen fork and dropped directly into the serving bowl. The slow passage from the cooking water to the bowl is all that's needed for a perfectly drained spaghetti that is neither too watery nor too dry.

The cooking time for homemade pasta varies according to thickness, shape, and degree of dryness. It ranges from a few seconds to 6 minutes.

With respect to hard pasta, I do want to emphasize that even though it is made with the same durum flour, the texture and even the taste change greatly from one cut to another. Therefore, the cuts are not always interchangeable. When a recipe calls for pasta cooked al dente, it means slightly underdone, although not quite hard. Pasta that is not mushy is not only more pleasant to the palate but definitively more digestible.

Basic Recipe for Homemade Pasta

ricetta base per pasta fatta in casa

2½ to 3 cups unbleached flour

4 eggs, slightly beaten

Mound part of the flour on a large board or other working surface and make a well at the center. Pour in the eggs. With the aid of a fork, mix the eggs and flour very gradually until a soft paste is formed. With your fingers mix in enough additional flour to make a firm, but not too hard, dough. Knead for about 5 minutes, or until the dough is smooth. Place in an unfloured dish; cover with an inverted dish and let rest in the refrigerator for about ½ hour.

Take half the dough, knead it lightly, and shape into a ball. Place on a well-floured board. With the palms of your hands flatten the ball, keeping the round shape, and sprinkle with flour. With the rolling pin, begin to thin the disk out in all directions, trying not to lose the round shape. Continue to sprinkle with flour as it becomes necessary, so that the dough does not stick to the rolling pin. As soon as the disk of dough is thin enough to be rolled *around* the rolling pin do so. Starting from the end farthest from you, begin to roll the dough toward you, using small, even strokes back and forth, at the same time as you swiftly slide your hands inward toward the center and outward to the edges of the pin. When the sheet is all rolled around the pin, *push* the pin away from you to your arm's length; then vigorously *roll* it back toward you, so that one side of the sheet flaps several times over the board. Turn the pin 90 degrees and unroll the sheet from it. Repeat as many times as needed for the desired thinness. Repeat with the other half of the dough and use as directed in each individual recipe.

serves from 6 to 16, depending on the different uses made of it

Homemade Pasta Made by Hand-Operated Machine

pasta fatta in casa a macchina

Make a dough, using the method described in the previous recipe, or by mixing eggs and flour in a bowl. Knead over a well-floured board, adding flour until you have a very firm dough. There is no need to make it smooth because the machine will take care of that. Place in an unfloured dish; cover with an inverted dish and let rest in the refrigerator for about ½ hour.

Take one-quarter of the dough at a time and begin the thinning. With the rollers set at the first slot (farthest apart), feed the dough between the rollers while turning the crank. If some of the dough sticks to the rollers or to the machine, that means the dough is too soft and more flour must be added. Fold and feed with the rollers set at the same slot 3 to 4 times, until the sheet comes out in one piece (but not too smooth). Move on to the second slot and feed the sheet only once. Keep on moving until the desired thinness is obtained. For *lasagne* or *fettuccine*, you will stop at the next to the last slot. For *taglierini* or *calzonicchi*, go through the last slot once, wait a few seconds, and then feed the sheet into the last slot again. (Pasta made with only eggs and flour is very elastic and tends to shrink. However, the second time through it keeps its shape better.)

Repeat with the remaining pasta, using one-quarter of the original quantity each time. Use as directed in each individual recipe.

serves 6 to 16, depending on the different uses made of it

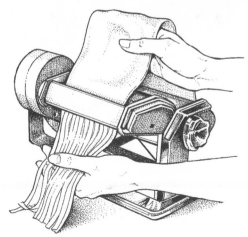

Ziti in White Sauce

maccheroni colla besciamella

This is a typical dairy pasta specialty served as a first course in the homes of the Jews from Padua, where I first tasted it.

1 pound ziti
½ cup butter
5 tablespoons unbleached flour
2 cups hot milk
1 cup heavy cream
½ cup freshly grated Parmesan cheese
Salt
White pepper

Cook the pasta according to the directions on the package. Meanwhile, prepare a white sauce with 5 tablespoons butter, the flour and milk, as described on page 273. Remove the sauce from the heat; add the heavy cream, Parmesan cheese, and salt and pepper to taste.

Drain the ziti and combine with the 3 remaining tablespoons butter. Add the white sauce and mix well.

Transfer to an overproof, buttered serving dish and place in a 450°F oven for 9 to 10 minutes.

serves 6

Rigatoni with Butter and Cheese

le pastone

This is the one dish liked by everybody in my mother's household. In fact, when nothing else seemed to appeal to any of us, Mother would make *Le Pastone*, and—lo and behold!—the dreaded "I'm not hungry" wouldn't be heard anymore.

6 quarts water
1-pound package imported Italian rigatoni
3 tablespoons salt
¾ cup unsalted butter, at room temperature

Bring the water to a boil. Add the rigatoni and salt and stir with a long-handled spoon until boiling resumes. Cook, uncovered, stirring occasionally, for 15 to 20 minutes or until the pasta is quite tender but not mushy.

Heat a large bowl and slice the butter into it. Take ¼ cup boiling water from the pasta pot and add to the bowl. Stir to melt the butter.

1 cup freshly grated imported Parmesan cheese

Drain the pasta and immediately pour it over the butter. Toss until all the pasta is coated with butter. Sprinkle Parmesan cheese over it and toss again until the pasta is coated with cheese. Serve immediately.

serves 6

Thin Egg Noodles with Artichokes
tagliolini coi carciofi

6 medium artichokes
½ cup olive oil
Salt
Freshly ground black pepper
Homemade pasta made with 4 eggs and 2½ to 3 cups flour
6 quarts water

Trim the artichokes as described on page 40, making sure to remove any choke. Cut the trimmed artichokes into very thin wedges. Heat the oil in a large skillet and add the artichokes. Season with salt and pepper to taste.

Cook over moderately high heat, stirring frequently for approximately 5 minutes. Lower the heat to medium and cook, stirring occasionally, another 5 to 10 minutes, depending on the freshness of the artichokes.

Roll the dough thin and cut into *tagliolini* as fine as possible.

Bring the water with 2 tablespoons salt to a boil. Add the *tagliolini* and stir. When boiling resumes, cook 2 minutes.

Drain and transfer to the skillet with the artichokes. Toss until the tagliolini are coated with oil and the artichokes are well distributed.

serves 6

Thin Egg Noodles with Brusco Sauce

taglierini col brodo brusco

> In some parts of Italy, Jews serve *taglierini* on the eve of Yom Kippur as a first course. It is generally served cold and can be served as a refreshing summer side dish. It is also ideal for Shabbat meals since it can be prepared a day ahead of time. I make it both hot and cold and find it good either way.

Homemade pasta made with 3 eggs and 2 cups flour

4 quarts water

2 tablespoons salt

½ cup *Olio di Arrosto* (page 126)

1½ cups Brusco Sauce (see following recipe)

Roll the pasta as thin as you can. If you roll it by hand, cut the roll, with a very sharp knife, into the thinnest slices possible. Toss the slices to unravel the *taglierini* and spread over a clean cloth to dry completely.

If you use the pasta machine, repeat the last thinning twice and cut with the smaller cutters.

Bring the water to a boil. Add the *taglierini* and salt and cook just until boiling resumes (a few seconds). Drain and place on a large plate. Add the oil and quickly toss to coat the *taglierini*. Set aside to cool for ½ hour. Combine with the Brusco Sauce and serve.

serves 6

Brusco Sauce

brodo brusco

>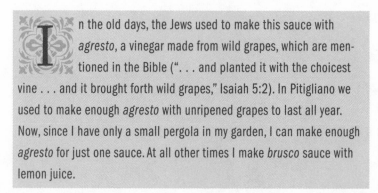
> In the old days, the Jews used to make this sauce with *agresto*, a vinegar made from wild grapes, which are mentioned in the Bible (". . . and planted it with the choicest vine . . . and it brought forth wild grapes," Isaiah 5:2). In Pitigliano we used to make enough *agresto* with unripened grapes to last all year. Now, since I have only a small pergola in my garden, I can make enough *agresto* for just one sauce. At all other times I make *brusco* sauce with lemon juice.

1 egg	Gently beat together the egg, egg yolk, and lemon juice. Grad-
1 egg yolk	ually add the stock, stirring. Pour into the top of a double boiler
Juice of 1 lemon	and cook over hot water, stirring constantly, until thickened.
1 cup beef stock	The sauce should have the consistency of a custard, without

1 egg

1 egg yolk

Juice of 1 lemon

1 cup beef stock

Gently beat together the egg, egg yolk, and lemon juice. Gradually add the stock, stirring. Pour into the top of a double boiler and cook over hot water, stirring constantly, until thickened. The sauce should have the consistency of a custard, without separating. Remove from the heat before it begins to boil and set aside to cool.

yields 1½ cups

Meat Sauce

sugo di carne

½ cup *Olio di Arrosto* (page 126)

1 medium onion, quartered

1 medium carrot, peeled and cut up

1 stalk celery, strings removed, cut up

1 large sprig Italian parsley

1 pound lean ground beef

½ cup dry white wine

⅔ cup tomato paste

1½ cups beef broth or water

Salt

Place the oil in a large saucepan. Chop the onion, carrot, celery, and parsley together, very fine. Add to the saucepan with the oil and lightly brown for 2 to 3 minutes, stirring occasionally.

Add the meat and brown thoroughly, stirring frequently.

Add the wine and raise the heat to let the wine evaporate completely.

Add the tomato paste and cook over high heat for 1 to 2 minutes, stirring frequently.

Add the beef stock or water and cook, covered, over very low heat for ½ hour to 45 minutes, stirring occasionally. Add salt to taste. The sauce should be nice and thick; if it looks too liquid, cook it a few minutes longer until it loses its excess liquid.

yields 3 cups / serves 6

Tortellini in Heavy Cream

tortellini alla panna

15 dozen *Tortellini
Vegetariani*
(see following recipe)
6 quarts boiling water
3 tablespoons salt
1 pint heavy dairy cream
1 cup freshly grated Italian
Parmesan cheese

Drop the tortellini into a large pot with the rapidly boiling water. Add the salt and stir gently. When boiling resumes, lower the heat and cook, uncovered, 5 to 6 minutes. Drain well.

Heat the cream in a large skillet, but do not allow it to boil. Add the drained tortellini and gently stir over moderate heat, until most of the cream has been absorbed by the tortellini. Turn off the heat, add half the Parmesan cheese, and stir to combine. Serve immediately with the remaining Parmesan cheese in a separate dish.

serves 6

Vegetarian Tortellini

tortellini vegetariani

1 pound fresh green beans
Olive oil
2 cloves garlic
Salt
Freshly ground black pepper
¾ cup water
Dash or two nutmeg
1 tablespoon freshly
chopped Italian parsley
¾ cup walnut meats,
chopped fine
¾ cup freshly grated Italian
Parmesan cheese
Homemade pasta made
with 4 eggs and 3 cups flour

Trim and wash the green beans and place in a saucepan with 1 tablespoon oil, garlic, salt, pepper, and water. Cook over moderate heat, uncovered, for 5 to 10 minutes, depending on the quality and freshness of the beans. Let cool, then puree in a blender or processor. Transfer to a medium bowl and add the nutmeg, parsley, walnuts, and Parmesan cheese. Mix to combine.

Take half the pasta and roll it thin. Cut into 2-inch squares. Spread ¼ teaspoon filling diagonally on each square; fold into a triangle along the line of the filling and fold once more. Lift the little stuffed roll and wrap it around your finger; squeeze the farthest points together. Toss on a large floured cloth where tortellini fit without touching. Continue until you have finished the first half of the pasta, then repeat with the second half until you have used up either the pasta or filling or both.

yields approximately 15 dozen

Meat Tortellini

tortellini di carne

Olive oil
½ medium onion, sliced
½ clove garlic, sliced
½ chicken breast, cubed
¼ pound lean veal, cubed
Salt
Freshly ground black pepper
2 boiled chestnuts (see following recipe), mashed
1 teaspoon Bac-Os, crushed
2 tablespoons beef broth
2 tablespoons breadcrumbs
1 egg, slightly beaten
Homemade pasta made with 4 eggs and 3 cups flour

Heat 2 tablespoons oil in a medium skillet with the onion and garlic. When the garlic becomes lightly golden, add the meats and small amounts of salt and pepper and cook over moderate heat about 10 minutes, stirring occasionally. Remove from the heat and chop very fine. Transfer to a medium bowl and combine with the other filling ingredients. Taste and correct seasoning if necessary.

Take half the pasta and roll it thin. Cut into 2-inch squares. Spread ¼ teaspoon filling diagonally on each square; fold into a triangle along the line of the filling, and fold once more. Lift the little stuffed roll and wrap it around your finger; squeeze the farthest points together. Toss over a large floured cloth where tortellini can fit without touching. Continue until you have finished the first half of the pasta, then repeat with the second half until you have used up either the pasta or filling or both.

yields about 15 dozen

Boiled Chestnuts

ballotte

2 pounds fresh chestnuts (4 to 6 dozen)
1 tablespoon salt
Water

Place the chestnuts in a saucepan with the salt and enough water to cover. Bring to a boil, then reduce the heat and simmer, covered, for 45 minutes.

With a sharp knife cut each chestnut in half, not quite going through the bottom, so that the halves remain attached to one another. Serve immediately and let each person scoop out the pulp with a small spoon or a dull butter knife.

serves 6

Meat Tortellini with Mushroom Sauce

tortellini di carne ai funghi

15 dozen *Tortellini di Carne*
(page 145)

6 quarts boiling water

3 tablespoons salt

Mushroom Sauce
(see following recipe)

Drop the tortellini into a large pot with the rapidly boiling water. Add the salt and stir gently. When boiling resumes, lower the heat and cook, uncovered, 5 to 6 minutes.

Meanwhile, heat the sauce in a very large skillet. Drain the tortellini and transfer them to the skillet with the sauce. Shake the skillet, then gently stir until the tortellini are well coated with sauce. Serve immediately.

serves 6

Mushroom Sauce

salsa di funghi

½ ounce imported dried
porcini mushrooms

1 cup warm water

2 pounds small,
firm white mushrooms

6 tablespoons olive oil

2 tablespoons finely
chopped onion

1 clove garlic, minced

1 tablespoon freshly
chopped Italian parsley

¼ teaspoon dried savory

1 teaspoon salt

¼ teaspoon freshly ground
black pepper

2 tablespoons tomato paste

½ cup dry white wine

Soak the dried mushrooms in the warm water for 10 minutes. Lift them with a fork, reserving the water. Remove and discard any parts that still have sand attached and coarsely chop.

Wash, drain, and thinly slice the fresh mushrooms.

Place the oil, onion, garlic, parsley, savory, salt, and pepper in a saucepan, and sauté for ½ minute. Add the dried and fresh mushrooms and cook over moderately high heat for 5 minutes, stirring frequently. Add the tomato paste and wine and cook over high heat, stirring, until the alcohol has evaporated, about 2 minutes.

Add the reserved water from the soaked mushrooms, taking care not to include any sand that might remain at the bottom of the cup. Cook over high heat 5 minutes longer or until the liquid is greatly reduced.

yields about 3 cups / serves 6 to 8

Spinach Panzotti

panzotti di spinaci

> **P**anzotti look like overgrown tortellini. Like tortellini they are somewhat laborious to prepare because they require wrapping by hand one by one. However, you can master this art with a little practice, and the rewards will be great.

2 pounds small-leaved spinach

Salt

2 tablespoons butter

1 small onion, chopped fine

1 small clove garlic, minced

¼ teaspoon powdered marjoram

⅔ cup ricotta, moisture reduced

⅔ cup freshly grated Italian Parmesan cheese

2 eggs, slightly beaten

Homemade pasta made with 4 eggs and 3 cups flour

Use only the leafy parts of the spinach. Rinse in cold water as many times as necessary to rid the leaves of any sand. Place in a large pot with no water other than the water retained by the leaves from washing. Add a pinch of salt and cook covered over high heat for 5 to 6 minutes. Drain and squeeze all the water out. Chop the spinach very fine.

Heat the butter in a skillet and sauté the onion and garlic in it for approximately 1 minute. Add the spinach, marjoram, and 1 teaspoon salt and cook, stirring, 2 minutes more or until the spinach looks quite dry. Transfer to a bowl and combine with the ricotta, Parmesan cheese, and eggs. Taste and correct seasoning if necessary.

Roll the pasta to medium thinness (one half at a time). Cut into 3-inch squares. Fill each square with 1 teaspoon of filling mixture, and fold diagonally into triangles. When the triangles are all lined up, take one and fold once more in the same direction; then pick up the two ends and bring them together. Press firmly to seal. Repeat with the rest of the stuffed triangles until they have all become *panzotti*, big bellies.

yields 7 to 8 dozen

Spinach Panzotti with Walnut Sauce

panzotti di spinaci con salsa di noci

7 to 8 dozen *Panzotti* (page 147)

3 tablespoons salt

6 quarts rapidly boiling water

2½ cups Walnut Sauce, at room temperature (see following recipe)

Add the panzotti and salt to the rapidly boiling water, and cook, uncovered, 3 to 4 minutes or until desired tenderness.

Warm a large serving bowl and place half the sauce into it. Drain the panzotti and add to the bowl. Add the remaining sauce and toss gently just until all the panzotti are coated. Serve immediately.

serve 6 to 8

Walnut Sauce

salsa di noci

This sauce is a delightful complement to any pasta dish, but it is especially suited for *Panzotti di Spinaci.*

2 cups healthy walnut meats

Boiling hot water

½ cup milk

¾ cup cold water

¼ cup granulated sugar

¼ teaspoon cinnamon

¼ teaspoon salt

⅓ cup freshly grated Italian Parmesan cheese

Soak the walnut meats in boiling hot water to cover for 1 hour or longer. Drain and rinse in cold water. Place in the work bowl of a blender or processor and start the motor. With the motor still on, add the milk, cold water, sugar, cinnamon, and salt and process until you have a cream. Add the Parmesan cheese and process just to mix.

yields about 2 cups / serves 6

Squash Ravioli with Sage Oil

tortelli di zucca alla salvia

2½ pounds butternut
squash
½ cup chopped onion
Olive oil
Salt
Freshly ground black
pepper
1 tablespoon freshly
chopped Italian parsley
1 egg, slightly beaten
1 egg yolk
Homemade pasta made
with 4 eggs and 2½ to
3 cups flour
¼ cup firmly pressed sage
leaves
¼ cup dry white wine
6 quarts water

Peel the squash and cut in half, lengthwise. Remove all the seeds and scrape to remove the stringy parts as well. Cut into approximately 1-inch cubes and place in a skillet with the onion, 2 tablespoons oil, 1 teaspoon salt, and a dash or two of pepper. Add ¼ cup water and cook over moderate heat, covered, for 15 minutes. Uncover and continue to cook, stirring, until most of the liquid has evaporated and the squash is reduced to a coarse puree.

Remove from the heat and let cool a little. Add the parsley, egg, and egg yolk, and stir to combine. Return to a very low heat and stir until the egg has lost its rawness and the puree has thickened.

Take one quarter of the dough and roll it thin. Place it over a floured cloth and lightly brush the surface with a pastry brush dipped in cold water to maintain moisture. Take half the filling and place mounds of it in straight lines about 2 inches apart. Roll thin another quarter of the pasta and place it loosely over the mounds. Press around the mounds with your fingers. With an Italian pastry wheel, press along the furrows, cutting and sealing at the same time. Repeat with the remaining pasta and filling.

Place ¾ cup oil, sage, and small amounts of salt and pepper into a large skillet. Heat the oil and sauté the sage for 1 minute or two. Sprinkle with wine and cook until the wine has completely evaporated. Remove and discard the sage, but retain the salt and pepper together with the oil.

Bring the water with 3 tablespoons salt to a boil. Add the ravioli and cook 5 minutes, or until desired tenderness. Drain thoroughly and add to the skillet with the sage oil. Stir until all the ravioli are coated with oil and serve.

serves 6 to 8

Adele's Homemade Ravioli

i tortelli della pora adele

Adele was a Christian girl who lived in the Jewish Ghetto and had always worked as a mother's helper in Jewish families. Even after she had grown up, had married, and had children of her own, she was willing to help Mamma whenever she was asked. One day, a few weeks before we set out for the woods to escape the Nazi fascists, she knocked at our door with a bundle hidden under her shawl. Upon entering the kitchen, she cautiously walked toward the table and put her bundle on it. Then she painstakingly unfolded the large cloth napkin and revealed an enormous plate of steaming homemade ravioli.

It was a punishable crime to help the Jews at that time, and a double crime to provide them with food other than what was allotted by the rationing system. Yet Adele knew that we often went hungry, and, bless her, she cared for us. She wouldn't have been able to enjoy the special meal she had prepared for her family had she not shared it with us. We dove into the plate like vultures, oblivious of Adele who stood there watching us with her sweet satisfied smile.

When we came back from our odyssey nearly one year later, Adele was no longer among the living—a victim of the bombings. Even though tortelli prepared in this manner are by no means Adele's invention, in honor of her generous gesture we have called them "Adele's Tortelli" ever since.

1 pound small-leaved bulk spinach	Use only the leafy part of the spinach, discarding all stems. Wash in cold water as many times as needed so that no trace of sand remains. Place in a pot with no water other than the water retained from washing. Add a pinch of salt and cook, covered, 5 to 6 minutes. Lift with a fork and squeeze all the water out. (It helps to wrap the spinach in a piece of cheesecloth and then to wring it.) Chop the spinach very fine.
Salt	
Olive oil	
1 small onion, chopped fine	
Freshly ground black pepper	Heat 2 tablespoons oil in a skillet with the onion and sauté for about 1 minute. Add the spinach and small amounts of salt and pepper. Cook over low heat, stirring frequently, approximately
2 cups ricotta, moisture reduced	

1 tablespoon freshly chopped Italian parsley

½ cup shredded Pecorino Toscano or Muenster cheese

1 egg, slightly beaten

1 egg yolk

Dash or 2 nutmeg

Homemade pasta made with 4 eggs and 3 cups flour

6 quarts water

3 cups tomato sauce (page 152)

2 minutes, or until the spinach is quite dry. Transfer to a bowl and combine with the ricotta, parsley, Pecorino or Muenster cheese, egg, egg yolk, and nutmeg. Taste and correct seasoning if necessary.

Take one quarter of the dough, roll it thin, and place over a floured cloth. With a pastry brush dipped in cold water, lightly brush the top of the sheet to maintain moisture. Take half the filling mixture and place mounds of it on the sheet in straight lines about 2 inches apart, measuring from the center of the mounds. You should obtain 4 to 5 dozen of them. Roll out another quarter of the dough and place loosely over the mounds. Press the dough around the mounds with your fingers. With an Italian pastry wheel, press along the furrows, cutting and sealing at the same time. Continue to make the ravioli with the remaining pasta and filling.

Bring the water to a boil. Add the ravioli and 3 tablespoons salt. Stir gently until boiling resumes. Cook, uncovered, 4 to 5 minutes, or until desired tenderness. Drain well and dress with hot tomato sauce.

serves 6 to 8

Classic Tomato Sauce

salsa di pomodoro classica

½ cup extra virgin olive oil

1 large clove garlic, minced

½ medium onion, chopped fine

1 small carrot, peeled and chopped

1 small stalk celery with leaves, chopped fine

1½ teaspoons salt

¼ teaspoon freshly ground black pepper

¼ teaspoon dried oregano

3 cups fresh or canned peeled tomatoes, drained and chopped

1 tablespoon finely chopped Italian parsley

Heat ¼ cup oil in a large saucepan. Add the garlic, onion, carrot, celery, salt, pepper, and oregano and sauté over moderately high heat, stirring, until the herbs have acquired a golden color.

Add the peeled tomatoes, lower the heat, and cook uncovered, stirring from time to time, ½ hour or until the sauce is thick and flavorful.

Remove from the heat, add the parsley and the remaining oil and stir.

yields approximately 3 cups / serves 6 to 8

Purim Ravioli

ravioli di purim

I suppose that the tradition of making spinach ravioli on Purim originated because Purim comes in the season when spinach is tender, flavorful, and abundant. Now we can make spinach ravioli throughout the year, but they never taste as good as they do around Purim.

2 pounds small-leaved bulk spinach

Salt

2 tablespoons olive oil

1 small onion, quartered

1 small carrot, peeled and coarsely chopped

½ chicken breast, cubed

Freshly ground black pepper

1 tablespoon unbleached flour

Homemade pasta made with 4 eggs and 2½ cups flour

6 quarts water

3 cups Marinara or Meat Sauce (pages 154 and 143)

Remove the roots and stems from the spinach and save for later use (see *Testine*). Rinse the spinach in cold water as many times as necessary to rid it of any sand. Place in a pot with no water other than the water the spinach retains from washing. Add a pinch of salt and cook, covered, for about 5 minutes. Transfer to a colander and set aside to drain.

Place the oil, onion, carrot, and chicken breast in a large skillet. Add 1 teaspoon salt and ⅛ teaspoon pepper and cook over moderate heat for 4 to 5 minutes, stirring frequently. Add the spinach and cook, stirring, 5 minutes longer or until most of the liquid has evaporated. Add the flour and stir 1 more minute. Remove from the heat; cool for 5 to 6 minutes, then chop very fine.

Roll half the dough paper thin and place over a floured cloth. With a feather brush dipped in cold water lightly brush the top to maintain moisture. Place mounds of the spinach mixture on the dough in straight lines about 2 inches apart (measurements are from the center of the mounds), making 8 to 9 dozen. Roll out the other half of the dough paper thin and place loosely over the sheet with the mounds. Press the dough around the mounds with your fingers. With an Italian pastry wheel, press along the furrows, cutting and sealing at the same time.

Bring the water to a boil. Add the ravioli and 3 tablespoons salt. Stir until boiling resumes. Cook 4 to 5 minutes, uncovered. Drain and dress with marinara or meat sauce.

serves 6 to 8

Marinara Sauce

salsa marinara

¼ cup olive oil

3 large cloves garlic

2½ cups canned or fresh peeled tomatoes, drained and chopped

½ teaspoon crushed red pepper

½ teaspoon salt

¼ teaspoon dried oregano

1 tablespoon freshly chopped Italian parsley

¼ cup extra virgin olive oil

Heat ¼ cup oil in a saucepan with 1 clove garlic and sauté until the garlic is golden brown. Discard the garlic, add the tomatoes, pepper, salt, and oregano and cook over low heat, uncovered, for ¾ to 1 hour, stirring occasionally.

A moment before removing from the heat, add the parsley, extra virgin olive oil, and the remaining 2 cloves garlic passed through a garlic press, and stir.

serves 6

Crusty Fettuccine (Pharaoh's Wheel)

tagliolini colla crocia (ruota di faraone)

 agliolini colla Crocia is traditionally served on Shabbat B'shallach in all parts of Italy, and is associated by Italian Jews with the passage of the Israelites through the Red Sea and their deliverance from the Egyptians, although the preparation of it, and even the name, varies from place to place.

Homemade pasta made with 4 eggs and 2½ to 3 cups flour

6 quarts water

3 tablespoons salt

Roll the dough not too thin and fold as you would for a jelly roll, 2½ inches wide. Cut ⅙-inch-wide slices and toss to unfold the noodles.

Bring the water to a boil. Add the *tagliolini* and salt; when boiling resumes, cook for 1 minute.

3 cups Meat Sauce (page 143)

½ cup diced Pickled Tongue or beef salami or Beef Sausage

¼ cup chicken fat or bone marrow

½ cup dark, seedless raisins (optional)

½ cup whole almonds (optional)

½ cup *pignoli* (pine nuts) (optional)

Drain and place in a large bowl with the meat sauce and the diced cold cuts. Toss quickly to distribute the dressing evenly.

Place in a round ovenproof baking dish, well greased with fat. If using raisins and nuts, make layers, alternating the pasta with a mixture of raisins and nuts. Bake in a 350°F oven for 1 to 1½ hours, or until a nice crust is formed on all sides. Invert over a serving dish and bring to the table.

serves 6 to 8

Crusty Fettuccine with Mushroom Sauce

tagliolini colla crocia ai funghi

Homemade pasta made with 4 eggs and 2½ to 3 cups flour

6 quarts water

3 tablespoons salt

3 cups Mushroom Sauce (page 146)

Olive oil

Roll the dough not too thin and cut into fettuccine.

Bring the water to a boil. Add the pasta and salt; when boiling resumes, cook for 1 minute.

Drain well, place in a large bowl with the mushroom sauce, and toss quickly to distribute the sauce evenly. Loosely cover with a clean towel and set aside for a few hours.

Heat 3 tablespoons oil in a large frying pan. Pour half the dressed fettuccine in the pan and flatten down with a spatula. Cook over very low heat, shaking the pan from time to time, until a golden crust is formed at the bottom. Turn with a dish and cook until golden on the other side. Repeat with the other half of the fettuccine.

serves 6 to 8

Vermicelli Primavera

This dish has become so popular in America that it doesn't require any translation. You can use any pasta with primavera sauce, but I find that the marriage between such a delicate sauce and vermicelli, or fidelini, or even capellini, is the most successful. The vegetables one chooses to use also can vary according to season and taste. Here is only one example.

6 tablespoons unsalted butter

½ cup small cauliflower florets

½ cup small broccoli florets

½ cup shredded carrots

¼ cup shelled tiny peas

¼ cup diced pink tomato

Salt

White pepper

1½ tablespoons unbleached flour

1½ cups hot milk

4 quarts water

1 pound vermicelli, fidelini, or capellini

½ cup freshly grated Italian Parmesan cheese

Heat the butter in a large skillet. Add the vegetables and small amounts of salt and pepper, and sauté for 1 minute, stirring frequently. Add the flour, stir, and cook another 2 minutes. Add the hot milk all at once and stir to prevent lumps. Cook 3 more minutes, stirring occasionally.

Bring the water to a rapid boil. Add the pasta and 2 tablespoons salt at the same time. Stir and cook 1 to 6 minutes (depending on the cut of the pasta) or until the pasta is *al dente*. Drain very well and transfer to the skillet with the primavera sauce. Add half the cheese and toss over the heat until well coated. Serve immediately with the remaining cheese in a separate dish.

serves 4 to 6

Linguine with Tomato and Basil Sauce

linguine al pomodoro e basilico

4 tablespoons olive oil

2 large cloves garlic, crushed

2 pounds ripe, firm tomatoes, peeled and cut up or one 2-pound can peeled plum tomatoes, drained and cut up

Salt

Dash or two ground red pepper

¼ cup firmly packed whole tiny or shredded large basil leaves

4 tablespoons extra virgin olive oil

4 quarts water

1 pound linguine

Heat the oil in a large saucepan. Add the garlic and sauté until golden, then discard.

Add the tomatoes, 1½ teaspoons salt, and a dash or two red pepper and cook over moderately high heat, stirring frequently, 6 to 7 minutes.

Add the basil and cook 1 minute longer. Remove from the heat and add the extra virgin olive oil.

Meanwhile bring the water to a rapid boil. Add the pasta and 2 tablespoons salt at the same time. Stir until boiling resumes. Cook over moderately high heat for 10 minutes or until desired tenderness.

Place the tomato and basil sauce into a heated serving bowl. Drain the linguine very thoroughly and add to the bowl with the sauce. Toss until all the pasta is coated with sauce and serve.

serves 4 to 6

Penne with Angry Sauce

penne all'arrabbiata

4 quarts water

1 pound penne *lisce*

2 tablespoons salt

2 cups Angry Sauce (recipe follows)

½ cup grated Romano cheese (optional)

Bring the water to a boil. Add the penne and salt and stir until boiling resumes. Cook, uncovered, 7 minutes, stirring occasionally. Meanwhile place the sauce in a large pot and heat through.

Drain the penne thoroughly and add to the pot with the sauce. Cook, stirring from time to time, 5 additional minutes, or until the pasta is slightly underdone and coated by a thick sauce.

If you opt for the cheese, use less salt or no salt at all in the cooking water since Romano is quite salty itself. Add half the cheese a moment before removing from the heat and stir to mix. Serve immediately with the remaining cheese in a separate dish.

serves 6

Angry Sauce
salsa arrabbiata

 rrabbiata, angry, in this case means spicy and hot. The sauce is so "angry" that it bites your tongue.

½ cup olive oil

½ to 1 teaspoon crushed red pepper

½ teaspoon salt

¼ teaspoon dried oregano

¼ teaspoon powdered sage

2 large cloves garlic, passed through a garlic press or minced

6 anchovy fillets

½ cup very dry red wine

2 cups peeled ripe tomatoes or canned peeled tomatoes, drained and coarsely chopped

Heat the oil in a saucepan over moderate heat; add the pepper, salt, oregano, sage, garlic, and anchovies and stir a little. When the garlic looks golden (but not browned) and the anchovies are almost melted, add the wine and raise the heat to let the alcohol evaporate.

Add the tomatoes and cook, over medium heat, for 10 to 15 minutes, stirring occasionally. Use immediately or cool before storing in a tightly covered jar in the refrigerator where it keeps for several weeks without the need to freeze it.

yields approximately 2 cups

Spaghetti with Pesto Sauce

spaghetti al pesto

4 quarts water

2 tablespoons salt

1 pound spaghetti

1½ cups pesto sauce
(see following recipe)

½ cup freshly grated Italian
Parmesan cheese

Bring the water to a rapid boil. Add the salt and spaghetti at the same time to prevent the water from slowing down. Cook *al dente*.

Meanwhile, warm a serving bowl and place half the sauce into it. Drain the spaghetti not too dry and transfer into the bowl with the sauce. Add the remaining sauce and toss quickly to combine. Serve immediately with Parmesan in a separate dish.

serves 4 to 6

Processor or Blender Pesto

pesto col frullatore

1 cup firmly packed fresh
basil leaves

6 large sprigs Italian
parsley, stems removed

2 cloves garlic, coarsely
cut up

½ cup *pignoli* (pine nuts) or
walnut meats

¾ cup extra virgin olive oil

½ cup grated Italian
Parmesan cheese

¼ cup grated Sardo or
Romano cheese

Salt

Freshly ground black
pepper

If you must, wash the basil leaves and pat them dry with paper towels. However, if the basil is clean, do without washing, since water will cause it to darken.

Place the basil in the processor together with the parsley and garlic. Process just until all is chopped fine. Add the nuts and chop a few seconds longer.

Transfer to a sauce bowl. Add the oil and the two cheeses and stir to combine. Add salt and pepper to taste and store in the refrigerator, where it will keep fresh up to 2 weeks. Let it stand at room temperature for at least 1 hour before using.

NOTE: If you don't own a food processor but have a blender, you might have to add ½ cup water to the bowl before processing. The parsley will help preserve the bright green. In any case, use as soon as possible.

yields approximately 1½ cups

Spaghetti with Tuna Sauce

spaghetti al tonno

This is a delightful summer first course. When I went to see a friend in Leghorn to get her marvelous old Jewish recipes, she prepared an all-fish lunch, starting with this tasty spaghetti. She told me that she always serves it when she has unexpected guests since it is so easy to prepare, yet so delicious. Indeed my husband and I found that meal, served on the terrace of her villa overlooking the Tyrrhenian Sea, absolutely heavenly.

4 quarts water

One 1-pound package imported Italian regular spaghetti

2 tablespoons salt

Tuna Sauce, hot (recipe follows)

1 cup freshly grated imported Parmesan cheese (optional)

Bring the water to a boil. Add the spaghetti and salt and cook *al dente* (slightly underdone and chewy). Begin to taste for the proper texture after 10 minutes and every minute thereafter.

Drain and dress with half the tuna sauce. Serve immediately with the remaining sauce in a separate sauce dish. Cheese should also be served separately because not everyone likes Parmesan with fish.

serves 6

Tuna Sauce for Spaghetti

salsa di tonno per spaghetti

1 clove garlic

2 large sprigs Italian parsley

1 tablespoon shredded fresh basil leaves, or 1 teaspoon dried

¾ cup olive oil

Salt

¼ teaspoon crushed hot red pepper

One 6½-ounce can light chunk tuna packed in oil, drained and chopped

2 heaping tablespoons tomato paste

½ cup dry red wine

2 cups canned peeled tomatoes, drained and chopped

Finely chop together the garlic, parsley, and basil. Place half this mixture in a saucepan with half the oil. Add ¼ teaspoon salt and the red pepper and cook over medium heat for 1 minute or two (do not let the garlic get brown). Add the tuna and tomato paste and stir with a wooden spoon 1 minute more. Add the wine and stir, over high heat, until the tomato paste is dissolved. Add the tomatoes and cook 5 minutes longer. Taste for salt and correct if necessary.

Remove from the heat and add the remaining herb mixture and the remaining oil.

serves 6

Macaroni Timbale

timballo di maccheroni

Unbleached flour
¼ cup sugar
Salt
¼ cup butter, chilled
1 egg, slightly beaten
2 egg yolks
1 pound firm white mushrooms, washed and sliced
1 tablespoon coarsely chopped Italian parsley
1 small clove garlic, minced
Freshly ground black pepper
Olive oil
½ cup water
2 teaspoons dehydrated minced onion
1 cup freshly shelled or frozen tiny peas
½ pound elbow macaroni, short ziti, or rigatoni
Butter
1½ cups hot milk
¼ cup grated Parmesan cheese
½ cup shredded mozzarella cheese

Sift together 1¼ cups flour, the sugar, and ¼ teaspoon salt. Shred the chilled butter over the mixture, then add 1 egg and 1 egg yolk; quickly mix and form into a ball. Place in a small dish, cover with an inverted dish, and let rest in the refrigerator for at least ½ hour.

Place the mushrooms, parsley, garlic, small amounts of salt and pepper, and 2 tablespoons oil in a saucepan. Cook covered over moderate heat approximately 10 minutes, stirring occasionally.

In a separate saucepan, place the water, onion, 2 tablespoons oil, and small amounts of salt and pepper. Bring to a boil and cook 2 minutes. Add the peas, cover, and cook over moderately high heat 5 more minutes.

Cook the macaroni according to the manufacturer's directions. Drain not too dry and place in a bowl. Add the cooked mushrooms and cooked peas with all their juices and toss to combine.

Heat 3 tablespoons butter with 2 tablespoons flour in a small skillet. Cook 2 minutes, stirring with a wire whisk. Add the hot milk all at once and stir vigorously. Cook 4 minutes longer, stirring occasionally.

Take half the pastry from the refrigerator, form into a ball, and roll it into a disk about 14 inches in diameter. Line a buttered 10-inch pie dish with pastry. Add alternate layers of macaroni and white sauce, sprinkling each layer with the two cheeses. Roll the remaining pastry thin and adjust loosely over the macaroni. Nicely seal and crimp the two disks of pastry together along the border. With a sharp knife make a few slits on top to allow the steam to escape during baking. Beat the remaining egg yolk with 1 teaspoon water and brush the top with the mixture. Bake in a preheated 350°F oven for 30 minutes, or until the top is nicely browned. Serve hot.

serves 6

Tagliatelle Jewish Style (Noodle Kugel)
tagliatelle all'ebraica

Homemade pasta made with 2 eggs and 1½ cups flour or ¾ pound fresh fettuccine

3 quarts water

1½ tablespoons salt

2 tablespoons sugar

2 eggs, slightly beaten

1 cup milk

2 cups ricotta, moisture reduced

½ cup dark, seedless raisins

½ cup *pignoli* (pine nuts)

Grated rind of 1 lemon

¼ teaspoon cinnamon

Dash ginger

4 tablespoons butter

¼ cup fine breadcrumbs

Roll the dough thin and cut into tagliatelle with the largest cutter. Bring the water to a boil. Add the tagliatelle and salt. As soon as boiling resumes, drain the pasta well and place in a large bowl. (If you use store-bought fresh egg noodles cook half the time recommended by the manufacturer.) Add all the other ingredients except the butter and breadcrumbs and mix well to combine.

Butter an ovenproof lasagna dish and coat it with breadcrumbs. Transfer the tagliatelle into it, flatten with a rubber spatula, and dot with butter. Bake in a preheated 350°F oven for approximately 30 minutes. Serve hot or at room temperature.

serves 6

Green Lasagna

lasagne verdi

Many years ago I invited some friends to lunch to try my kosher green lasagna. At first they declined my invitation (being strictly orthodox, they seldom accepted invitations to eat in other people's homes). But when I insisted that I would buy everything new—from pots and pans to tablecloth and dishes—they accepted. They came early, so I prepared everything with their help. We had a lot of fun, and they liked my lasagna so much that they asked to stay for supper to eat the leftovers. Of course I was flattered and delighted that they stayed.

½ cup cooked spinach leaves, drained

2 eggs, slightly beaten

2½ to 3 cups flour

6 quarts water

Salt

4 tablespoons olive oil

3 cups tomato sauce (page 152)

3 cups cheese sauce (page 166)

½ cup freshly grated imported Parmesan cheese

Squeeze most of the liquid out of the spinach. Chop very fine to the consistency of a smooth paste. Make a dough with the spinach, eggs, and flour as needed, following the general directions for homemade pasta. Roll it thin, sprinkling often with flour to avoid sticking. Cut into strips about 5 × 8 inches.

Bring the water to a boil with 3 tablespoons salt. Cook a few strips at a time for 2 minutes, uncovered. Remove from the boiling water with a slotted spoon and drop into a basin of cold water. Drain and spread over a slightly damp cloth.

Coat the bottom of a lasagna baking dish with 2 tablespoons oil and ¼ cup tomato sauce. Place in it one layer of pasta; lightly cover it with tomato sauce and dollops of cheese sauce. Sprinkle with some Parmesan cheese and continue to make layers until you have used up all the pasta and the sauces. Sprinkle the top with the remaining oil and bake in a 400°F oven for approximately 20 minutes. Serve with the remaining Parmesan cheese in a separate dish.

serves 6

Mother's Tomato Sauce

salsa di pomodoro della mamma

hildren usually don't like to see pieces of tomatoes and vegetables floating in their sauce (we certainly didn't!), so our mother used to prepare tomato sauce the following way.

½ medium onion, sliced

½ cup olive oil

3 pounds ripe firm tomatoes, coarsely cut up or 1 large can (2 pounds 3 ounces) peeled plum tomatoes

1 small carrot, peeled and cut up

2 sprigs Italian parsley

1 clove garlic

1 teaspoon salt

3 large basil leaves, or ½ teaspoon dried basil

1 stalk celery with leaves, coarsely cut up

Place the onion and half the oil in a saucepan and cook until the onion is lightly browned.

Add the tomatoes, carrot, parsley, garlic, salt, basil, and celery. Cook, covered, over moderate heat, stirring occasionally, for ½ hour, or until the vegetables are very soft.

Strain through a food mill, taste for salt, and adjust if necessary. (If the sauce is too thin, place on the heat again to thicken.) Remove from the heat, add the remaining oil, and stir.

NOTE: For a marinara or more piquant sauce, just before adding the last oil, add ¼ teaspoon crushed hot red pepper and 1 clove garlic passed through a garlic press or chopped very fine.

yields 3 cups / serves 6 to 8

Cheese Sauce

salsa di formaggi

his recipe lists the cheeses one should use for this very versatile sauce. However, it can be prepared, as I often do, with any kind of cheese. Leftover cheeses are perfect for it.

3 tablespoons butter
3 tablespoons unbleached flour
2 cups hot milk
1 cup cubed mozzarella cheese
1 cup cubed fontina
1 cup cubed provolone

In a heavy-bottomed saucepan, melt the butter over low heat. Add the flour and stir until well combined with the butter. Add the hot milk all at once and keep stirring until the sauce is smooth and thick. Add the cheeses and stir until all the bits are melted. Keep warm until you are ready to use it.

NOTE: If you don't use the sauce right away, you may keep it in the refrigerator for one day. Then leave it at room temperature for several hours before placing it over very low heat and stirring constantly to make sure that it does not stick to the bottom of the pan and burn.

yields about 3 cups

Matza Lasagna with Meat Ragù and Mushroom Sauce

mazzagne con ragù e salsa di funghi

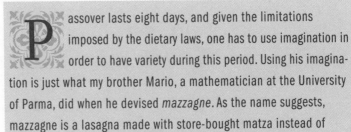assover lasts eight days, and given the limitations imposed by the dietary laws, one has to use imagination in order to have variety during this period. Using his imagination is just what my brother Mario, a mathematician at the University of Parma, did when he devised *mazzagne*. As the name suggests, mazzagne is a lasagna made with store-bought matza instead of the characteristic wide noodles.

Olive oil

2 cups mushroom sauce (page 146) and 1 cup Beef Ragù (page 182)

8 egg matzòt

1 cup beef or chicken broth

Cover the bottom of a lasagna baking dish with a thin film of oil. Make alternate layers of sauces and uncooked matza, ending with a sauce. Pour the broth over the prepared matza lasagna, cover with aluminum foil, and let rest in the refrigerator for 1 hour, or until the matza is quite soaked.

Place in a preheated 350°F oven, covered, for 10 minutes. Remove the foil and bake another 10 to 15 minutes.

serves 6 to 8

Matza Lasagna with Pesto Sauce
mazzagne al pesto

2 cups pesto sauce (page 159)

8 egg matzòt

2 cups ricotta sauce (recipe follows)

1 cup milk

Coat the bottom of a deep square baking dish slightly larger than the matza with pesto.

Make alternate layers with the uncooked matza, pesto sauce, and dollops of ricotta sauce. Continue to make layers until you have exhausted all the ingredients. End with the ricotta sauce. Pour all the milk over the prepared mazzagne, cover with aluminum foil, and bake in a preheated 350°F oven for 30 minutes. Serve hot or at room temperature.

serves 6 to 8

Passover Ricotta Sauce
salsa di ricotta per pesach

4 tablespoons unsalted butter

6 tablespoons Passover cake flour

1½ cups hot milk

1 cup ricotta

Heat the butter and flour in a saucepan and cook 2 minutes, stirring frequently. Add the milk all at once, and cook another 2 minutes, stirring vigorously with a wire whisk.

Add the ricotta and simmer, stirring, until the ricotta is almost completely melted.

yields approximately 2 cups

Polenta

olenta is a staple in northern Italy and among all peasants. In my parents' household we seldom had polenta because my mother was from Rome where this rustic meal was not very popular among the Jews. But during the war, among the farmers who gave us shelter and food, not only did we eat polenta with them every day but we learned to love it!

Polenta was not only a staple; it was a ritual. Every morning, rain or shine, all the men of the extended family would get up at daybreak and leave the house without any breakfast to take care of the morning chores. The older children and some of the women would go along to help. The women in charge of the household remained to take care of the younger children, clean the house, set the gigantic table and, above all, make polenta.

The fire on the hearth, which had been dormant during the night under a blanket of ashes, was rekindled with pieces of hemp straw and new twigs. The big *paiuolo* (a copper kettle lined with tin that resembled an inverted bowler hat) was filled three-quarters of the way with water and hung on the hook of the big round chain coming down from the chimney. When the water began to let off steam (but was not yet boiling), the woman in charge of the polenta would throw in a handful of coarse salt, then pour a steady stream of cornmeal in with one hand while stirring constantly with a long cylindrical stick in the other hand. When the mixture was thick enough to coat the stick, more twigs were placed under the *paiuolo* to raise the flame and the mixture cooked and thickened for about 20 minutes more. By this time there was no danger of lumps forming, and the woman, red in the face and with an aching back, could relax for a moment. She would then throw handfuls of cornmeal into the *paiuolo* every now and then, stirring after each addition. When the mixture was so thick that the stirring could be performed only by tilting the *paiuolo* and rotating the stick in an elliptical up and down motion, the polenta was done. The *paiuolo* was removed from the hook and placed on a stand away from the heat. With a wooden spatula dipped in cold water, the polenta was separated from the sides of the *paiuolo*. More hemp straw and twigs were put on the fire to raise the flame. The *paiuolo* was again hooked onto the chain for one last moment in order to let the high heat separate the polenta from the bottom of the kettle. Then the woman's strong, capable hands would hold the *paiuolo* so that it could be turned onto a wooden board, and a smoky golden polenta would drop down in the form of a beautiful round cake.

At this point, as if by magic, everyone who had been working in the stables and in the fields would walk in to wash and to eat the first meal of their long workday.

In recent years, polenta has found its way among people with more sophisticated palates both in Italy and in America, and it is finally recognized for the true delicacy it is.

Some people here in America associate polenta with corn mush. But aside from their c orn derivation, the two dishes have very little in common as far as texture, versatility, and even flavor are concerned.

In this country as a married woman, I got into the ritual of making polenta when the first snow whitened the grounds, and made it again once or twice during the cold season. It was a laborious task I could not afford to undertake too often. Eventually, I devised a simpler method of cooking it than the one used by the Italian peasants, and I now enjoy polenta in its many forms quite often.

Polenta—Basic Recipe

3 cups yellow cornmeal

6 cups water

1 tablespoon salt

Mix 2 cups cornmeal with 2 cups cold water. Bring 4 cups water with the salt to a boil. Gradually drop the corn mixture into the boiling water while stirring with a large wooden spoon. (I brought a special wooden spatula from Italy. If you can't find one in specialty stores, use a 20-inch section from a new, unpainted wooden broomstick, washed with bleach and rinsed thoroughly.) Continue to stir until boiling resumes. Simmer for 10 minutes, stirring frequently. Add the remaining cornmeal a handful at a time while stirring vigorously. Cook 10 minutes more, stirring occasionally, to ensure the polenta does not burn or stick to the bottom of the pot.

Remove from the heat. With a flat wooden spatula dipped in cold water, separate the mass of polenta from the walls of the pot, gently tapering it toward the center. Dip the spatula in cold water very frequently, so that the polenta doesn't stick to it.

Return the pot to the burner and raise the heat very high for 1 to 2 minutes without stirring. The hot steam will separate the polenta from the bottom of the pot, although some will stick to the bottom at this point. (As soon as you have poured the polenta, place the pot under the faucet and half fill it with cold water. When you are ready to clean the pot, you will find that the polenta that stuck to it will easily peel off.)

Holding the pot firmly, turn it over a wooden board in one swift motion. A cheese-like round cake of polenta will come down. Cover with a clean kitchen towel and let rest 2 to 3 minutes before slicing.

To slice freshly made polenta, hold a 20-inch piece of white string at tension between your thumbs and forefingers. Slide it under the cake of polenta to the thickness of the slice you want to cut (generally ½ to 2 inches). Still holding the string with both hands, pull it upward so that, in passing through, it cuts one slice. Give one slice at a time and keep the remaining polenta covered to maintain heat.

Serve with *Ciccio e Cavolo Riccio, Spezzatino, Gulyás, Baccalà colla Cipolla,* or ricotta.

NOTE: Cutting polenta with a string is part of the fun. After it gets cold and firm, however, you must use a sharp knife. Keep leftover polenta refrigerated no longer than a day; you may freeze it for longer periods, but although the flavor remains more or less the same, the texture is definitely no longer like the fresh one.

serves 6 or more

Polenta with Cheese

polenta col cacio

Cacio is the generic term for cheese. In this case, however, the term *cacio* had a very specific connotation. It meant cheese that was freshly made from sheep's milk, and used before it had a chance to form a crust. This cheese is formally called *Pecorino fresco*, not to be confused with *Pecorino Romano* or *Sardo*, which are both aged and very sharp. Pecorino fresco is not treated to last. It is mild, soft, and has a delicious creamy consistency. If finding Pecorino fresco is a bit of a problem, Muenster cheese is a satisfactory substitute.

1 cake freshly made polenta (page 170)

¼ cup unsalted butter, melted

4 cups shredded Pecorino fresco or Muenster cheese

As soon as the polenta has been turned onto the wooden board, cover it with a clean kitchen towel for a couple of minutes. Then cut ½-inch slices with the string. When you have cut the first slice, pull it gently with your fingers toward you to separate it from the rest of the cake, and quickly place it in a large heated and buttered serving plate. Repeat until you have made a first layer of slices. Brush with melted butter and smother with cheese. Continue to make layers until you have finished all the ingredients. Serve immediately.

NOTE: For a more rustic polenta, omit the butter, serve each slice coated with cheese individually, and pass the pepper mill.

serves 6

Baked Polenta

polenta pasticciata

 olenta pasticciata, despite its peasant origins, appeals to a refined palate. It can be served as a *primo* in a dairy meal, but it can stand alone as a main course as well.

½ cake cold polenta *fina*

2 tablespoons olive oil

2 cups mushroom sauce (page 146)

4 cups cheese sauce (page 166)

1 cup freshly grated imported Parmesan cheese

With a sharp knife cut the polenta into ¼ to ½-inch slices. Oil the bottom of an ovenproof baking dish and cover it with slices of polenta in a single layer. Spread some mushroom sauce and cheese sauce over it. Continue to make layers until you have used up all the ingredients. End with the cheese sauce. Place in a 350°F oven for ½ hour or until the top begins to brown. Serve hot and pass a separate dish of Parmesan cheese.

NOTE: For a white *Polenta Pasticciata* for Shavuot, make polenta with white cornmeal and omit the mushroom sauce.

serves 6 to 8

Shavuot Baked White Corn Polenta

polenta bianca pasticciata per shavuot

3 cups white cornmeal

6 cups cold water

1 tablespoon salt

Unsalted butter

4 tablespoons unbleached flour

2 cups hot milk

Prepare the polenta as described on page 170. Let it cool for several hours or overnight.

Make a white sauce with 4 tablespoons butter, the flour, and hot milk. (You can prepare the white sauce the traditional way: sauté the butter and flour for a couple of minutes, then add the hot milk all at once while stirring vigorously with a wire whisk and cook a few more minutes. Or, you can use the blender white sauce, page 245.)

1 pound mozzarella di bufala, shredded

1 cup freshly grated Italian Parmesan cheese

With a sharp knife, cut the polenta into ½-inch slices. Place one third of the slices in a well-buttered baking dish and smear with one third of the white sauce. Sprinkle one third of the shredded cheese and continue to make layers until you have used up all the ingredients, except for the Parmesan cheese. Dot with butter and place in a 350°F oven for 30 minutes or until the top begins to brown. Serve hot with the Parmesan cheese in a separate dish.

serves 8

Toasted Polenta

polenta abbrustolita

1 cold cake of polenta (page 170)

2 tablespoons butter

4 cups ricotta, at room temperature

1 cup hot honey

With a sharp knife cut the polenta into ½-inch slices. Line up on a well-buttered baking sheet. Place on the rack closest to the broiler and broil for 6 minutes or until the tops get dark brown. Turn the slices and brown the other side.

Transfer to a hot serving plate. Spread the ricotta over the slices, then pour the hot honey over the ricotta. Serve immediately.

NOTE: You can serve the toasted polenta, ricotta, and hot honey separately, so that the family or the guests may help themselves to as much ricotta and honey as they wish.

serves 8

Fried Polenta

polenta fritta

½ cake day-old cold
polenta (page 170)
1 cup olive or other
vegetable oil for frying

Cut the polenta into ½-inch slices with a sharp knife. Heat the oil in a frying pan (preferably nonstick) and fry the slices in a single layer for 5 to 6 minutes on each side, or until a golden crust is formed. Transfer to paper towels to drain excess oil. Sprinkle with salt and serve as a snack.

NOTE: For a more elegant *Polenta Fritta* to be served as a side dish, make polenta as described on page 170 up to when the polenta is ready to be removed from the heat. Instead of making a bulky cake out of it, spread it ½-inch thick over an oiled surface. When it is cold, cut with cookie cutters into disks, diamonds, stars, etc., and proceed as above. Omit the salt.

serves 4 to 6

Couscous and Gnocchi

cuscussù e gnocchi

Couscous

Cuscussù

Cuscussù, the very symbol of Italian Jewish cuisine, is also the symbol for very complicated cooking (see the introduction to *Minestre*). Its lengthy preparation, however, never discouraged the Jewish cooks, who not only made it for their families but also for dinner parties and for fund-raising purposes (my husband and I were once among the paying guests at a *cuscussù* evening organized by the temple members of Florence for a benefit). *Ode al Cuscussù*, by the distinguished poet Angiolo Orvieto, is an eye-opener. In his twenty stanzas the poet describes the day, from early morning to Vespers, in which he and his wife prepare the *cuscussù*. The directions he gives, interspersed with words of praise and love for his wife and longing for his Middle Eastern forefathers who brought this fabulous dish to Italy, make the preparations seem like a breeze.

There are, of course, many shortcuts one can use to make a couscous (such as using precooked cereal, frozen or canned vegetables, etc.). However, I make couscous only once in a while and for that time I like to have the authentic dish. The only way I shorten the time of preparation is by cooking the meats and vegetables ahead of time (on a rainy weekend, for example) and leaving them in the freezer. In fact, when I make stuffed artichokes, stuffed cabbage, stuffed celery, etc., I put the leftovers in the freezer until I have enough for one couscous. The cereal I use is the long-cooking type, which you can find in fine grocery stores. The following is the authentic family recipe.

2 pounds long-cooking couscous

Salt

½ cup olive oil

1 cup cold water

2 cups spongy beef bones

1 stalk celery

1 small onion

1 small carrot, peeled

¼ teaspoon whole peppercorns

¼ cup olive oil

½ onion, sliced

2 cloves garlic, sliced

2 stalks celery, cut up

2 carrots, peeled and cut up

7 to 8 pounds of a variety of vegetables (cabbage, savoy cabbage, cauliflower, Swiss chard, etc.), washed and cut up

2 large ripe tomatoes, peeled (page 52) and cut up

2 cups cold water

Freshly ground black pepper

½ recipe *Fagiolini Conditi* (page 294)

1 recipe *Carciofi Ripieni* (page 194) or *Sedani Ripieni* (page 192)

½ recipe Chicken Breast Balls (page 228)

Hot *Thurshi* sauce (page 177)

4 hard-boiled eggs, cut into 6 wedges

Place the couscous and 4 teaspoons salt in a large bowl. While stirring with a wooden spoon (or beaters if you have a dough maker), gradually add the ½ cup oil and the cold water and continue to stir until all the water has been absorbed by the couscous. Set aside while you prepare the pot for the broth.

Wash the bones and put into the pot—the bottom part of the couscoussier. Add 1 tablespoon salt, whole celery, onion, carrot, peppercorns, and cold water to cover, about 2 quarts. Bring to a rapid boil, then lower the heat to a gentle simmer.

Stir the couscous again and transfer to the steamer—the top part of the couscoussier. Cover this with its lid, place on top of the simmering pot, and forget about it for 2½ to 3 hours.

Take the couscous from the steamer and pour it into the original bowl. Strain the broth and put 1 cup of it into the couscous bowl before placing the broth in the refrigerator to cool. Stir the couscous to mix and to undo any lumps.

Wash the pot and place the ¼ cup oil, sliced onion, garlic, celery, and carrots into it. Sauté a couple of minutes, stirring frequently; then add all the vegetables, including the tomatoes. Add 2 cups cold water and salt and pepper to taste. Bring to a boil, then reduce the heat. Return the couscous to the steamer, cover, and place over the pot with the vegetables. Simmer for 1½ to 2 hours. During this period, ladle some of the vegetable liquid from the lower pot and baste the couscous with it 2 or 3 times.

Before serving, defat and reheat the broth, after adding the chicken balls. Reheat all the prepared stuffed vegetables.

Place the couscous in a large bowl and fluff it with a fork. Place all the other ingredients in separate serving dishes. Serve the broth in individual cups.

serves 12 or more

Sauce for Couscous

thurshi

2 pounds any yellow
squash except butternut,
which is too sweet

1 cup water

1 teaspoon salt

⅛ teaspoon cayenne pepper

1 teaspoon caraway seeds

½ cup olive oil

Juice of 1 lemon

2 cloves garlic

Pare the squash and cut in half. Remove and discard all the seeds and the fibrous parts. Cube and place in a saucepan with the water. Cover and cook over low heat for 25 to 30 minutes, stirring occasionally. When the squash is reduced to a puree, remove from the heat.

Add the salt, pepper, caraway seeds, oil, and lemon juice.

Squeeze the garlic through a garlic press or chop very fine and add to the sauce. Stir to combine. Serve hot with couscous.

NOTE: Traditionally, this sauce is served only with couscous, but I like to serve it also with a Combination of Boiled Meats (page 187) or as a dip with appetizers.

serves 6

Potato Gnocchi

gnocchi di patate

nocchi should not necessarily be translated into "dumplings" just because by these we mean lumps made of flour, semolina, potatoes, or other, dumped and boiled in water, and served with Parmesan or other cheeses and/or a variety of other sauces. *Gnocchi alla Romana,* for example, cannot be translated as dumplings at all because they are not dumped and cooked in any liquid but baked. In my opinion, they are not dumplings but the aristocracy of *gnocchi.*

4 pounds baking potatoes

3 cups unbleached flour

6 quarts water

Salt

½ cup butter, melted

1 cup freshly grated imported Parmesan cheese

3 cups tomato sauce (page 152)

Boil or steam the potatoes until very soft. Peel while still hot and mash or force through a sieve. Add enough flour to make a soft dough. Knead 2 minutes on a floured board. Cut into 6 or 8 pieces. Roll each piece into a ¾-inch rope. Cut the ropes into 1½-inch pieces. Continue to sprinkle the dough with flour if it becomes too sticky. With gentle pressure, roll each piece over a slotted spoon or the back of a cheese grater to make grooves.

Bring the water to a boil. Add 3 tablespoons salt and one-quarter of the *gnocchi.* As soon as boiling resumes and the *gnocchi* float to the surface, remove with a slotted spoon and place in a serving dish. Dress with some of the butter, cheese, and tomato sauce. Repeat until you have cooked all the *gnocchi.*

Let rest 5 minutes for the flavors to come together.

serves 6

Small Potato Gnocchi with Gorgonzola Cheese

gnocchetti di patate al gorgonzola

nocchetti is one of the many culinary inventions of Giovanna's. Yet Giovanna is not a professional cook. She is one of those amazing persons who can do anything well. Giovanna is a professor of English literature in the English department at the University of Bologna; as a literary critic specializing in the Gothic and Romantic novel, she has published many acclaimed works in the field, in Italian as well as in English. And as a native Bolognese, she has an innate flair for cooking.

Giovanna is not Jewish, but she knows about the Jewish dietary laws, and when I asked her for a contribution for my new book, she came up with this delightful dish.

3 pounds baking potatoes

¼ cup freshly grated Italian Parmesan cheese

1 egg, slightly beaten

2½ cups unbleached flour

4 quarts water

Salt

1 pint heavy cream

¼ pound Gorgonzola cheese, crumbled

⅓ cup chopped walnut or pecan meats

Boil or steam the potatoes until very soft. Peel while still hot and mash or force through a sieve. (Do not use a blender or food processor.) Add the Parmesan cheese and stir to cool a little. Add the egg and stir to combine. Add enough flour to make a soft dough. Knead 2 minutes on a floured board. Cut into 6 or 8 pieces. Roll each piece into a ½-inch rope. Cut the ropes into ½-inch bits, sprinkling with flour to prevent sticking.

Bring the water with 2 tablespoons salt to a boil. Add one quarter of the *gnocchetti*. As soon as boiling resumes and the *gnocchetti* float to the surface, remove with a slotted spoon and place in a colander to drain. Continue with the remaining *gnocchetti*.

Heat the heavy cream in a large skillet without letting it boil. Add the *gnocchetti* and gently stir until they have absorbed the cream. Remove from the heat, sprinkle the Gorgonzola over the *gnocchetti*, and stir once more. Pour on a heated serving plate, sprinkle the top with the chopped nuts, and serve.

serves 6

Farina Gnocchi Roman Style

gnocchi di semolino alla romana

The authentic recipe for this delicious variation on *gnocchi* calls for *semolino grosso*, a coarse-grained flour made from durum wheat. The only semolina I have been able to find here in the United States is the fine type, which is not suitable for this type of *gnocchi*. I therefore use farina, which is precooked and gives a somewhat different, but still very good, *gnocchi*.

4 cups milk
¾ teaspoon salt
¾ cup unsalted butter
1¼ cups farina
1 cup freshly grated imported Parmesan cheese
2 egg yolks

Place the milk in a large saucepan with the salt and 1 tablespoon butter over low heat. When the milk begins to smoke, drop the farina in all at once and stir vigorously with a wooden spatula or a wire whisk. Cook, stirring, for 2 minutes. Remove from the heat. Add half of the remaining butter and half the grated Parmesan and stir to combine. Add the egg yolks and mix very well. Pour over a buttered surface and spread to ½-inch thickness. Let cool thoroughly. Melt the remaining butter.

With a pastry cutter or wet knife, cut the solid farina into disks, squares, or diamonds and arrange in layers in a buttered baking dish, sprinkling each layer with butter and cheese. Place in a preheated 400°F oven for 20 minutes or until the top begins to brown.

serves 6

Passover Sfoglietti with Meat Sauce

sfoglietti per pesach al ragù

foglietti is a homemade pasta that can be used during the eight days of Passover. Pasta, in general, is not allowed on Passover. However sfoglietti—which was devised by the Italian Jews, who would not give up their taste for pasta even during Passover—differs from other pastas in two ways. It is made with the same flour that is used to make matza, and it is baked as soon as it is rolled thin to prevent leavening. Pasta that has been prebaked has a different texture from ordinary pasta, and this difference provides a delightful gourmet experience.

4 eggs, slightly beaten

3 cups Passover flour

4 quarts water

2 tablespoons salt

3 cups hot ragù sauce (see following recipe)

Mix the eggs with enough flour to make a rather hard dough. Divide into 16 pieces. With a rolling pin or with machine rollers, roll each piece very thin, toss on a baking sheet, and bake immediately in a 550°F oven (higher if your oven goes to more than 550°F) for approximately 2 minutes. Turn over and bake 1 minute longer. Sfoglietti should be well dried but not browned. Remove from the oven, cool, and break into large, uneven pieces.

Bring the water to a boil; add the sfoglietti and salt and cook, uncovered, 3 to 4 minutes. Drain and dress with hot sauce. Serve immediately.

NOTE: *Sfoglietti* can be prepared ahead of time and stored for later use in a plastic bag after they are thoroughly cooled and broken up. They will keep fresh for the eight days of Passover and beyond.

serves 6

Beef Ragù
ragù di manzo

Olive oil

1 small onion, minced

1 medium carrot, peeled and diced

1 stalk celery, chopped

¾ pound lean ground beef

½ pound lean ground veal

Salt

Freshly ground black pepper

1 whole clove

1 heaping tablespoon tomato paste

½ cup dry white wine

1 cup clear beef broth

1 clove garlic, minced

1 tablespoon freshly chopped Italian parsley

In a medium saucepan, place 6 tablespoons oil, the onion, carrot, celery, and the two meats and brown on moderately high heat, stirring frequently, until all is quite dark.

Add the salt and pepper to taste, 1 whole clove, and the tomato paste and stir thoroughly. Add the wine and raise the heat to let the wine evaporate completely. Add the broth, lower the heat, and simmer, covered, for ½ hour, or until the sauce is thick and flavorful. Add the garlic and parsley and 2 tablespoons fresh oil, and stir.

yields approximately 3 cups / serves 6 to 8

Crêpes Florentine

crespelle alla fiorentina

 These crêpes taste better if you can make them with *Pecorino fresco* which differs from region to region. In Florence, we used *Pecorino Toscano*. Muenster cheese is an acceptable substitute.

2 pounds small-leaved bulk spinach or two 10-ounce packages frozen spinach

3 tablespoons olive oil

1 medium onion, chopped fine

½ pound white mushrooms, finely chopped

2 tablespoons freshly chopped Italian parsley

Salt

Freshly ground black pepper

Dash nutmeg

Unsalted butter

Unbleached flour

Milk

1½ cups shredded Pecorino fresco or Muenster cheese

6 eggs, slightly beaten

Remove the stems from the spinach and wash the leaves until no trace of sand remains. Cook without any additional water other than the water retained from washing. Drain, get rid of most of the liquid, and finely chop.

Heat the oil in a large skillet. Add the onion and sauté 2 minutes. Add the spinach, mushrooms, and parsley; lightly season with salt, pepper, and nutmeg and sauté 3 more minutes. Remove from the heat.

Make a white sauce by heating 6 tablespoons butter with 6 tablespoons flour. Add 2 cups hot milk all at once and stir vigorously with a wire whisk while cooking for 4 to 5 minutes. Take 1 cup white sauce and ½ cup cheese and add to the spinach mixture; stir and set aside.

Make a batter combining the eggs, 1½ cups milk, 1½ cups flour, and 1 teaspoon salt. Heat 1 tablespoon butter in an 8-inch skillet. Add ⅓ cup batter and tilt the skillet in a rotating motion to spread the batter evenly. Cook for 1 to 2 minutes or until firm, with the bottom slightly brown. Invert on a clean, damp cloth on the table. Repeat, using less butter to grease the pan, until you have used up the batter (12 or more crêpes).

Divide the spinach mixture among the crêpes, spread over each one, and roll up. Arrange in a well-buttered ovenproof dish in a single layer.

Add 1 cup milk to the remaining white sauce, mix in the remaining cheese, and pour over the crêpes. Bake in a preheated 375°F oven for ½ hour. Remove from the oven and let stand 5 to 10 minutes before serving.

serves 6

BEEF, VEAL, LAMB, AND POULTRY

carne

ven though I have encountered many vegetarians among the Italian Jews during my search for ancient Italian Jewish recipes, and in spite of the fact that the Italian Jewish cuisine's emphasis is on vegetable rather than animal proteins, I have been able to collect a surprising number of recipes for preparing meat deliciously.

In the process I have discovered that the Italian Jews made great use of chopped meats. The majority of the exceptionally tasty meat items in my collection are prepared with one type or another of ground meat, be it beef, veal, lamb, or poultry. Because it is easy to stretch ground meat by adding eggs, bread, etc., I suspect that ground meat was used to lower the cost of meals. However, another, more compelling reason is that it is consistent with the demand of our religious tradition, which often requires preparation of meals several days ahead of time, for example, before Shabbat and other holidays. Stews can also be made ahead of time and preserved for a few days without refrigeration, but ground meat provided a much greater variety of menus.

I also noticed that ground meats were very often prepared with a vegetable. Again, it might have been more economical this way, but mainly it provided diversity. *Polpettone al Limone*, for example, have nothing in common in the way of taste and texture with stuffed artichokes, although both dishes are made with ground beef.

And, of course there are quite a few outstanding meat dishes that are not made with ground meat. *Prosciutto d'Oca*, for example, is a superb way to prepare meat.

Beef

bue

A Combination of Boiled Meats

bollito misto

Sometimes during a holiday dinner, a plate with three or four kinds of meat, which had been used to make the *Brodo delle Feste*, would appear on the table. *Bollito Misto*, however, is not to be confused with those meats. It is a delicious dish, made for its own sake, whether the broth resulting from it is used or not. The types of meat used vary from community to community, but for a luxurious *bollito*, beef tongue and beef sausage are never missing. If home-made beef sausages (*Salsicce di Manzo*) are not part of your cooking repertoire, knockwurst or kosher salami is quite an acceptable substitute. *Bollito Misto* may be served with mayonnaise, *Brusco* Sauce, and a number of other sauces.

2 quarts water
1 stalk celery, cut up
1 small carrot, peeled and sliced
½ medium onion
1 bunch Italian parsley stems (leaves removed) tied in a bouquet
1 tablespoon salt
¼ teaspoon whole peppercorns
2 whole cloves

Bring the water to a boil with the vegetables, herbs, and seasonings. Add the beef, beef tongue, and sausages. (If you use knockwurst or salami, boil it in a separate saucepan until swollen and tender.) Boil, covered, for about 1 hour. Add the turkey and continue to boil, covered, for ½ hour. Add the veal and calf foot and boil, covered, another ½ hour. Finally, add the chicken and cook, covered, until the chicken is tender.

If some meats are cooked sooner than others, remove them to a warm plate and reheat with the rest just before serving. Remove the second skin from the tongue and place all the meats on a wooden tray. Serve every person a portion of each meat.

1½ pounds muscular
beef meat

½ beef tongue or 1 veal
tongue, peeled

6 beef sausages or knock-
wurst or one 12-ounce
kosher salami

1 turkey leg and thigh

1½ pounds lean veal

1 calf foot, cut up

½ small chicken

NOTE: For a good, flavorful *bollito*, do not simmer the meats but, rather, boil them quickly.

To peel the tongue, place directly over the heat on top of the stove or very close to the broiler rack in the oven for 5 minutes, turning very often on all sides. This will cause the skin to blister, which makes it easy to remove.

serves 12

Meat Loaf
polpettone di manzo

2 pounds lean ground beef

2 eggs, slightly beaten

Seasoned breadcrumbs

Salt

Freshly ground black
pepper

2 hard-boiled eggs, shelled

½ cup olive oil

1½ cups tomato sauce
(page 152)

½ cup warm water

1 large clove garlic, sliced

1 tablespoon freshly
chopped Italian parsley

In a large bowl, combine the meat, beaten eggs, ¼ cup bread-crumbs, and salt and pepper to taste. Mix well. Spread half the mixture over an oiled piece of plastic wrap. Place 1 hard-boiled egg at the center. With the help of the plastic wrap, enclose the egg inside the meat, trying to avoid pockets of air, and form a large, egg-shaped loaf. Roll in the breadcrumbs. Repeat with the remaining meat mixture, egg, and breadcrumbs.

Heat 4 tablespoons oil in a large nonstick skillet and fry the two loaves in it until nicely browned on all sides. Remove to a fish poacher or large saucepan. Add the tomato sauce and warm water and cook over moderate heat, covered, for 30 minutes, turning the loaves occasionally. Make sure the loaves don't stick to the bottom of the pan. Add the remaining oil, garlic, and parsley and cook 5 minutes longer. Remove from the heat and let cool for 5 to 6 minutes.

Slice carefully so that the egg remains in its place. Arrange the slices on a hot serving plate and pour the gravy over them.

serves 6 to 8

Lemon Meat Loaf

polpettone al limone

2 slices stale bread, diced (use any of the homemade breads)
2 eggs, slightly beaten
2 large lemons
2 pounds lean ground beef
1 tablespoon freshly chopped Italian parsley
1 teaspoon salt
¼ teaspoon freshly ground black pepper
¼ cup fine breadcrumbs (page 311)
Olive oil
1 tablespoon unbleached flour
½ cup cold water

In a large bowl, combine the bread, eggs, and the juice of 1 lemon. Stir until the bread is thoroughly soaked. Add the meat, parsley, salt, and pepper and mix well. With oiled hands shape the meat mixture into 2 oval loaves; roll in the breadcrumbs.

Heat ¼ cup oil in a skillet and fry the two loaves in it until nicely browned on all sides.

Dissolve the flour in the cold water and add to the skillet. Cook, covered, over moderate heat for approximately 45 minutes, turning the loaves and scraping the bottom of the skillet occasionally. Remove the loaves, slice, and arrange the slices on a hot serving plate.

Add the juice of the second lemon to the skillet, stir to mix, get the brown bits from the bottom of the pan, and pour this gravy over the meat. It is excellent hot or cold.

serves 6

Meatballs Jewish Style

polpette alla giudia

1½ slices White Bread (page 310)
1½ pounds lean ground beef
2 eggs, slightly beaten
Salt
Freshly ground black pepper

Soak and cook the bread until it becomes pap. (Place the bread, covered by water, in a small saucepan and let it soak for 5 minutes. Drain the excess water, place the saucepan over high heat and cook, stirring, until the bread has become a pap, the consistency of cooked cereal.)

In a medium bowl, combine the meat, eggs, and the cooked bread; add salt and pepper to taste, the parsley, garlic, and cinnamon. Mix well. With oiled hands shape the mixture into

1 tablespoon freshly
chopped Italian parsley

¼ teaspoon garlic powder

2 dashes cinnamon

½ cup fine breadcrumbs
(page 311)

Olive oil

1 cup water

½ cup white wine vinegar

approximately 30 oval balls and roll them in the breadcrumbs.

Heat ½ cup oil in a large frying pan; add the meatballs and fry in a single layer, shaking the pan frequently, until browned on all sides. Repeat until all the balls are fried.

Transfer to a clean skillet, add the water and vinegar and cook, covered, over low heat for 30 minutes. Add 3 tablespoons olive oil, stir, and serve.

NOTE: Even though spaghetti and meatballs appear to be such a happy marriage for most Americans, the combination is totally unknown to Italians (including Jews). Meatballs are served alone or with a number of vegetables—the most popular of which is green peppers (see the following recipe).

serves 6

Meatballs and Peppers

polpette coi peperoni

2 pounds green peppers

4 tablespoons olive oil

1 large yellow onion, sliced

4 cups fresh, ripe peeled
tomatoes (page 52)
or canned

Salt

Freshly ground
black pepper

30 fried meatballs (see
preceding recipe)

¼ cup dry white wine

Wash and core the peppers. Cut into strips lengthwise. Place in a large saucepan with the oil, onion, tomatoes, and small amounts of salt and pepper. After the meatballs are fried, transfer them to the saucepan with the peppers. Cook, covered, over low heat for about ½ hour. Add the wine and cook over moderately high heat, stirring frequently, 15 minutes longer, or until most of the liquid has evaporated and the stew is in a thick, savory sauce.

NOTE: For a real treat, serve this dish with freshly baked Tuscan bread or *Sfilatini*.

serves 6

Meat and Potato Patties

polpettine di carne e patate

 his dish was obviously born to make use of leftover meat. Its plebeian origin notwithstanding, it is a very pleasant dish you can serve with a soup and/or a tossed salad for lunch or even at dinner.

1½ cups cooked meat, cubed

2 to 3 medium boiling potatoes, cooked, peeled, and mashed

2 eggs, slightly beaten

1 tablespoon freshly chopped Italian parsley

1 small clove garlic, minced

Dash nutmeg

Salt

Freshly ground black pepper

1 cup fine breadcrumbs (optional)

Vegetable oil for frying

Grind the meat and combine with the potatoes, eggs, parsley, garlic, and nutmeg. Add salt and pepper to taste and mix very well.

Spoon by the heaping tablespoon onto your oiled hands and shape into round patties. Roll in fine breadcrumbs and pat to remove excess. (This is exactly how the recipe was given to me. However, I have made these patties without rolling them in breadcrumbs and they are fine that way as well.)

Heat the oil in a large skillet and fry until golden brown on both sides. Serve immediately.

serves 6 to 8

Stuffed Celery

sedani ripieni

T his is another of the stuffed vegetable dishes that were originally created to go with the famous couscous, but they are so delicious that they have earned a status of their own as a main course. The most popular of these is stuffed artichokes, but stuffed celery, cauliflower, or zucchini is also good.

1 large bunch of celery

Salt

1 slice stale bread, soaked and cooked into a pap (page 43)

1 pound lean ground beef

3 eggs

2 tablespoons freshly chopped Italian parsley

Freshly ground black pepper

½ cup unbleached flour

Olive oil

1 clove garlic, minced

1½ cups fresh, ripe peeled tomatoes (page 52), cut up, or 1½ cups canned tomatoes

Separate the celery stalks and remove the stringy fibers. Cut into thirty-six 2½-inch pieces. Place in a saucepan with 1 teaspoon salt. Add water to cover, bring to a boil, and cook, covered, for 25 to 30 minutes. Drain and let cool.

Place the cooked bread and meat in a bowl. Add 1 egg, 1 tablespoon parsley, 1 teaspoon salt, and ⅛ teaspoon pepper. Mix well to combine. Divide into 18 small balls.

Place one ball between two pieces of celery and press so that they hold together. Roll in the flour and lay on a piece of wax paper. Continue until all the meat and celery have been used.

Beat the remaining eggs with a pinch of salt. Heat ½ cup oil in a frying pan; dip the stuffed celery in the beaten egg and fry until golden on all sides. Place in a large skillet in a single layer. Add the garlic, tomatoes, 3 tablespoons oil, the remaining parsley, and small amounts of salt and pepper. Place over medium heat and cook, covered, for 25 to 30 minutes.

NOTE: You may prepare stuffed celery a day ahead of time. Reheated a moment before serving, it actually tastes better than when served immediately after cooking.

serves 4 to 6

Stuffed Cabbage

cavoli ripieni

1 pound ground lean beef

2 eggs, slightly beaten

¼ cup coarse Breadcrumbs (page 311)

¼ cup beef broth or water

Salt

⅛ teaspoon freshly ground black pepper

⅛ teaspoon garlic powder

2 tablespoons freshly chopped Italian parsley

4 cups water

24 cabbage leaves (1 large head)

6 tablespoons olive oil

2 cups fresh, ripe peeled tomatoes (page 52) or canned tomatoes, drained

2 tablespoons tomato paste

1 clove garlic, sliced

In a medium bowl, combine the meat, eggs, breadcrumbs, and broth. Add 1 teaspoon salt, pepper, garlic powder, and 1 tablespoon parsley. Mix well and set aside for 15 to 20 minutes.

Bring 2 cups water to a boil in a large pot. Add 1 teaspoon salt and cabbage leaves and boil for 3 to 4 minutes. Drain and spread out over a slightly damp kitchen towel for a couple of minutes to cool.

Place a ball of the meat mixture on each cabbage leaf. Fold the sides over the meat; then roll, tucking under. Arrange in a large skillet. Add the oil, tomatoes, tomato paste diluted in 2 cups water, and salt and pepper to taste. Simmer, covered, for 45 minutes.

Add the garlic and remaining parsley and cook, uncovered, 15 minutes longer, or until the rolls are in a thick savory sauce.

serves 4 to 6

Stuffed Artichokes

carciofi ripieni

Stuffed artichokes are one of the ingredients that went into the famous couscous. In my parents' household couscous (*cuscussù*) was seldom made because of the elaborate preparations involved. Stuffed artichokes, however, were made again and again in the spring, when artichokes were in season, because it is a delicious dish in its own right, and we all loved it.

6 medium artichokes

Juice of 1 lemon

1 pound lean ground beef

1 slice stale bread, soaked in water and cooked into a pap (page 43)

3 eggs

½ teaspoon garlic powder

Salt

Freshly ground black pepper

½ cup unbleached flour

Olive oil

2 large ripe peeled tomatoes (page 52), or 2 cups canned peeled tomatoes

½ cup tomato juice

1 clove garlic, minced

1 small onion, minced

1 tablespoon freshly chopped Italian parsley

Prepare the artichokes as described on page 40. Cut each into 8 pieces, remove and discard the choke, if there is any, and drop into a bowl of water containing the juice of 1 lemon. Drain and pat dry with a clean kitchen towel.

In a medium bowl, combine the meat, pap, 1 egg, garlic powder, 1 teaspoon salt, and ⅛ teaspoon pepper. Mix well. Divide into 24 oval balls. Place each ball between two pieces of artichoke, pressing so that they hold together. Roll in the flour and lay on a piece of wax paper.

Beat the 2 remaining eggs with a pinch of salt. Heat 1 cup oil in a frying pan, dip the stuffed artichokes in the beaten egg and fry in the hot oil until golden brown on all sides. Arrange in a large skillet, preferably in a single layer. Add the tomatoes and tomato juice. Season with 4 tablespoons olive oil, garlic, onion, parsley, and salt and pepper to taste. Place over medium heat and cook, covered, for 20 to 30 minutes, or until the sauce is nice and thick.

serves 4 to 6

Meats and Kale for Polenta

ciccio e cavolo riccio

 iccio (pronounced chee-cho) is another way of saying *carne*, meat, especially a variety of fried meats. *Cavolo riccio*, kale, generally accompanies the fried meats, but any green leafy vegetable such as spinach or dandelion also goes well with it.

2 pounds fresh small-leaved kale

1 cup water

Salt

Olive oil

12 bite-size frankfurters

12 balls or 1-inch pieces *Luganega* (page 197)

Six ¼-inch slices kosher salami

6 chicken livers, soaked in cold water

1 clove garlic, minced

1 cake freshly made Polenta (page 170)

Remove the stems and larger leaves from the kale. Rinse and place in a large pot with the water and ½ teaspoon salt. Cook over high heat, covered, for 10 minutes or until tender. Transfer to a colander to drain.

In a large skillet place 6 tablespoons oil, frankfurters, *luganega*, and salami. Gently fry until the meats are lightly browned.

Drain the chicken livers. Remove and discard the fat and discolored parts. Cut the livers in half and add to the skillet with the meats. Fry an additional 5 minutes, stirring. Remove from the heat and transfer the meats to a hot serving plate, leaving the oil in the skillet.

Add the garlic to the skillet and sauté until lightly golden. Add the cooked kale and sauté, stirring occasionally, 5 more minutes, or until the kale is crisp and dry. Transfer to the plate with the meats. Serve with hot slices of polenta.

serves 6 to 8

Tuscan Cholent

hammin toscano

This is an ancient recipe which, unlike *Hammin di Pesach*, does not call for matza and was not served on any particular holiday. It is, however, ideal for Shabbat because it can be prepared well in advance and then kept warm overnight either on low heat or in the oven. Cholent is the Ashkenazic counterpart of this *Hammin*.

2 pounds Swiss chard or spinach

1 egg, slightly beaten

¼ cup coarse breadcrumbs (page 311)

3 tablespoons chicken broth

Salt

Freshly ground black pepper

1 pound ground chicken breast

½ cup olive oil

1 small onion, thinly sliced

1 clove garlic, minced

1 tablespoon freshly chopped Italian parsley

3 fresh sage leaves or 1 teaspoon dried

2 cups dried cannellini or great Northern beans

4 cups warm water

1½ pounds flank steak

2 hard-boiled eggs, sliced

Trim and cut the Swiss chard into large pieces. Rinse thoroughly and cook, covered, with no water other than the water retained after washing, for 5 minutes.

Combine the beaten egg with the breadcrumbs and chicken broth. Add ½ teaspoon salt, dash of black pepper, and ground chicken. Mix well and let rest 10 minutes. Form many tiny balls.

In a large crock pot or enameled pot, place 4 tablespoons oil, onion, garlic, parsley, and ½ teaspoon salt. Cook over medium heat, stirring frequently, until the garlic is golden. Drain the Swiss chard, add to the pot, and stir. Gently place the meatballs over the chard; cover the pot, and simmer for 15 to 20 minutes, shaking, but not stirring. Transfer the contents of the pot to a dish and set aside.

Add the remaining ¼ cup oil and sage to the pot. Rinse the beans with warm water several times and add to the pot. Add 1 teaspoon salt and 2 cups warm water and bring to a boil. Lower the heat and simmer, covered, for 25 to 30 minutes, or until most of the liquid has evaporated. Transfer the beans temporarily to a dish, but retain the oil.

Trim all fatty parts from the steak and lightly season with salt and pepper on both sides. Add to the pot with oil and brown on both sides. Return the beans to the pot, add 2 cups warm water, and bring to a boil. Immediately lower the heat to a minimum and let simmer very gently, covered, for at least 5 hours.

Before serving, return the Swiss chard and chicken balls to the pot and let heat through. Slice the steak. Arrange *Hammin* on a hot serving plate starting with the vegetables. Place the sliced steak over the vegetables. Surround with the chicken balls and slices of hard-boiled eggs.

serves 8 to 12

Venetian Beef Sausage

luganega

This beef sausage is not intended to be preserved for long periods as other sausages are: it should be consumed within four or five days. However, it tastes better if kept for three or four days in the refrigerator before using it. It is not necessary to stuff it into casing and it is, therefore, very easy to prepare.

2 pounds lean beef cubes
½ pound white beef fat (optional)
1 clove garlic, passed through a garlic press
1½ tablespoons salt
1 teaspoon freshly ground black pepper
⅛ teaspoon ground cloves

In a meat grinder or food processor, grind the meat (together with the fat if desired). Add the seasoning and process a few more seconds to combine.

Roll out in the form of a rope, or make small balls with it. Arrange over a large plate in a spiral, or, if you make balls, spread in a single layer. Store, uncovered, in the refrigerator, where it will keep four or five days without spoiling. During this period turn it once to allow the bottom side to dry.

Serve as an appetizer in an antipasto platter or cooked with a vegetable as in the following recipe.

NOTE: The original recipe, given to me by a Venetian Jew whose family has resided in Venice for centuries, called for fat. However, I never use fat in my ground meat, and the flavor of my version, if not the texture, is superior.

serves 6

Venetian Beef Sausage and Beans

luganega coi fagioli

1 cup dried white beans

5 cups hot water

1 teaspoon salt

1 clove garlic, husk on

2 large sage leaves

Olive oil

Luganega of the preceding recipe

2 heaping tablespoons tomato paste, diluted in 1 cup warm water

Remove any debris from the beans. Rinse twice in warm water. Place in a large saucepan with the hot water and salt. Bring to a boil; then reduce the heat and simmer, covered, for 45 minutes.

Add the garlic and sage. After 5 minutes add 4 to 5 tablespoons olive oil, luganega cut into bite-size pieces, and the diluted tomato paste. Simmer, uncovered, shaking the pan from time to time, for ½ hour or until the sausage is fork tender and the beans are done but not mushy. The sauce should be thick and savory. Remove the garlic and sage before serving.

serves 8

Stuffed Flank Steak

rotolo di carne ripieno

Olive oil

1 small onion, chopped fine

1 small carrot, peeled and shredded

One 5-inch stalk celery, chopped fine

1 slice day-old bread

¼ cup beef broth or water

½ pound ground veal

1½ teaspoons salt

¼ teaspoon black pepper

1½ pounds flank steak

1 clove garlic, slightly crushed

Place 2 tablespoons oil, the onion, carrot, and celery in a small saucepan over medium heat and cook 2 minutes, stirring. Remove from the heat and add the bread and broth or water. After a minute or two, place over high heat and cook 2 minutes, or until most of the liquid has evaporated. Transfer to a bowl. Add the ground veal, salt, and pepper and mix to combine.

Remove all the fat and skin from the flank steak. Rub with garlic on both sides and lay it on a working surface. Shape the ground meat mixture into an oval ball about as long as the width of the steak; place at the center of the steak. Roll the steak and place in an oiled loaf pan, seam side down. With a sharp knife, gash the top against the grain, brush it with oil, and place in a 375°F oven for 1 to 1½ hours, or until fork tender.

serves 6

Beef and Potato Stew

la tegamata

a Tegamata was one of the family dinners that was considered too rustic to be served on a festive occasion. I find it so delightful, however, that I do not hesitate to serve it at dinner parties. Fall is the season for tiny new potatoes, but in other seasons I use large potatoes either diced or made into small balls with a melon scoop.

2½ pounds lean beef, cut into 1½-inch cubes

½ cup dry red wine

1 small carrot, peeled and diced

1 small onion, minced

½ teaspoon dried rosemary leaves

¼ teaspoon ground cloves

½ cup olive oil

2 teaspoons salt

⅛ teaspoon crushed hot red pepper

2 cups ripe peeled tomatoes (page 52)

1 small clove garlic, sliced

20 small new potatoes or 4 cups potato balls or cubes

Place the meat in a bowl with the wine, carrot, onion, rosemary leaves, and cloves. Let it marinate in a cool place for several hours or overnight, stirring occasionally.

Drain, reserving the marinade, and place in a pot with half the oil and salt and red pepper. Brown on all sides. Add the marinade and cook over high heat for 3 minutes.

Reduce the heat. Add the tomatoes, cover, and simmer for 1½ hours. Add the remaining oil, garlic, and potatoes. Cook until the potatoes are tender but not overdone.

NOTE: My mother used to say, *"La Tegamata è buona fatta e mangiata,"* it is good, that is, if eaten as soon as it is done. But I find that it is also delicious when it is prepared ahead of time and reheated before serving.

serves 6 to 8

Roast Beef

arrosto di manzo

1 clove garlic, crushed

3 pounds boneless rib roast, trimmed

1 teaspoon salt

¼ teaspoon freshly ground black pepper

⅛ teaspoon ground cloves

½ teaspoon dried rosemary leaves

½ cup dry white wine

1 cup olive oil

1½ cups sliced zucchini, mushrooms, or artichokes

Rub the crushed garlic all over the meat. Evenly season with salt, pepper, clove, and rosemary. Place in a small bowl, add the wine, and let rest in a cool place for several hours or overnight, turning once.

Transfer the meat to a small saucepan where it fits snugly. Reserve the marinade left in the bowl. Add the oil to the meat and cook over high heat, turning, until well browned on all sides. Add the reserved marinade. After 2 to 3 minutes, lower the heat and cook, uncovered, 20 minutes longer, turning occasionally. If the meat becomes too dry, add a few drops of water. Remove from the heat, pour most of the oil into a skillet, and reserve. Cover the pan and let rest for a few minutes.

Meanwhile, quickly stir fry the sliced vegetables in the reserved skillet with oil. Slice the roast and strain the gravy over it. Serve surrounded by stir-fried vegetables.

serves 6

Goulash with Polenta

gulyàs colla polenta

2½ pounds boneless beef shank

½ cup olive oil

1 clove garlic, crushed

2 bay leaves

1 teaspoon dried rosemary leaves

1 cup diced onion

Salt

¼ teaspoon crushed red pepper

One 6-ounce can tomato paste

2 cups beef broth or water

2 quarts water

2 cups coarse cornmeal

Cut the meat into 1-inch cubes. Place the oil, garlic, bay leaves, and rosemary leaves in a large skillet. Sauté, stirring, until the garlic is browned. Sprinkle with water a couple of times to release the flavors from the herbs. With a fork, remove and discard the herbs. Add the onion and sauté until soft. Add the meat, 2 teaspoons salt, and red pepper and brown, stirring, 5 minutes. Add the tomato paste and sauté, stirring, another 2 minutes. Add 1 cup beef broth or water and cook, covered, 2 hours, adding more liquid as necessary. Keep cooking while the polenta is being made.

Start the polenta by bringing the water with 1 tablespoon salt to a rapid boil. Lower the heat, add the cornmeal all at once, and stir vigorously. Cook 20 minutes, stirring frequently to prevent sticking. Spoon the polenta directly into each individual dish and top with a portion of goulash.

serves 6 to 8

Veal and Other Calf Meats

vitello

Veal Scaloppine with Lemon and Parsley

piccata di vitella

1½ pounds veal *scaloppine*, sliced thin

3 tablespoons flour

2 teaspoons salt

¼ teaspoon freshly ground black pepper

4 tablespoons olive oil

¼ cup chicken broth or water

Juice of 1 large lemon

2 tablespoons freshly chopped Italian parsley

With a meat mallet or the blade of a heavy cleaver, pound the *scaloppine* until paper thin. Combine the flour, salt, and pepper and lightly coat the *scaloppine* with the mixture.

Heat the oil in a large skillet and add the *scaloppine* in a single layer. Brown over high heat approximately 1½ minutes on each side; remove to a hot serving plate. Repeat until all the *scaloppine* are browned.

Add the broth or water to the skillet and simmer 1 minute while scraping the glaze with a wooden spoon. (For an excellent cold dish, return the *scaloppine* to the skillet when you add the broth and simmer for 10 to 15 minutes. Transfer to a serving dish, add the lemon juice and parsley, and let stand a few hours at room temperature.) Remove from the heat; add the lemon juice and parsley, stir, and pour over the *scaloppine*. Serve immediately.

serves 6

Veal and Romaine Lettuce

scaloppine colla lattuga

 ncient Roman Jewish cuisine often combined a salad vegetable with a protein dish such as fish, meat, or eggs. This recipe is a delicate combination of veal and romaine lettuce.

1½ pounds thinly sliced veal *scaloppine*

2 teaspoons salt

¼ teaspoon freshly ground black pepper

¼ cup unbleached flour

6 tablespoons olive oil

2 pounds romaine lettuce

2 tablespoons chicken fat or bone marrow

¼ cup dry white wine or vermouth

With a meat mallet or the blade of a heavy cleaver, pound the *scaloppine* very thin, then cut into 1-inch-wide strips. Lightly season with salt and pepper on both sides. Dredge with the flour and pat to remove excess.

Heat 4 tablespoons oil in a large skillet and brown the *scaloppine* over high heat 1 to 2 minutes on each side. Place on a hot serving dish and set the skillet, with drippings, aside.

After discarding the outer, bruised leaves, wash the lettuce thoroughly and pat dry with paper towels. Shred and place in a salad bowl. Season with small amounts of salt and pepper and the remaining olive oil; mix well.

Grease a large ovenproof pan with the chicken fat or marrow and arrange the *scaloppine* and lettuce in alternate layers. Start with half the veal, then half the lettuce; add the remaining *scaloppine* and end with the remaining lettuce.

Add the wine to the skillet and simmer 1 to 2 minutes while scraping the glaze; pour over the lettuce. Bake in a 375°F oven for 25 to 30 minutes. Serve hot and do not neglect the gravy at the bottom of the pan.

serves 6

Veal Scaloppine with Mushrooms

scaloppine ai funghi

¼ ounce dried, imported porcini mushrooms

½ cup warm water

¾ pound firm white mushrooms

6 tablespoons olive oil

Salt

1 clove garlic, sliced

1 tablespoon freshly chopped Italian parsley

1½ pounds veal *scaloppine*, sliced thin

¼ teaspoon freshly ground black pepper

½ cup unbleached flour

Soak the dried mushrooms in the warm water. Trim, wash, and slice the white mushrooms. With a fork, lift the soaked mushrooms from their bath, reserving the water. Cut into very small pieces and place in a saucepan with the sliced mushrooms. Add 3 tablespoons oil, ½ teaspoon salt, the garlic, and parsley; add the reserved water, taking great care not to include any of the sand that might be at the bottom. Cook over moderately high heat for 4 to 5 minutes.

Sprinkle the *scaloppine* with 2 teaspoons salt and the pepper and dredge with flour. Heat the remaining oil in a large skillet and lightly sauté the *scaloppine* for 1 minute on each side. Add the prepared mushrooms and simmer 5 minutes, scraping the bottom of the skillet. Let steep in the skillet ½ hour before serving.

serves 6

Veal Scaloppine with Madeira Wine

scaloppine al madera

This is one of the finest recipes in my repertoire. It is a blessing for dinner parties because it may be prepared one day in advance and its taste is actually enhanced.

1½ pounds veal *scaloppine*, sliced very thin

1½ teaspoons salt

¼ teaspoon freshly ground black pepper

Sprinkle the *scaloppine* with salt and pepper; dredge with flour and pat to shake off the excess.

Heat the oil in a large skillet with the onion and cook over moderate heat until the onion is golden brown. Temporarily remove the onion to a dish. Add the *scaloppine* to the skillet and brown for 2 minutes on each side.

½ cup unbleached flour

6 tablespoons olive oil

1 medium onion, minced

1 clove garlic, minced

1 tablespoon freshly chopped Italian parsley

½ cup Madeira wine

1½ cups tomato juice or 2 tablespoons tomato paste, diluted in 1½ cups water

Return the onion to the skillet; add the garlic, parsley, and Madeira and cook over high heat for 1 to 2 minutes. Add the tomato juice or diluted tomato paste and simmer, covered, for 5 to 7 minutes longer. If the veal is of a good quality, it should not take any longer to be cooked through and tender. If prepared in advance, simply heat through before serving.

NOTE: If you use tomato juice, use only 1 teaspoon salt, since the juice already contains salt.

serves 6

Breaded Veal Chops

cotolette impanate

6 rib veal chops, about 1 pound each

1 teaspoon salt

3 tablespoons unbleached flour

2 eggs, slightly beaten

1 cup seasoned breadcrumbs (page 311)

¾ cup olive oil

6 small sprigs parsley

1 lemon, sliced, or cut into 6 wedges

Separate the rib bone from any attached meat or skin so that the rib is bare. Trim off all fat and gristle from the chops. With a meat mallet or the blade of a heavy cleaver, pound the meaty rosettes until they are considerably enlarged and very thin. Combine the salt and flour and lightly coat the meat with the mixture. Holding by the bare rib, dip each chop in the beaten egg and dredge with breadcrumbs.

Heat the oil in a large, heavy skillet and fry the chops over moderately high heat for 2 minutes on each side or until golden brown. Transfer to a hot serving dish and garnish with parsley and lemon slices or wedges.

serves 6

Veal Tuna Style

vitello tonnato

Some believe that *Vitello Tonnato* is a veal dish with tuna sauce. Others take the word *tonnato* to mean that veal is cooked the way tuna fish is before it is canned. Whatever the origin of this dish, it is a delicate and tasty cold entree. Since the version made with tuna sauce has been presented in many other Italian cookbooks, I offer the version that does not call for tuna fish, but treats the veal as if it *were* tuna fish.

2 pounds lean boneless veal

1 clove garlic, sliced lengthwise into 4 pieces

4 anchovy fillets

1 tablespoon salt

¼ teaspoon freshly ground black pepper

3 tablespoons olive oil

1 medium onion, sliced

2½ cups water

Sauce (recipe follows)

Parsley sprigs

Make 4 small shallow cuts at different points on the surface of the meat. Insert 1 slice of garlic in each cut. Cover each garlic piece with an anchovy fillet and lightly tie all around with a white string so that the fillets and garlic remain in place. Sprinkle the meat with all the salt and pepper.

In a small saucepan in which the piece of meat can fit snugly, place the oil and sliced onion. Add the meat and brown on all sides, turning the meat frequently.

Add the water and bring to a rapid boil. Lower the heat and cook, covered, for 1¾ to 2 hours. Uncover and boil down until the liquid is reduced by half.

Transfer the meat to a glass, ceramic, or plastic container and strain all the liquid over it. Let cool, then store in the refrigerator for several hours or overnight.

Drain, remove the string, and cut into very thin slices. Arrange the slices on a serving plate in layers, covering each layer with the sauce. Cover with plastic wrap and refrigerate again. Allow to stand 1 hour at room temperature before serving. Garnish with parsley sprigs and serve with a cold rice salad.

serves 6

Sauce for Veal Tuna Style

salsa per vitello tonnato

1 egg
1 egg yolk
Juice of 1 lemon
2 tablespoons tiny capers packed in vinegar, drained
¼ teaspoon dry mustard
6 anchovy fillets
1½ cups olive oil
2 tablespoons concentrated liquid from the meat, if necessary

Place the egg, egg yolk, half the lemon juice, capers, mustard, and anchovy fillets in a blender. Set at medium-high speed and blend while adding oil and the remaining lemon juice alternately. The sauce should have the consistency of a very liquid mayonnaise. If it is too thick, add some of the concentrated meat liquid. Use as directed on the veal slices.

Veal Shanks with Peas

ossibuchi coi piselli

6 slices veal shank (about 4½ pounds)
Unbleached flour
1 clove garlic
2 sprigs Italian parsley
2 large basil leaves
¼ cup chopped onion
1 carrot, peeled and diced
6 tablespoons olive oil
2 teaspoons salt
2 dashes nutmeg
¼ teaspoon freshly ground black pepper

Cut the skin at 2 or 3 points around the circumference of the *ossibuchi* so that the skin, on shrinking, does not bunch the meat out of shape. Lightly flour the shank pieces on all sides.

Chop the garlic, parsley, and basil together very fine and place half of this mixture in a large skillet together with the onion, carrot, and oil. Sauté, stirring, 1 to 2 minutes. Add the *ossibuchi* in a single layer and brown 2 minutes on each side. Season with salt, nutmeg, and pepper. Add the wine and raise the heat to let the wine evaporate completely. Add the tomato paste and scrape the bottom of the skillet with a wooden spatula to loosen the stuck particles. Add 1 cup broth or water, shake the pan, and simmer, covered, 1½ hours, scraping the glaze occasionally.

Add the remaining liquid as it becomes necessary, but keep the *ossibuchi* in a thick, savory sauce at all times. When the meat

½ cup dry white wine

2 teaspoons tomato paste

2 cups beef broth or water

1 teaspoon grated
lemon rind

2 cups freshly shelled or
one 10 ounce package
frozen sweet tiny peas

begins to separate from the bone, add the remaining garlic mixture, lemon rind, and peas. Cook 10 more minutes, or until the peas are tender but not mushy and the sauce is thick and flavorful.

serves 4 to 6

Oven-Roasted Veal

vitella in forno

1 tablespoon salt

½ teaspoon freshly ground
black pepper

1 clove garlic, minced

1½ teaspoons
rosemary leaves

2 pounds lean veal leg in
one piece

Olive oil

1 large onion, coarsely
cut up

2 large carrots, peeled and
coarsely cut up

½ cup dry white wine

½ cup warm water

Combine the salt, pepper, garlic, and rosemary leaves on a piece of wax paper. Roll the piece of meat over this mixture until it is evenly coated on all sides.

Oil a shallow baking dish and spread the onion and carrots in it. Place the veal at the center; slowly pour ½ cup olive oil over the meat and vegetables. Place in a 450°F oven for 20 minutes.

Baste with the wine and return to the hot oven; after 3 minutes add the warm water. Turn the heat down to 300°F and bake another ½ hour or until fork tender. Remove from the oven and cover with a damp towel for 5 to 10 minutes.

Slice the meat and arrange on a hot serving plate. Strain the gravy and vegetables through a sieve and serve over the slices of meat.

serves 6

Piglet (Stuffed Breast of Veal)

chazirello (pancetta di vitella ripiena)

 Some time ago I received a telephone call from the widow of the historian Cecil Roth who asked me whether I knew why the Jews of Pitigliano called this delicious kosher dish *Chazirello*, piglet. I didn't know for certain, but I could imagine the reason. In early autumn, in the main piazza in Pitigliano, a big open-air fair took place in which almost everything—from shoes to dry fruit, from livestock to toys, from yard goods to wines, from earthenware to grains—was sold. In the middle of the square loomed a pushcart that sold hot slices of *porchetta*, a stuffed roasted piglet that sent forth delicious aromas. The Jews, who refrained from eating pork to obey their dietary laws, were envious of their fellow Pitiglianesi and invented this dish, which of course doesn't use any pork, but is as fragrant and perhaps as tasty as its namesake.

4 pounds breast of veal (with bones)

2 cloves garlic, crushed

Salt

Freshly ground black pepper

1 teaspoon fennel seeds

½ boneless, skinless chicken breast

¾ pound cubed lean beef

2 thick slices stale bread, cooked into a pap (page 43)

1 egg, slightly beaten

¼ cup raw, unsalted pistachio nuts or walnut meats

Dash or two nutmeg

1 teaspoon fresh or ½ teaspoon dried rosemary leaves

Open the pocket of the breast of veal completely as you open a book, or have your butcher do it. Painstakingly remove and discard as much fat as possible. Rub with garlic on both sides, then sprinkle with salt and pepper to taste. Spread the open breast, rib side down, over a working surface and sprinkle with fennel seeds.

Grind together the chicken breast and beef. Combine the ground meats with the pap, egg, nuts, nutmeg, and salt and pepper to taste and mix well. Spread this mixture over the rib half of the open breast, then close the other half over it. Sew the sides closed using needle and thread, or fasten all around with a string. Sprinkle all over with rosemary leaves and place in a baking pan, rib side down. Bake in a 350°F oven for 2½ hours or until quite browned and crisp.

Remove from the oven, cover with a clean kitchen towel, and let stand 10 minutes before slicing.

serves 6

Jellied Veal

vitella in gelatina

2 pounds boned veal
shoulder

1 tablespoon salt

¼ teaspoon freshly ground
black pepper

2 tablespoons olive oil

1 clove garlic

½ calf foot

1 lemon, sliced
or cut into wedges

4 to 5 sprigs American
curly parsley

Sprinkle the veal with salt and pepper and form into a roll. Tie all around with a string and place in a casserole with the oil and garlic. Slowly brown on all sides, over moderate heat, for about 10 minutes. Discard the garlic and add the calf foot. Add water to cover and simmer, covered, for 1½ hours or until the veal is quite tender. Transfer the roll to a dish to cool.

Boil the calf foot another hour or until the broth is greatly reduced.

Remove the string from the roll and slice. Arrange the slices in a somewhat deep serving plate. Strain the broth through a fine sieve and pour over the slices. Place in the refrigerator until firm. Garnish with lemon and parsley sprigs.

NOTE: The calf foot is also delicious. You may want to cut the meaty parts and add them to the strained broth.

serves 6

Veal Stew

spezzatino di vitella

2 pounds boneless leg of
veal, cut into 1½-inch cubes

2 pounds veal breast, cut
into 1½-inch cubes

2 teaspoons salt

¼ teaspoon ground red
pepper

1 dash ground cloves

Sprinkle the veal cubes with the salt, red pepper, cloves, cinnamon, and flour.

Heat the oil in a large saucepan with the onion and carrot. Add the veal and cook over moderately high heat, stirring, until all the pieces of veal are browned. Add the wine and cook over high heat 1 to 2 minutes.

Lower the heat, add the lemon peel and tomatoes and simmer, covered, for approximately 1 hour, stirring occasionally.

2 dashes cinnamon

1 tablespoon unbleached flour

¼ cup olive oil

1 medium onion, sliced thin

1 medium carrot, peeled and diced

½ cup dry white wine

One ½ × 2-inch piece lemon peel, shredded

2 cups diced peeled tomatoes with their juice, fresh or canned

1 clove garlic, minced

1 tablespoon freshly chopped Italian parsley

(Should the sauce become too dry, add a few tablespoons water. However, this is unlikely to happen, and at any rate, veal should cook in a thick, flavorful sauce at all times.) A few minutes before removing the stew from the heat, add the garlic and parsley and stir.

serves 6

Cold Calf Tongue
lingua di vitello fredda

1 calf tongue (about 2 pounds)

1 tablespoon salt

¼ teaspoon whole peppercorns

⅛ teaspoon ground cloves

2 bay leaves

Green Sauce (recipe follows)

In a saucepan just large enough to contain the tongue snugly, place the tongue, salt, peppercorns, ground cloves, and bay leaves. Add enough warm water to cover and bring to a rapid boil. Cook, covered, over moderately high heat, for approximately 2 hours.

Transfer the tongue to a cutting board. As soon as it is cool enough to handle, remove and discard the skin, and trim all the fatty parts. Cool thoroughly before slicing into thin slices.

Arrange on a serving plate; spread the sauce over it. Cover the plate with plastic wrap and place in the refrigerator for several hours to allow the tongue to absorb the flavors of the sauce.

serves 4 to 6

Green Sauce

salsa verde

1 cup firmly packed
Italian parsley leaves

1 small clove garlic

1 tablespoon capers,
drained

1 small hard-boiled egg,
shelled

1 tablespoon breadcrumbs

1 tablespoon lemon juice

1 tablespoon wine vinegar

¼ cup olive oil

Salt and pepper to taste

Finely chop together the parsley, garlic, and capers. Transfer to a sauce bowl. Mash the egg and add to the bowl. Add the breadcrumbs, lemon juice, and vinegar and let stand for a few minutes.

Add the oil and small amounts of salt and pepper to suit your taste, and mix well.

yields about ½ cup

Calf Tongue and Onions in a Sweet-and-Sour Sauce

lingua e cipolline in agro-dolce

2½ pounds calf tongue

Olive oil

1 small carrot, peeled
and sliced

1 stalk celery, coarsely
chopped

2 bay leaves

1 large sprig Italian parsley,
coarsely chopped

2 teaspoons salt

Trim the tongues of all fat that can possibly be removed. Place them under a broiler or in a toaster oven, turning once, until the skins begin to burn and blister. As soon as the tongues can be handled, peel them, then rinse thoroughly under cold water and pat dry.

In a pot just large enough to contain the tongues snugly, heat 3 tablespoons oil. Add the carrot, celery, bay leaves, and parsley and sauté 2 minutes. Add the tongues and season with salt and cloves. Lightly brown, turning once or twice, for 3 to 4 minutes. Add the peppercorns and enough hot water to cover and simmer, covered, for about 1 hour. Transfer the tongues to a

⅛ teaspoon ground cloves

¼ teaspoon whole peppercorns

Hot water

2 pints pearl onions, peeled and soaked in cold water

½ cup dark seedless raisins

2 tablespoons raw sugar

1 tablespoon red wine vinegar

cutting board and remove any peel that remains. Strain and defat the broth and reserve.

Drain the onions and place in a saucepan with 3 tablespoons oil. Brown, stirring frequently, for about 5 minutes. Add the raisins, sugar, vinegar, and reserved broth to the onions.

Slice the tongues and add to the saucepan. Cook, uncovered, for ½ hour or until most of the liquid has evaporated and the meat and onions are in a dense, savory sauce. This is excellent hot or at room temperature.

serves 6

Calf Liver Grandma Sara Style

fegato di vitella della nonna sara

 My mother believed that some of the nutrients in food were lost by overcooking. To overcook liver would not only rob it of nutrients but make it hard and chewy. She would, therefore, serve it simply marinated in lemon juice and olive oil, and then seasoned with salt, pepper, and parsley. Not all of us liked the texture of the raw liver, though, and the following recipe is a more acceptable version.

2 pounds calf liver, sliced very thin

1 teaspoon salt

¼ teaspoon freshly ground black pepper

2 tablespoons olive oil

1 small onion, chopped fine

2 tablespoons lemon juice

2 tablespoons freshly chopped Italian parsley

Lightly season the calf liver slices with salt and pepper on both sides. Place the oil and onion in a large skillet and cook over moderate heat until the onion is soft. Add the liver, cover the skillet, and simmer for 3 minutes. Add the lemon juice and parsley and cook 1 to 2 minutes longer. Serve immediately.

serves 6

Lamb

agnello

Roast Leg of Lamb with Potatoes
agnello in forno con patate

1 leg of lamb
(6 to 7 pounds)
or ½ baby lamb, about the
same weight

12 medium potatoes

3 tablespoons olive oil

3 teaspoons salt

¾ teaspoon freshly ground
black pepper

1 small clove garlic, minced

1 teaspoon dried
rosemary leaves

1 clove garlic,
slightly crushed

Leave the lamb at room temperature. Peel the potatoes and cut lengthwise into 4 to 6 pieces each. Place in a bowl and season with 2 tablespoons oil, 1 teaspoon salt, half the pepper, minced garlic, and half the rosemary leaves. Toss well and set aside.

Remove the excess fat from the lamb. Rub all its surface with the crushed garlic clove and then with the remaining tablespoon oil. Season with the remaining salt, pepper, and rosemary leaves and place at the center of a large roasting pan. Distribute the seasoned potatoes around it and bake in 550°F oven for 30 minutes. Decrease the temperature to 350°F and cook for another 45 minutes.

Keep in mind that overcooked lamb acquires an unpleasant flavor and it is better—as it happened in my first experience quite by accident—to have it quite done on the surface but slightly underdone on the inside.

serves 6 to 8

Braised Lamb Shanks

cianchetti di agnello brasati

6 meaty lamb shanks

Olive oil

Salt

Freshly ground black pepper

2 cloves garlic, minced fine

2 teaspoons rosemary leaves

½ cup dry white wine

½ cup hot broth or water

Wash the shanks thoroughly and pat dry. Rub with olive oil, then sprinkle with salt and pepper, garlic, and rosemary. Set aside in a cool place, covered, for several hours.

Place in a large saucepan with ½ cup olive oil and brown over moderate heat on all sides for 10 to 15 minutes. Add the wine and raise the temperature for 1 minute, then lower to minimum, cover the pan tightly, and simmer for 1 hour, or until the shanks are fork tender. Check every 15 minutes or so and add the broth or water by the tablespoonful as it becomes necessary.

Transfer the shanks to a hot serving plate and strain the gravy over them before serving.

serves 6

Rib Lamb Chops with Artichokes

braciolette di agnello coi carciofi

3½ pounds small rib lamb chops

4 tablespoons olive oil

2 teaspoons salt

¼ teaspoon freshly ground black pepper

2 large cloves garlic, sliced

3 tablespoons coarsely chopped Italian parsley

3 cups hot water

10 medium fresh artichokes, or 2 boxes frozen artichoke hearts

Trim the lamb ribs of all their fat. Place in a large skillet with the oil, salt, pepper, garlic, and parsley. Sauté over low heat for 3 to 4 minutes. Add 1 cup hot water and simmer, covered, for approximately 45 minutes. Add another cup of hot water and cook another half hour, or until the lamb is of desired tenderness.

Meanwhile, trim the artichokes as described on page 40 and cut into 6 wedges each. (If you use frozen artichokes, leave the packages at room temperature when you begin to cook the lamb.)

Add a third and final cup hot water and the artichokes and cook, uncovered, until the artichokes are tender but not mushy. Raise the temperature, if necessary, to reduce the liquid so that the lamb and artichokes are in a savory sauce.

serves 6

Lamb and Artichoke Medallions

medaglioni di agnello e carciofi

12 medium-thick rib lamb
chops

3 medium artichokes

2 lemons, juice and rind

Salt

Freshly ground black pepper

2 tablespoons freshly
chopped Italian parsley

1 small clove garlic, minced

1 cup unbleached flour

3 eggs, slightly beaten with
a pinch of salt and a dash
of pepper

1 cup seasoned
breadcrumbs (page 311)

Olive oil

Sauce for medallions
(recipe follows)

Use only the central rosettes of the ribs and reserve the bones and scraps for the sauce. With a meat mallet or with the blade of a heavy cleaver, pound the meat rosettes thin. Arrange on a working surface in a single layer.

Clean and trim the artichokes (see page 40), then cut each lengthwise into 4 slices (remove the choke, if there is any), and spread out on the working surface next to the meat.

Lightly season the meat and artichokes with small amounts of salt, pepper, parsley, and garlic. Combine one meat rosette with one artichoke slice, seasoned sides together, and gently press. Coat with the flour, patting to remove excess. When all the cutlets are ready, dip in the beaten egg, roll in breadcrumbs, and fry in hot oil for 2 minutes on each side or until golden on both sides. Serve as is or with the hot sauce on a separate sauce dish.

serves 4 to 6

Sauce for Medallions

salsa per medaglioni

Bones and scraps
from previous recipe

Salt

2½ cups water

4 tablespoons olive oil

Place the lamb bones and scraps in a saucepan with 1 teaspoon salt and the water. Bring to a boil, then reduce the heat and simmer gently, covered, for 45 minutes to 1 hour. Strain and defat the broth.

Heat the oil in a saucepan, add the flour and sauté, stirring, 2 minutes. Add the wine and lamb stock and stir vigorously to prevent lumps from forming. Cook 2 minutes.

3 tablespoons
unbleached flour

2 tablespoons dry white wine

½ medium clove garlic,
minced fine

1 tablespoon freshly
chopped Italian parsley

Freshly ground black pepper

2 egg yolks

2 tablespoons lemon juice

Remove from the heat and add the garlic, parsley, pepper, and egg yolks, stirring after each addition.

Return to the heat and cook 1 to 2 minutes longer, stirring frequently. Just before serving add the lemon juice and mix well.

yields approximately 2 cups

Baby Goat for Passover

capretto per pesach

 kid is the baby goat, just as a lamb is the baby sheep. Many make the mistake of confusing the two, but kid meat is much more tender and delicate than lamb. If you cannot find kid, you can try this dish with lamb, but be sure to get a small spring lamb.

3 pounds kid chops

3 tablespoons olive oil

1½ teaspoons salt

¼ teaspoon freshly ground
black pepper

1 clove garlic, minced

3 to 4 stems Italian parsley
(leaves removed),
tied in a bouquet

1½ cups cold water

2 egg yolks

Juice of 1 lemon

Place the chops in a skillet with the oil, salt, pepper, garlic, and the parsley bouquet. Add the cold water and simmer, covered, for 1 hour or until the meat is fork tender. Discard the parsley bouquet.

Mix the egg yolks and lemon juice; turn the heat off and add the mixture at once. Shake the skillet to mix the sauce. Serve immediately.

serves 6

Lamb, Meatballs, and Spinach for Passover

hammin di pesach

The word *hammin* (or *hammim*) is derived from the Hebrew adjective *ham*, or warm, which describes certain dishes that are kept warm for prolonged periods (see *Hammin Toscano*). In various parts of Italy, the name *hammin* was given to different recipes. In Pitigliano, however, *hammin* was *the* classic one-course meal for Passover that both rich and poor used to make. The only difference between the two versions was in the cuts of meats used. Poor people used breast of lamb (which, by the way, is very tasty) and meatballs made with beef (when the cost of ground beef was a fraction of the cost of chicken). People who didn't have to worry about cost used tiny rib chops from baby lamb and chicken balls.

1 chicken breast (2 halves), ground

4 tablespoons olive oil

1 egg, slightly beaten

2 tablespoons matza meal

8 cups chicken broth

Salt

Freshly ground black pepper

Dash nutmeg

2½ pounds breast of lamb or rib lamb chops

2 cloves garlic, sliced

2 large sprigs Italian parsley, coarsely chopped

1 cup warm water

2 pounds small-leaved bulk spinach, cooked and slightly drained

4 regular *matzòt*, broken into large pieces

Combine the ground chicken, 1 tablespoon olive oil, egg, matza meal, and 2 tablespoons broth in a small bowl. Add salt, pepper, and nutmeg to taste and mix well.

In a large pot, place the lamb with the remaining oil; sprinkle with 1 teaspoon salt and ¼ teaspoon pepper and lightly brown for 2 to 3 minutes. Add the garlic, parsley, and the warm water.

Form many tiny balls with the ground chicken mixture and gently add to the pot with the lamb. Cover and simmer for 1 to 1½ hours. Add the spinach and 1 teaspoon salt and simmer, covered, 15 minutes longer.

Transfer the lamb chops, half the spinach, and most of the gravy to a hot serving dish and keep warm.

Add the remaining broth to the pot and bring to a boil. Add the matza pieces and cook 4 to 5 minutes. Turn the heat off and let stand 5 minutes before serving as a soup. Serve the lamb and spinach as the main dish.

serves 6 to 8

Lamb Loaves

polpettoni d'agnello

Polpettoni d'agnello is a relatively simple dish to prepare. Yet it tastes delicious, and I never hesitate to serve it on special occasions. It is a favorite at Passover, when lambs are still young and artichokes and other vegetables are tender.

1 leg of lamb, the meaty shank portion (about 4 pounds), boned

2 teaspoons salt

¼ teaspoon freshly ground black pepper

1 cup olive oil

¼ cup dry white wine

Remove all the fat and skin from the meat and grind it, or have your butcher grind it for you. Season with salt and pepper and mix well. Divide into two portions and shape each portion into an oval ball. In order to avoid air pockets inside the loaves, roll a piece of plastic wrap around the meat, hold it at the two ends and push the meat together.

Place the two loaves, with all the oil, in a saucepan just large enough to contain them. Brown on all sides, uncovered, over moderate heat, for 30 minutes.

Transfer the loaves to a cutting board and slice as soon as they are cool enough to handle. Arrange the slices on a hot serving plate.

Pour most of the oil from the saucepan into a container and save for a later use. (You may use the reserved oil to make *Carciofi Trifolati*, to sauté your favorite steamed vegetable, or see *Olio di Arrosto*, page 126.) Add the wine to the saucepan and simmer for 1 to 2 minutes, scraping the glaze. Pour over the slices and serve.

serves 6

Lamb Balls with Mushrooms

polpettine di agnello coi funghi

4½ pounds lean
boneless lamb

Salt

Freshly ground black
pepper

Olive oil

1 pound small white mush-
rooms, sliced very fine

¼ teaspoon dried savory

½ cup dry white wine

Grind the lamb with 2 teaspoons salt and ⅛ teaspoon pepper. Shape into tiny balls.

Heat ½ cup oil in a large skillet and fry half the balls, shaking the skillet frequently, until browned on all sides. With a slotted spoon transfer to a warm dish and set aside. Repeat with the remaining balls, adding fresh oil to the skillet as necessary. Pour most of the oil into a new skillet (reserve the one where you fried the balls). Add the mushrooms, savory, and salt and pepper to taste and stir-fry over moderately high heat for 5 minutes.

Add the wine to the old skillet and simmer for 1 to 2 minutes, scraping the glaze. Transfer the balls and mushrooms to this skillet and heat through over moderately high heat, stirring frequently, until most of the liquid has evaporated.

serves 6

Poultry

pollame

Pot-Roasted Cornish Hens

pollastrini arrosto morto

 This is a delicious alternative to Roast Chicken for Sabbath, with the advantage that it can be prepared a few hours ahead of time.

3 small Cornish hens

3 teaspoons salt

½ teaspoon freshly ground black pepper

1 tablespoon dried sage leaves or ½ teaspoon powdered sage

6 tablespoons olive oil

3 small cloves garlic

1 small onion, sliced

1½ cups long-grain rice

3 cups hot chicken broth

Wash the Cornish hens and remove as much fat as possible. Sprinkle with the salt, pepper, and sage inside and out. Place in a large pan with 3 tablespoons oil and garlic and brown on all sides for 5 to 10 minutes. Lower the heat, cover the pan tightly, and cook, without adding any liquid, for 30 to 45 minutes, turning occasionally. Leave on the lowest heat until ready to serve.

Half an hour before mealtime, cook the onion in the remaining oil until dark brown, then discard. Add the rice to the oil and cook, stirring, 3 to 4 minutes. Add the stock or broth and cook, covered, without stirring, another 15 minutes. Spread over a large hot serving plate.

Cut the hens in half lengthwise and arrange, skin side up, over the rice. There will be plenty of tasty gravy in the pan in which the hens were cooked. Strain, heat, and pour it over the hens and rice. Serve immediately.

serves 6

Roast Chicken for Sabbath

pollo arrosto per shabbàt

This is the dish served in my family on Friday evening, right after lighting the candles and blessing the wine and the bread at the onset of Sabbath.

2 broiler-fryers, about 2½ pounds each

2 tablespoons salt

Freshly ground black pepper

4 large fresh or 2 teaspoons dried sage leaves

2 large cloves garlic, with husk on

8 large baking potatoes

2 teaspoons fresh or 1 teaspoon dried rosemary leaves

2 teaspoons garlic salt

4 tablespoons olive oil

Wash the chickens thoroughly and pat dry with paper towels. Remove as much fat as you can and tuck the wings under. Sprinkle the cavity of each chicken with ½ tablespoon salt and approximately ½ teaspoon pepper. Place 2 fresh sage leaves or 1 teaspoon dried sage leaves and 1 clove garlic inside each chicken. Sprinkle the outside with ½ tablespoon salt and about ½ teaspoon pepper and place in a large baking pan, making sure the chickens do not touch each other.

Peel the potatoes, wash and cut lengthwise into 6 pieces each. Place in a bowl and season with the rosemary leaves, garlic salt, oil, and ¼ to ½ teaspoon pepper. Toss to allow seasoning to coat the potatoes evenly. Pour around the chickens in a single layer, if possible. Place in a 450°F oven for 25 minutes. Lower the heat to 350°F and bake the chickens for 45 minutes to 1 hour longer.

serves 6 to 8

Stuffed Roast Chicken

pollo arrosto ripieno

1 teaspoon dried sage leaves

1 teaspoon dried rosemary leaves

Olive oil

1 medium onion, chopped

½ pound lean ground veal

2 chicken livers, cut up

Salt

Freshly ground black pepper

Dash nutmeg

1 cup chicken broth

2 slices white bread, toasted

2 stalks white celery, diced

4 medium mushrooms, sliced

1 egg, slightly beaten

1 medium roasting chicken (about 4 pounds)

1 large clove garlic, slightly crushed

1 teaspoon fennel seeds

Place the sage and rosemary in a piece of cheesecloth and tie with a string.

In a medium skillet, heat 2 tablespoons oil over moderate heat. Add the onion, veal, and livers (previously soaked in water until no trace of blood is visible). Sprinkle with small amounts of the salt, pepper, and nutmeg. Cook, stirring frequently, for 3 minutes. Add the chicken broth and cheesecloth bouquet and simmer, covered, for ½ hour. Remove and discard the bouquet and transfer the contents of the skillet to a bowl. Add the toasted bread and let it soak thoroughly. Add the celery, mushrooms, and egg and mix well.

Rub the inside and outside of the chicken with garlic. Sprinkle the inside with fennel seeds and rub the outside with olive oil. Place the stuffing into the chicken cavity and season the outside with salt and pepper to taste.

Place in an uncovered roasting pan, breast side up, in a preheated 500°F oven for 30 minutes. Lower the temperature to 350°F and cook 1½ hours longer.

serves 6

Classic Chicken Cacciatora

pollo baruch

Baruch was my father's Hebrew name, and I named this recipe after him because he prepared it with his own personal touch, which made everything taste delicious. Of course, the chickens he prepared were not mass-produced, but were raised in the fields where they could run and scratch and scrape the dirt for food. Their meat was firm, tasty, and fat free. But even the chickens we have today, cooked this way, become very tasty.

2 small chickens (totaling 3½ to 4 pounds), cut up into small pieces

1 large onion, thinly sliced

4 tablespoons olive oil

1 tablespoon salt

½ teaspoon freshly ground black pepper

½ cup dry red wine

2 heaping tablespoons tomato paste, diluted in 1 cup water

½ cup oil-cured black olives

Remove and discard the backs and necks (you can use them to make soup) and as much fat as you can from the chicken pieces. Place in a large skillet with the onion and oil and brown on medium heat, stirring occasionally, for 20 to 30 minutes. Add the salt and pepper, stir, then add the wine. Raise to high heat and cook for 5 minutes. Add the diluted tomato paste and olives. Cover and simmer for 15 minutes. Serve piping hot.

serves 6 to 8

Chicken and Potato Patties

polpettine di pollo e patate

2½ cups cooked chicken, diced

1 pound all-purpose potatoes, steamed, peeled, and mashed

3 eggs, slightly beaten

1 tablespoon freshly chopped Italian parsley

½ small clove garlic, minced

Dash nutmeg

Salt

Freshly ground black pepper

Olive oil for frying

Grind or chop the chicken very fine and combine with the potatoes, eggs, parsley, garlic, and nutmeg. Add salt and pepper to taste and mix well.

With oiled hands, shape the mixture by the tablespoonful into round patties.

Heat ½ cup oil in a large skillet and fry the patties, turning and adding oil if necessary, until they are golden brown on both sides. Serve immediately.

serves 6

Fried Chicken for Chanukah

pollo fritto per chanukà

 During the eight days of Chanukah, Jews the world over eat all kinds of fried foods. This custom commemorates and celebrates "the miracle of the oil" at the rededication of the Temple of Jerusalem by the Maccabee brothers in 165 B.C.E. It is said that the oil they found for the eternally burning lamp was just enough to last one day, but miraculously it lasted eight days—long enough to allow them to make and sanctify a fresh supply. *Pollo Fritto* is a classic dish in Jewish Italy.

1 small frying chicken, cut up into small pieces

1½ teaspoons salt

¼ teaspoon freshly ground black pepper

¼ teaspoon nutmeg or cinnamon

½ teaspoon garlic salt

Juice of 1 lemon

Olive oil

½ cup unbleached flour

2 eggs, slightly beaten

1 lemon, cut into 6 wedges

Riso Coll'Uvetta (page 128)

Sprinkle the chicken pieces evenly with the salt, pepper, nutmeg, and garlic salt. Place in a bowl with the lemon juice and 2 tablespoons olive oil and set aside in the refrigerator to marinate for several hours or overnight. Toss once in a while to ensure evenness of seasoning.

Heat 1 cup oil in a large skillet. Roll the chicken pieces in the flour, dip in eggs, and fry in the hot oil over high heat for 1 to 2 minutes. Lower the heat and fry for 15 minutes longer or until the pieces are golden (but not brown) on all sides. Serve with lemon wedges and *Riso Coll'Uvetta*.

serves 4 to 6

Chicken Breast Patties with Celery Fingers

pizzette di petto di pollo coi sedani

3 boneless, skinless chicken breasts (6 halves)

½ cup coarse breadcrumbs (page 311)

¼ cup chicken broth

2 eggs, slightly beaten

1 tablespoon freshly chopped Italian parsley

Salt

Freshly ground black pepper

6 stalks celery, cut into 2 × ½-inch pieces

3 tablespoons olive oil

2 cloves garlic, minced

2 cups cold water

Remove the tendons from the chicken breasts and grind or chop fine. In a medium bowl, combine the breadcrumbs, chicken broth, eggs, and parsley. Add the ground chicken and salt and pepper to taste, and mix well.

In a large skillet, place the celery pieces, oil, garlic, and cold water. Add small amounts of salt and pepper and simmer, covered, until the celery is soft, 15 to 20 minutes.

With wet hands, make 18 patties out of the ground chicken mixture and gently add to the skillet. Cover tightly and simmer for 15 minutes longer. Uncover and boil down the excess liquid.

serves 6

Chicken Galantine

pollo in galantina

his elegant form of chicken must be made ahead of time. Its preparation is somewhat complicated, but, like many recipes in this collection that are time consuming, the result is worth the trouble.

1 medium stewing chicken (about 4 pounds)

Salt

Freshly ground black pepper

½ cup dry white wine

¼ pound chicken hearts, diced

¾ pound lean veal

4 quarts cold water

1 small onion, cut in half

1 small carrot, peeled

1 stalk celery

1 sprig Italian parsley

4 to 5 whole peppercorns

2 whole cloves

2 slices stale bread cooked into a pap (page 43)

2 eggs, slightly beaten

Dash nutmeg

¼ cup shelled and peeled fresh pistachio nuts

2 black truffles, diced

1 hard-boiled egg, cut into 4 lengthwise wedges

With a sharp knife make an incision lengthwise in the skin of the chicken along the backbone. With your fingers and the help of the knife, loosen the skin from the meat of the fowl (the fat will help you achieve your end) and "undress" the chicken. When you reach the wings, cut the joints from the inside, detaching them from the breast, but leaving the whole wings attached to the skin. Lightly sprinkle the skin with salt and pepper on both sides and place in a bowl with the wine. Add the diced hearts.

Carve and dice the breast; add to the bowl and set aside. Carve all the other meat, scraping the bones (reserve the bones) and grind together with the veal.

In a large pot, place the water, 2 tablespoons salt, the reserved bones, onion, carrot, celery, parsley, peppercorns, and cloves. Bring to a boil, then simmer, covered, for about 1 hour.

Meanwhile prepare your galantine. Combine the ground meats with the cooked bread, beaten eggs, salt and pepper to taste, and a dash of nutmeg. Mix well. Add the diced breast, hearts, pistachios, and truffles and mix again. Spread the chicken skin on a working surface with the inside facing up. Place the ground meat mixture on the skin and inside the legs. Arrange the hard-boiled egg pieces in 4 different spots. Bring the skin together and sew it closed using a large, threaded needle. Be sure the neck and leg holes are sewn. Poke the skin all over with the needle, then add to the simmering broth. Cook, covered, for approximately 2½ hours, adding a little hot water at a time if it becomes necessary in order to keep the fowl submerged at all times.

Transfer the stuffed skin to an oval dish, cover with an

inverted dish, and place a light weight on it. Let stand at room temperature until thoroughly cool, then place in the refrigerator for several hours or overnight.

Boil the broth down to approximately 2 cups. Strain through a damp linen cloth and pour into a loaf pan; refrigerate to form a gelatin. Slice the chicken, but keep the slices together for the whole chicken effect. Unmold the gelatin and cut into even slices. Surround the "whole" chicken with gelatin slices and bring to the table.

NOTE: If you don't find fresh pistachio nuts, replace them with walnut meats rather than using dried pistachio nuts, which have lost their beautiful green. Also, if truffles are not available, use ¼ ounce dried imported porcini mushrooms, soaked in ¼ cup warm water for 10 minutes, drained and diced.

serves 6 to 8

Chicken Breast Balls

polpette di petto di pollo

You will be happy to have *polpette* in the freezer for unexpected guests. All you have to do is add them to your favorite stewed vegetable and simmer until heated through. Or another suggestion would be to heat the chicken balls over low heat for half an hour while you prepare a *Risotto Semplice* and a green salad. But you will find, I am sure, many uses for these very tasty chicken balls.

3 boneless, skinless chicken breasts (6 halves)
2 eggs, slightly beaten
¾ cup coarse breadcrumbs (page 311)

Remove and discard all tendons and fat from the chicken breasts. Grind or chop very fine and place in a bowl. Add the eggs, breadcrumbs, parsley, and ⅓ cup chicken broth. Season with salt and pepper and mix to combine.

In a large skillet that can go into the freezer and directly

1 tablespoon freshly chopped Italian parsley

Chicken broth

1 teaspoon salt

⅛ teaspoon freshly ground black pepper

4 tablespoons olive oil

1 large clove garlic, slightly crushed

from the freezer to the range, heat the oil with garlic. Shape the ground meat mixture into 20 oval or round balls and brown in the oil on all sides. Discard the garlic and add 1½ cups broth. Cover the skillet tightly and simmer for 15 to 20 minutes.

Let stand at room temperature until cool, then place a piece of aluminum foil between the skillet and lid so that it is almost airtight and place in the freezer until ready to use.

serves 6

Chicken and Artichoke Cutlets

cotolette di pollo e carciofi

6 medium fresh artichokes

2 lemons, juice and rinds

2 boneless chicken breasts (4 halves)

2 tablespoons freshly chopped Italian parsley

Salt

Freshly ground black pepper

1 cup unbleached flour

3 eggs, slightly beaten with a pinch of salt

1 cup fine breadcrumbs

Olive or other vegetable oil for frying

1 lemon, cut into 6 wedges

Clean the artichokes and slice lengthwise into 4 slices each. Place the artichokes into a bowl of water containing the lemon rinds and juice (see page 40).

Cut the chicken breasts into 24 small pieces and flatten down with the blade of a cleaver or a meat mallet. Line up on a working surface and season only the top side with parsley and small amounts of salt and pepper.

Cover the seasoned side of each cutlet with 1 artichoke slice and gently press down.

Coat with the flour, patting to remove the excess; dip in the beaten egg, and roll in the breadcrumbs. Fry in the hot oil, a few at a time, until golden on both sides. Serve with lemon wedges.

serves 6

Cold Chicken with Green Sauce

pollo freddo in salsa verde

1 boiled young fowl, boned

Nutmeg

1 cup firmly packed parsley leaves

2 tablespoons tiny capers, drained

2 tablespoons breadcrumbs or matza meal

2 tablespoons wine vinegar

2 hard-boiled eggs

Olive oil

Salt

Freshly ground black pepper

Tomato Roses (optional; page 52)

Chill the chicken in the refrigerator for several hours. Slice thin and arrange the slices on a platter. Sprinkle with small amounts of grated nutmeg, cover with plastic wrap, and return to the refrigerator.

Place the parsley in a processor and process until the parsley is chopped fine. Add the capers and process a few seconds. Add the breadcrumbs, vinegar, and hard-boiled eggs and process just until the eggs are chopped but not reduced to a puree. Add ¼ to ½ cup oil and salt and pepper to taste. Blend for a second.

Take the chicken platter from the refrigerator and spread the sauce over the chicken, leveling with a rubber spatula. Cover with plastic wrap again and keep refrigerated until ready to serve. Garnish with tomato roses.

NOTE: If you opt for tomato roses, make them and place on the plate a moment before serving, since they lose their crispness in the refrigerator.

serves 6

Roast Turkey

tacchino arrosto

12- to 15-pound hen turkey, at room temperature

2½ cups water

1 large clove garlic, slightly crushed

2 tablespoons olive oil

1 tablespoon dried rosemary leaves

2 tablespoons salt

2 teaspoons freshly ground black pepper

Stuffing (recipe follows)

Remove the giblets and neck from the turkey. Place the neck and gizzard in a saucepan with the water and a little salt. Bring to a boil, then simmer, covered, for 1½ hours. Strain and use for the stuffing.

Wash the turkey inside and out and pat dry with paper towels. Remove as much fat as possible; then rub the entire turkey surface with the garlic clove. Sprinkle with oil and rub with your hands to coat the surface evenly. Sprinkle with rosemary, salt, and pepper and set aside in a shallow pan, loosely covered with aluminum foil, until the broth is ready.

Prepare the stuffing and fill the cavity of the neck, tucking the skin under. Fill the large cavity and close with a wire gadget or with pins and twine. Place, uncovered, with breast up, in a 450°F oven for 30 to 45 minutes. Lower the temperature to 350°F and roast 1 to 1½ hours longer—no need to baste or turn. Remove from the oven and cover with a slightly damp kitchen towel. Let stand about 20 minutes before carving.

NOTE: If you have more stuffing than you can fit inside the bird, put the remainder in a covered, oiled baking dish, and place in the oven at 350°F as soon as you remove the turkey. The stuffing will be done when you have finished carving the turkey. The gravy that has formed in the roasting pan is delicious and should be served strained and heated, without thickening.

serves 12 or more

Poultry Stuffing

farcita per pollame

1 medium knob *finocchio* (fennel)

¾ cup olive oil

1 medium onion, diced

3 stalks celery, diced

3 cooking apples, peeled, cored, and diced

½ cup walnut meats, coarsely chopped

½ cup diced beef salami

6 cups seasoned bread croutons (page 309)

30 *mondine* (boiled chestnuts), peeled and broken up (2 cups)

2 cups turkey or chicken broth

Discard the tough, outer leaves and most of the green from the fennel. Thoroughly wash, then cut up into small pieces. Place in a skillet with the oil, onion, and celery and cook over high heat for approximately 3 minutes. Add the apples, walnut meats, and salami and cook, stirring, 1 more minute. Transfer to a bowl and let cool for 10 minutes.

Add the croutons and chestnuts and gently mix to coat the croutons with oil. (Up to this point, you may prepare your stuffing well in advance and keep refrigerated until you are ready to stuff the poultry. The stuffing of the poultry should be done at the very last moment before roasting, to avoid spoilage.) Add the broth and mix just enough to wet all the bread.

Place inside the poultry or cook separately in an oiled baking dish, covered, for 40 to 45 minutes at 350°F.

serves 12 (or for 12- to 15-pound bird)

Pot-Roasted Turkey Drumsticks

tacchino arrosto morto

 whole roasted turkey is the very symbol of affluence. When I was growing up in Italy, this luxury was known only to the royal family and a privileged few. All other people—those able to afford meat of any kind—bought turkey only by the parts. A wing was a desirable complement to other bony meats for a good broth; breast was used in place of veal for scaloppine; drumsticks made a tasty pot roast.

3 teaspoons salt

½ teaspoon black pepper

1 teaspoon dried sage leaves

1 teaspoon dried rosemary leaves

1 clove garlic, minced

6 small turkey drumsticks (3½ to 4 pounds)

Olive oil

½ cup dry white wine

Combine the salt, pepper, sage, rosemary, and garlic on a piece of wax paper. Roll the turkey legs over the mixture to coat them evenly. Place in a fish poacher without the rack or in a large saucepan. Sprinkle the remaining salt mixture over the legs, then add 1 cup olive oil. Set aside in the refrigerator for several hours or overnight.

Place over high heat and brown on all sides. Reduce the heat and simmer, covered, for about 20 minutes, turning the legs occasionally. Add the wine and cook, uncovered, until the liquid is completely gone. Sprinkle with cold water to generate steam. Repeat sprinkling as many times as needed for the meat to become fork tender.

serves 6

Turkey Breast with Egg Sauce
petti di tacchino in salsa d'uovo

2 pounds young turkey breast

½ cup unbleached flour

3 tablespoons olive oil

1 teaspoon salt

⅛ teaspoon white pepper

3 scallions, coarsely cut up

Three 2-inch-long stalks celery

1 medium carrot, peeled and coarsely chopped

1 small piece lemon peel

1½ cups warm water

3 egg yolks

Juice of 1 lemon

1 tablespoon chopped parsley

Cut the turkey breast into small strips. Quickly roll in the flour and pat to remove excess. Place in a casserole with the oil, salt, and pepper and cook over moderately high heat, stirring, just until the turkey pieces are lightly golden.

Add the scallions, celery, carrot, lemon peel, and warm water; cover the casserole and simmer for 1 to 2 hours, stirring occasionally.

Temporarily transfer the turkey pieces to a dish and strain the liquid and vegetables. Return the turkey and sauce to the casserole and bring to a boil.

Mix together the egg yolks and lemon juice. Pour the mixture over the turkey and immediately turn the heat off. Add the parsley and stir gently to combine.

serves 6

Turkey Loaf

polpettone di tacchino

1½ pounds ground dark turkey meat

1 cup seasoned breadcrumbs

2 eggs, slightly beaten

1 teaspoon minced garlic

1 teaspoon salt

⅛ teaspoon ground red pepper

2 teaspoons dehydrated minced onion

½ cup olive oil

2 sage leaves

1 teaspoon rosemary leaves

¼ cup dry white wine

2 tablespoons lemon juice

In a bowl place the turkey, ⅓ cup breadcrumbs, eggs, garlic, salt, red pepper, and onion and mix to combine. Spread the remaining breadcrumbs over a piece of wax paper. Divide the ground meat into two portions and form each into an egg-shaped loaf. Roll in the breadcrumbs until coated all over.

Heat the oil with sage and rosemary in a large skillet and place the two loaves in it. Thoroughly brown on all sides. Sprinkle a few drops of water to generate steam. When the loaves feel firm they are done, about 30 minutes in all.

Remove from the skillet to a heated serving plate. Add the wine and lemon juice to the skillet and sauté, scraping the bottom with a wooden spoon. Slice the loaves and pour the gravy over the slices.

NOTE: For Passover, substitute matza meal for breadcrumbs. However, since matza meal is not seasoned, you may want to mix it with ½ teaspoon Italian herb seasoning and ½ teaspoon garlic salt for a comparable flavor.

serves 6

Turkey Breast Pie for Passover

piccadigno di pesach

This delightful Passover dish must have been brought to Italy by Spanish refugees nearly five hundred years ago, since its name and preparation are close to the *Picadillo* of Spain and South America, which is usually made with beef.

2 regular *matzòt*

1½ cups cold chicken broth

1½ pounds turkey breast, cubed

½ cup olive oil

1 teaspoon salt

¼ teaspoon freshly ground black pepper

Dash nutmeg

1 bay leaf

2 large fresh or 1 teaspoon dried sage leaves

1 large clove garlic

½ teaspoon dried rosemary leaves wrapped in cheesecloth

¼ cup *pignoli* (pine nuts) or coarsely chopped walnut meats

2 eggs, slightly beaten

Matza meal

3 egg yolks

Break the *matzòt* directly into a shallow bowl and pour the broth over them.

In a large saucepan, place the meat and oil and season with salt, pepper, and nutmeg. Add the bay leaf, sage, garlic, and rosemary and sauté, stirring frequently, until the meat is dark brown on all sides. (If dried sage is used, enclose it in the cheesecloth with the rosemary.) Transfer the meat to a dish to cool.

Remove and discard the bay leaf, sage, garlic, and rosemary. Add the nuts to the saucepan with oil and sauté for 2 to 3 minutes.

Drain the excess liquid from the *matzòt*, but do not squeeze dry. Add the soaked *matzòt* to the saucepan and turn the heat off.

Grind the meat and return it to the saucepan. Add the beaten eggs and mix thoroughly.

Oil a 9-inch cake pan and sprinkle with matza meal. Pour the meat mixture into it; level with a spatula. With a small ladle make three depressions near the center and place 1 egg yolk in each depression. Bake in a 375°F oven for ½ hour.

serves 6

Duck in Orange Sauce

anatra all'arancia

1 medium duck
1 clove garlic, slightly crushed
Salt
Freshly ground black pepper
¼ cup orange marmalade
Olive oil
¼ cup frozen orange juice
4 seedless oranges, 2 unpeeled and 2 peeled, sliced

Remove as much fat as possible from the bird. Rub inside and out with garlic; generously season with salt and pepper. Spread the orange marmalade inside the cavity. Sprinkle the outside with olive oil and rub with your hands to coat evenly. Place in an uncovered roasting pan, breast side up, in a preheated 450°F oven for 30 minutes.

Baste with all the concentrated orange juice and arrange the unpeeled orange slices all around. Lower the temperature to 350°F and bake 1 hour longer.

Arrange the peeled orange slices on top of the duck and bake just until the orange slices are heated through.

serves 4 to 6

FISH

pesce

ish is a primary staple in Jewish cuisine because, being neither meat nor dairy, it is very versatile and can be used in either meat or dairy dinners (for example, a delightful *Antipasto di Pesce* can be served with either a meat or dairy meal). Many desserts contain milk or other dairy products and therefore cannot be served in a meal with meat. With fish, however, we can serve all sorts of dessert without violating the dietary laws.

The Jews of Eastern Europe had no easy access to saltwater fish and devised gefilte fish, which means "stuffed fish." The stuffing contained little fish scraps and lots of onion and other ingredients, thus stretching the precious fish.

The Jews of Italy had no such problem since the peninsula is surrounded by fish-laden seas. Fish was abundant and inexpensive. Instead of gefilte fish they made *Muggine in Bianco*, a poached striped bass (or similar) cooked in herb-flavored water, then cooled together with its own broth to make a delightful gelatin. I cool it inside a fish-form mold and when I unmold it, it resembles a whole fish. I smear it with mayonnaise and trim it with some of the marinated vegetables. Everybody loves this dish, not only my family members but also my guests (especially those with an Eastern European background).

A favorite is also *baccalà* (salted and dried cod) because it preserves without refrigeration, which was and is still is a great convenience. *Pezzetti di Baccalà,* a specialty of the Roman Jews, were once served ready-to-eat hot in one of the many specialty eating places, now almost destroyed by the German fury.

Fillets of Sole with Lemon for Sabbath

filetti di sogliole al limone del sabato

12 small fillets of sole
(1½ to 2 pounds)
Salt
Freshly ground black
pepper
Juice of 2 lemons
6 tablespoons olive oil
2 tablespoons coarsely
chopped Italian parsley
½ cup oil-cured
black olives

Wash the fillets and pat dry with paper towels. Sprinkle with salt and pepper to taste. Place in a large dish and smother with lemon juice. Place in the refrigerator to marinate for 8 to 12 hours. Remove from the refrigerator and let stand at room temperature for ½ hour. Drain all the liquid, sprinkle with oil and parsley and garnish with oil-cured olives.

If the idea of raw fish is not appealing, after removing the liquid place the dish on top of a pot containing boiling water for 5 minutes or until the fillets have lost their rawness, but are not quite cooked. Then sprinkle with oil and parsley and serve with black olives.

serves 6

Fish and Chicory Casserole

pesce e indivia

In Rome this dish is prepared with fresh anchovies and its true name is, in Roman Jewish dialect, *Aliciotti coll'Indivia*. Here, in North America, *aliciotti* (young fresh anchovies) are not available and we know anchovies only as the salted, canned ones found in stores. I find that small fillets of sole are an acceptable substitute for this most delicate and delicious fish. *Pesce e Indivia* is strictly Roman Jewish and practically unknown to other Italian Jews.

2 pounds fillets of sole
2 pounds chicory
3 teaspoons salt
¼ teaspoon freshly ground
black pepper

Wash the fillets and pat dry with paper towels. Cut lengthwise into small strips and dry again.

Discard the outer leaves from the chicory; cut or tear the rest into small pieces and wash thoroughly. Drain well, then pat dry with paper towels.

1 tablespoon freshly
chopped Italian parsley
1 large clove garlic, minced
very fine
½ cup olive oil

In an oiled baking dish, arrange the chicory and fish in alternate layers, seasoning each layer with salt, pepper, parsley, garlic, and oil; end with the chicory and seasoning. Bake in a 400°F oven for 35 minutes and serve.

NOTE: In summer you can serve this casserole cold and, although less crisp, it still retains its lovely flavor.

serves 6 to 8

Mayonnaise

salsa maionese

1 tablespoon lemon juice
1 teaspoon wine vinegar
1 egg yolk
¼ teaspoon salt
Dash white pepper
½ cup olive oil

Combine the lemon juice and vinegar in a little jug with a tiny spout.

Place the yolk in a small bowl with the salt and pepper. With a wooden spoon or with a small wire whisk, begin to work the yolk in a rotary motion until it becomes dark yellow and sticky, and air bubbles begin to form. Add a few drops of oil, stirring constantly. As the yolk mixture becomes too thick, add a few drops of the lemon-vinegar mixture. Since the oil thickens the sauce and lemon and vinegar thin it, continue to make the additions alternately. Beat at least 3 minutes after each addition.

NOTE: Should the sauce separate or curdle, start afresh with another egg yolk, in a clean bowl, with a clean spoon, adding the curdled mayonnaise in place of the oil and juice. Also, if you have a portable electric mixer, you can use one of the beaters instead of the spoon or whisk and the result will be the same.

yields ½ cup

Fish Pudding
budino di pesce

1 pound boneless, skinless fish, such as salmon, scrod, or haddock

2 tablespoons olive oil

½ teaspoon salt

¼ teaspoon white pepper

1 clove garlic, sliced

1 tablespoon chopped Italian parsley

¼ cup cold water

6 tablespoons unbleached flour

Butter

Milk

½ cup grated Italian Parmesan cheese

1 cup ricotta

3 eggs, slightly beaten

Dash or two nutmeg

Seasoned breadcrumbs

Place the fish in a skillet with the oil, salt, pepper, garlic, and parsley. Add the water and cook over low heat, covered, until the fish flakes easily, approximately 2 minutes. Drain and reserve the liquid.

In a heavy-bottomed saucepan, place the flour and 4 tablespoons butter. Cook, stirring constantly, until the mixture is pale tan. Add enough milk to the reserved fish liquid to make 2 cups and pour all at once into the saucepan. Stir vigorously with a wire whisk and cook, stirring frequently, 3 to 4 minutes. Remove from the heat, combine with the fish and cheeses and after a minute or two add the eggs and nutmeg. Mix well.

Pour into a buttered baking dish sprinkled with breadcrumbs. Flatten the top with a rubber spatula, sprinkle with breadcrumbs, and dot with butter. Bake in a 375°F oven, uncovered, for 20 minutes or until the top begins to brown.

NOTE: This is an ideal dish to be made when there is leftover cooked fish. The pudding, covered with plastic wrap and aluminum foil, can be frozen before baking, and baked unwrapped, without defrosting, only a few minutes longer than indicated above.

serves 6

Passover Fish Croquettes

crocchette di pesce per pesach

 efilte fish is traditionally served on Passover and other festivities in the home of the Ashkenazim. In Italy we had never heard of gefilte fish, even though fish was very much part of our festive meals. Here is a traditional fish dish for Passover that reminds us of gefilte fish.

1½ pounds boneless raw fish
¾ cup cold water
1 whole clove garlic
8 sprigs Italian parsley
3 tablespoons olive oil
Salt
Freshly ground white pepper
Dash or two nutmeg
3 tablespoons *pignoli* (pine nuts)
3 tablespoons non-dairy margarine
½ cup Passover cake flour
2 small eggs, slightly beaten
1 cup matza meal
Oil for frying

Cook the fish for 6 minutes with the water, garlic, parsley stems (chop and reserve the leaves), olive oil, and salt and pepper to taste. Discard the parsley stems and garlic, drain well (reserve the liquid and keep it hot), and place in a bowl with the chopped parsley leaves, nutmeg, and *pignoli*. In a small skillet heat the margarine and flour. Add the reserved hot liquid from the fish all at once and stir vigorously with a wire whisk. Cook 3 minutes, then add to the bowl containing the fish. Stir to cool a little, then add the eggs and mix well.

Spread the matza meal on a piece of wax paper. Form oval croquettes with the fish mixture and roll in the matza meal. Fry in hot oil until golden brown.

serves 6

Fish Stew

cacciucco

acciucco is most successful if you use different kinds of fish. Try mixing red snapper, sole, salmon, and scrod, some of which may be small and whole.

1 cup olive oil

½ teaspoon crushed red pepper

4 cloves garlic, 2 minced, 2 whole

1 heaping tablespoon tomato paste

½ cup dry red wine

4 cups diced freshly peeled tomatoes or canned peeled tomatoes

1 cup warm water

2 teaspoons salt

5 pounds assorted fish, including skin and bones, cleaned and gutted, cut into 2-inch cubes (or left whole if small)

12 diagonal slices *fruste* (page 328) or French bread, toasted

In a large pot, heat the oil with the red pepper and minced garlic. When the garlic is lightly golden, add the tomato paste and cook, stirring, 2 minutes. Add the wine and raise the heat for ½ minute. Add the tomatoes, warm water, and salt and cook 3 to 4 minutes. Add the fish, cover the pot tightly, and simmer for 10 minutes or until the fish is done.

Rub the whole cloves garlic on both sides of the toast and arrange the slices on a large, deep serving plate. Pour the stew over the toast and serve.

serves 6 to 8

Sole and Artichoke Casserole

filetti di sogliole e carciofi

1 lemon

9 medium fresh artichokes

1 clove garlic, minced

1 tablespoon freshly chopped Italian parsley

1½ teaspoons salt

¼ teaspoon freshly ground black pepper

1½ pounds fillets of sole

½ cup olive oil

¼ cup breadcrumbs

Squeeze the lemon and place the juice and rind halves into a basin with cold water. Trim the artichokes and drop them in the acidulated water. Drain and cut the artichokes lengthwise into thin slices and remove the choke if there is any. Place in a bowl and combine with half the garlic, half the parsley, half the salt, and half the pepper. Toss and set aside for a moment.

Wash the fillets and pat dry with paper towels. Cut into small strips, place in a bowl, and season with the remaining seasoning ingredients.

In an oiled baking dish, arrange the artichoke slices and sole strips in alternate layers, sprinkling each layer with oil. End with the fish, top with breadcrumbs and a drizzle of oil. Bake, uncovered, in a 400°F oven for 30 to 45 minutes. (Baking time depends on the size and freshness of the artichokes; if they are crisp and tender, do not bake for more than 30 minutes.) This is delicious hot or at room temperature.

serves 6

Fillets of Sole with Mushrooms

filetti di sogliole ai funghi

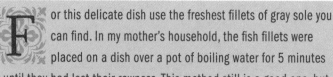

For this delicate dish use the freshest fillets of gray sole you can find. In my mother's household, the fish fillets were placed on a dish over a pot of boiling water for 5 minutes or until they had lost their rawness. This method still is a good one, but now I can use the microwave oven successfully. Fresh porcini mushrooms would be ideal, but fresh shiitake mushrooms are an excellent substitute.

1 pound fresh porcini or shiitake mushrooms
Olive oil
2 cloves garlic, sliced
Salt
Freshly ground white pepper
12 small fillets of sole (2 to 2½ pounds)
1 tablespoon freshly chopped Italian parsley

Remove and discard most of the stems and any parts that look sandy from the mushrooms. Clean the mushrooms with a cloth to remove any debris that might be left. Slice to ¼-inch thickness.

Heat 6 tablespoons oil in a large skillet. Add the mushrooms, garlic, and salt and pepper to taste and stir-fry for 2 to 3 minutes.

Oil a large microwave-proof serving dish and place the fillets into it in a single layer if possible. Cook in a microwave oven 1 to 2 minutes, or until the fish has lost its rawness. Drain any liquid that has formed in cooking, and cover with the mushrooms and all the condiments. Sprinkle with parsley and serve.

serves 6

Blender White Sauce

salsa besciamella col frullatore

2 cups hot milk
4 tablespoons butter
¼ cup unbleached flour
Dash nutmeg

Place the milk, butter, and flour in the cup of a blender and process at high speed for 5 seconds.

Pour into a saucepan and cook over moderate heat for 6 minutes, stirring frequently. Add the nutmeg and cook 1 minute longer.

yields about 2 cups / serves 6

Baked Fish

spigola arrosto

Almost any fish can be prepared this way, but the one we served on the night of Simchat Torah was *spigola*, one of the best fish to come from the Mediterranean Sea. Unfortunately, it is not found in North America. A very good substitute is red snapper (when it is really fresh), but I also use bluefish or a big slice of salmon.

1 whole red snapper (4 pounds) or 2 red snappers totaling 5 pounds

Salt

Freshly ground black pepper

6 anchovy fillets

Olive oil

¼ cup fine breadcrumbs (page 311)

2 tablespoons freshly chopped Italian parsley

1 teaspoon fresh or ½ teaspoon dried rosemary leaves

1 lemon, cut lengthwise into 6 wedges

Cut the fish open; wash thoroughly and pat dry with paper towels. Lightly season with salt and pepper and place, skin side down, in an oiled baking dish.

Heat the anchovies with 4 tablespoons oil and stir to make a paste. Remove from the heat, add the breadcrumbs and parsley and mix to combine. Spread this mixture over the fish. Place the rosemary leaves along the bone, without touching the flesh too much, since rosemary should give off fragrance, but not too strong a flavor.

Place in a 400°F oven and bake 20 to 30 minutes for smaller fish, 30 to 45 minutes for larger fish, or until the top is browned and the fish well dried. Serve garnished with lemon wedges.

serves 6

fried fish

pesce fritto

 ractically any type of fish can be fried, but small fish such as red mullet, smelts, trout, baby sole, whitings, butterfish, perch, or baby flounder are best for this dish.

3½ pounds small fish
¾ cup unbleached flour
1 cup cold water
Salt
1 cup vegetable oil for frying
Freshly ground black pepper
1 lemon, cut lengthwise into 6 wedges
6 sprigs of Italian parsley

Have the scales, gills, and organs removed from the fish at the store, but have them leave the heads on. Wash thoroughly and pat dry with paper towels. Dredge with the flour and shake to remove excess.

Have a bowl containing the cold water and 2 teaspoons salt at hand near the range. In a large skillet heat the oil to 375°F on a deep-frying thermometer. Take one floured fish at a time, dip in salted water, and drop in hot oil. Keep the fish in the pan in a single layer. Fry, turning a few times, until golden and crispy on both sides.

Remove to paper towels to drain. Place on a serving plate and sprinkle with salt and pepper to taste. Garnish with lemon wedges and sprigs of parsley and serve immediately.

serves 6

Marinated Fish

pesce marinato

Pesce Fritto can be marinated and served as an appetizer, as a tasty lunch, or as part of a festive dinner. It can be prepared ahead of time and actually tastes better after a few days.

3½ cups red wine vinegar

3 large cloves garlic, with husk on

6 bay leaves

6 large fresh or 2 teaspoons dried sage leaves

1 teaspoon dried rosemary leaves

1 teaspoon crushed red pepper

3½ teaspoons salt

2½ teaspoons sugar

Fried Fish (see preceding recipe)

¼ cup olive oil

In a large pot combine the vinegar, herbs, pepper, salt, and sugar. Bring to a boil and cook for 3 minutes. Add the fish and almost immediately (15 to 20 seconds) turn the heat off. Transfer to a glass or ceramic container and let cool 1 to 2 hours. Add the oil, cover, and store in the refrigerator where it will keep for several weeks.

serves 6, or more if used as an appetizer

Tuna Loaf

polpettone di tonno

This recipe was given to me, along with many others, by Signora Jenny Bassani Liscia, the Leghorn friend who served Spaghetti al Tonno to my husband and me for lunch. The garden salad, the Tuscan olive oil, the vinegar, and the superb wines were all products of her farmland.

After lunch, we went over recipes together. When we came to this recipe, she assured me that it was better than any tuna fish loaf I had ever tasted. I couldn't wait to try it myself. It is indeed superior.

Two 7-ounce cans chunk tuna packed in oil

½ cup coarse breadcrumbs (page 311)

¼ cup grated Parmesan cheese

¼ teaspoon white pepper

3 eggs, slightly beaten

Cheesecloth

2 tablespoons olive oil

1 clove garlic

3 cups milk

1 teaspoon salt

Sauce for Tuna Loaf (recipe follows)

1 cup oil-cured black olives

1 lemon, sliced

Chop the tuna very fine and combine with the breadcrumbs, Parmesan, pepper, and eggs. Mix well. Shape the mixture into an oval loaf and wrap cheesecloth around it. Tie both ends of the cloth with a string.

In a saucepan heat the oil with the garlic. When the garlic is golden, add the tuna loaf, milk, and salt. Bring to a gentle simmering and cook, uncovered, shaking the pan frequently, for 30 minutes or until the liquid is reduced to about 4 tablespoons.

Transfer to a dish (save the liquid for the sauce), unwrap, cover with another dish, and store in the refrigerator for several hours or overnight.

Slice, arrange on a serving plate, and cover with the sauce. Garnish with olives and lemon slices and serve.

serves 6

Sauce for Tuna Loaf
salsa per polpettone di tonno

4 tablespoons liquid from Tuna Loaf

1 egg

1 tablespoon tiny capers packed in vinegar, drained

4 anchovy fillets

Dash white pepper

Juice of ½ lemon

1 cup olive oil

Strain the liquid and place it in a blender with the egg, capers, anchovy fillets, and white pepper. Blend on high speed for 10 seconds. Add the lemon juice and, while blending, slowly add the oil in a thin steady stream through the opening of the blender cover.

NOTE: If you have leftover sauce, use it over steamed vegetables.

yields about 1½ cups

Dried Codfish

baccalà

Baccalà is dried salted cod. When refrigeration did not exist in the advanced technological form of today, dried, smoked, or canned fish was the only kind that people who lived far from the sea could have. Baccalà was decidedly the most versatile fish because it could be restored almost to its original fresh state simply by soaking it in water. This, plus the fact that it was relatively inexpensive, made it the favorite preserved fish among inland peoples. Baccalà was very popular with the Jews of Italy, who prepared it in a wide variety of ways.

In Italy, *Alimentari* carry baccalà throughout the year (except for the hottest of summer days) already soaked and ready to be cooked. In the United States, soaked baccalà can be bought in only a few fish markets. Usually you will find baccalà in the dried form and, therefore, any meal that includes it should be planned one or two days ahead of time since it takes at least twenty-four hours for baccalà to be completely soaked and salt-free. This might be a slight inconvenience, but the fact that you can store it without refrigeration is no small advantage.

Baccalà, according to an ancient saying, is one of the three foods that get harder as they cook (the other two are liver and eggs). If, after cooking it properly, baccalà is hard, it is of poor quality and any attempt to make it softer by cooking it longer would be a total waste of time. Should this happen to you, use it for one of the many dishes that do not depend on texture and for which the flesh is chopped in preparation anyway. In fact, for economy's sake, I buy the best quality and best parts (thick, white boneless fillets) only for certain dishes, while for others the cheaper baccalà is good enough. For each of the following recipes, I suggest what type to buy. The best quality baccalà can be found in any reputable Italian grocery store and sometimes in fish markets. The ones of lesser quality are available in any supermarket, generally in the produce section.

If you are able to find already soaked baccalà, buy 1½ times the weight that you would for the dried type. In other words, every pound of dried baccalà yields approximately 1½ pounds soaked baccalà.

Baccalà Sticks

pezzetti di baccalà

ezzetti is an ancient Roman recipe. Until a few years ago, one could still see Roman Jews from all walks of life and from any part of the city eating *pezzetti* with gusto right on the street, outside one of the Jewish ghetto fried-food shops. The last time I visited the ghetto, in 1979, most of those shops were gone: some were replaced by fancy restaurants. Only the *Pizza Romana* shop remains the same as it was centuries ago, now operated by one of the descendants of the original owner. If your travels bring you to Rome, by all means go and taste this delicious dish made by the expert. I do every year before she, too, is forced by the changing world to endure the fate of all the others.

Returning to *pezzetti:* read the introduction to baccalà and buy the best quality available.

1 pound dried baccalà fillets
1 cup unbleached flour
2 teaspoons baking powder
½ teaspoon salt
1 cup cold water
2 tablespoons olive oil
1 cup or more vegetable oil
1 lemon, cut into 6 wedges or 1½ cups Sweet-and-Sour Sauce (see following recipe)

serves 6

Soak the fish for 24 to 36 hours, changing the water several times during this period.

When you are ready to prepare *pezzetti*, drain the baccalà and remove any skin or bones. Cut into pieces 6 inches × 1 inch and pat dry with paper towels. Combine the flour, baking powder, salt, water, and olive oil and beat with a fork until the batter is smooth.

Heat the vegetable oil in a medium skillet. Dip the pieces of fish in the batter and fry a few at a time, turning, until lightly golden on all sides. Serve piping hot with lemon wedges or accompanied by a sweet-and-sour sauce.

Sweet-and-Sour Sauce

salsa agro-dolce

This sauce can be served with a variety of dishes, but should be an inseparable companion to *Pezzetti di Baccalà* and boiled beef tongue.

3 tablespoons olive oil

1 large onion, thinly sliced

¼ cup *pignoli* (pine nuts)

1 cup tomato sauce (page 152)

2 tablespoons brown sugar

1 tablespoon wine vinegar

½ cup dark, seedless raisins

1 tablespoon potato starch

½ cup cold water

Place the oil, onion and *pignoli* in a saucepan and cook over low heat until the onion and nuts are lightly golden. Add the tomato sauce, sugar, vinegar, and raisins and simmer 3 to 4 minutes.

Dissolve the potato starch in the cold water and add to the sauce. Cook, stirring, until thickened. Serve hot.

yields about 2 cups

Creamed Baccalà

baccalà mantecato

1 pound dry baccalà or 1½ pounds already soaked baccalà

1 cup hot milk

½ cup fresh Italian parsley (stems removed)

1 large clove garlic, coarsely cut up

1½ cups olive oil

Salt

If you have dry baccalà, soak it in 4 quarts cold water for 24 to 36 hours, changing the water three or four times during this period. Remove any bones or skin, cut into 2-inch pieces, and place in a saucepan with cold water to cover. Bring to a boil and cook for 2 minutes. Drain well and, while still hot, place in a blender or food processor with the hot milk, parsley, and garlic. Process until chopped fine, gradually adding the oil. Blend just enough for a creamy paste to form. Add the salt and pepper to taste and blend a few seconds more to mix.

Transfer to a serving dish over a bed of sliced raw mushrooms.

serves 6

White pepper

1 pound small, firm mushrooms, sliced thin

NOTE: *Baccalà Mantecato* makes a superb hors d'oeuvre. For this purpose, pour it into an oiled 1-quart fish-shaped mold and place in the refrigerator for several hours or overnight. To unmold, dip the mold in hot water for a second, then invert over a serving plate (omit the mushrooms) and garnish with lemon slices and black olives.

serves 12 or more

Baccalà with Onions

baccalà colla cipolla

1½ pounds white baccalà

½ cup olive oil

6 medium white onions, sliced

Salt

Freshly ground black pepper

2 teaspoons unbleached flour

1 cup cold water

Soak the dry baccalà in cold water for 24 hours, changing the water several times during this period.

Heat the oil in a large saucepan. Add the onions, lightly season with salt and pepper, and cook over moderate heat, stirring occasionally, until the onions are limp and translucent.

Drain the baccalà and cut into 2-inch squares. Add to the pan with the onions, sprinkle with the flour, and stir. Add the water, bring to a boil, and cook for 7 to 8 minutes, shaking the pan often. Taste for salt and pepper and adjust if necessary.

NOTE: This dish is especially delicious if served with hot slices of polenta (page 170). Also, keep in mind that baccalà, even more so than fresh fish, becomes hard and stringy if overcooked.

serves 6

Fried Cod Fillets

filetti di merluzzo fritti

2 pounds cod fillets

1 cup unbleached flour

2 teaspoons baking powder

½ teaspoon salt

1 cup cold water

Olive oil

1 lemon, cut into wedges

Wash and pat dry the fillets. Remove any bones and cut into strips approximately 1½ × 5 inches.

Combine the flour, baking powder, salt, water, and 2 tablespoons oil and beat with a fork until the batter is smooth.

Heat 1 cup oil in a medium pan. Dip the pieces of fish in the batter and fry a few at a time, turning, until lightly golden on all sides.

Serve piping hot with lemon wedges.

serves 6

Red Snapper Jewish Style

triglie all'ebraica

Triglie all'Ebraica is traditionally served on the night of Yom Kippur. In Italy it is made with *triglie*, a medium red fish resembling red snapper. Here *triglie* are not available, and so I substitute small red snapper, which works just as well.

4 pounds small red snapper

2 teaspoons salt

1 teaspoon sugar

¼ cup red wine vinegar

½ cup olive oil

1 cup dark, seedless raisins

½ cup *pignoli* (pine nuts)

Wash the fish thoroughly and pat dry with paper towels. Lightly sprinkle all over with salt and arrange in an oiled baking dish in a single layer.

Dissolve the sugar in the vinegar and pour over the fish. Pour in the oil, then sprinkle with raisins and *pignoli*.

Cover with a piece of aluminum foil and bake in a 400°F oven for approximately 20 minutes. Remove the foil and bake another ½ hour or until all the liquid is gone and the snapper is golden.

serves 6

Jellied Striped Bass

muggine in bianco

This traditional Passover and Rosh Hashanah dish is a typical example of the difference between the Ashkenazic and Italian Jewish cuisine. *Muggine in Bianco* is the Italian counterpart of the popular gefilte fish patties. Striped bass is preferred for this dish because it produces more natural gelatin.

One 4-pound striped bass
1 small onion, sliced
1 carrot, sliced
1 stalk celery, coarsely cut up
1 lemon, sliced
¼ teaspoon whole peppercorns
Salt
White pepper
1 cup mayonnaise (page 240)

Have the fish cleaned at the store, making sure the gills are removed from the head. Have the head and bones separated from the meat, but take them home with the fish.

In a fish poacher or kettle, place the onion, carrot, celery, 1 slice of lemon, and peppercorns. Add the fish fillets, the head and bones. Add cold water to cover and ½ teaspoon salt and simmer, covered, for 10 to 20 minutes or until done. The fish is done when the eye pops out a little and the meat flakes. Remove from the heat.

Carefully pick up all the pieces of meat, avoiding any bones or vegetables, and arrange inside a fish mold or on an oval serving plate. Lightly season with salt, white pepper, and a few drops of lemon juice.

Strain the broth and return it to the stove. Let it boil down, uncovered, until the liquid is reduced to about a cup. Pour over the fish and chill until the gelatin is firm.

Unmold and cut in half lengthwise with a sharp knife. Then cut each half into 4 to 5 pieces diagonally, forming a fishbone pattern. Mask the cuts under a twirl of mayonnaise for the whole fish effect. Cut the lemon slices in half and arrange around the fish to resemble fins.

NOTE: This dish makes an unusual appetizer and a fine main course during hot summer days.

serves 6

Red Mullet with Sweet-and-Sour Sauce

triglie in agro-dolce

½ cup olive oil

1 medium onion, thinly sliced

2 cups peeled ripe tomatoes, coarsely cut up

1 teaspoon salt

¼ teaspoon crushed red pepper

¼ cup red wine vinegar

¼ cup raw sugar

½ cup dark, seedless raisins

¼ cup *pignoli* (pine nuts)

6 red mullets, gutted and cleaned but with heads left on

1 tablespoon finely chopped Italian parsley

Place the oil and onion in a large skillet and sauté until the onion is soft and translucent. Add the tomatoes, salt, and pepper and cook over moderately high heat, uncovered, for 6 to 7 minutes, stirring occasionally. Add the vinegar, sugar, raisins, and *pignoli* and cook, stirring, another 2 minutes.

Lower the heat to medium and add the fish in a single layer, if possible. Baste with the sauce and cook, covered, for 7 minutes. Uncover and simmer until the liquid is greatly reduced and the fish is in a thick flavorful sauce. Serve hot or at room temperature.

serves 6

VEGETABLES

verdura

D on't be surprised if vegetarian dishes constitute the bulk of my collection. Historically Jews have been vegetarians whenever kosher animal proteins were inaccessible, and also for ethical and economical reasons. More recently, health considerations have turned many away from fat and cholesterol-laden foods and toward a table on which vegetarian food plays a more prominent role.

Whether one is a vegetarian or not the practice of eating a non-meat meal and 5 or more servings of vegetables a day is recommended both by nutritionists and gourmet experts alike. From the nutritional point of view, we have been told time and again that there are lots of minerals and vitamins and fibers in vegetables that are indispensable for our well being. Any connoisseur, anyone who has an appreciation of good taste, will agree that vegetables add tremendously to the enjoyment of a dish. From a purely aesthetic viewpoint, there would be nothing less appealing, in my opinion, than a piece of meat or fish placed at the center of a dish without any *contorno*, or side dish, to enliven its dullness.

Sauces, sometimes, take the place of vegetables to give life to a dish. The French cuisine makes great use of complicated sauces, mostly based on butter. Other cuisines employ sauces laced with all sorts of spices for the same purpose. Also, the Italian Jewish cuisine makes use of sauces; however, they are very simple and almost always based on olive oil. Sauces can indeed make an otherwise lackluster dish very exciting. My husband, for one, says that boiled chicken is an excuse to enjoy *Salsa Verde* (page 212). However, for all their zest, sauces cannot take the place of vegetables as far as nutrition is concerned.

In compiling this collection, I realized that rosemary is widely used by the Italian Jews. I suspect that the reason is that the Jews who settled in Italy a few thousand years ago made their first home in Sicily where rosemary grows wild.

So, try some of the vegetable dishes that you are not familiar with, and enjoy some enticing gourmet experiences.

Artichoke—The Quintessential Staple of the Italian Jewish Table

Cynara scolimus, the celebrated artichoke, now available in practically every supermarket around the world, is a native of the Mediterranean regions and was virtually unknown to the rest of the world until the advent of rapid commercial transportation.

I call the artichoke "the flower of vegetables" for it is not only the most versatile vegetable in my repertory but because the edible part of the artichoke plant *is* the flower, when it is still in bud. These buds, if not picked immediately, will become tough and hairy, and therefore unpalatable, and eventually inedible.

In Italy there are several varieties of artichokes, each with its slightly different look, taste, and use. One variety looks like a pinecone, about 2 inches in diameter and 5 inches long, purple in color and so tender that it is best eaten raw. Another variety has the shape and size of a small chicken egg, and is generally used to make artichoke hearts in oil. Then there are the large, roundish *mamme*, which are tender and very tasty and are best boiled. There are other varieties—pointed and with thorns, rounded and with smooth tips, thin or fat—but they are all tender and flavorful.

The Italians attribute all sorts of magical and curative properties to artichokes. "They are good for your liver," "they make other foods taste better," and so on. I don't subscribe to these claims, but I do recognize artichokes for what they really are: an incredibly versatile delicacy.

Italians in general are fond of artichokes and prepare them in several ways. But Italian Jews made a staple of them, especially at Passover time, when they are in season, and invented a great number of ways to prepare them. Most of these preparations require a "cleaning," or preliminary trimming, so that what is left is all edible.

The ancient Roman Jews devised a brilliant technique for cleaning artichokes for their renowned *Carciofi alla Giudia*. The curious thing is that when I lived in Italy no one, including Jews from other parts of the country, knew how to clean artichokes the way the Roman Jews did. It is possible that the growing interest in exotic foods and the improvement in methods of communication may have prompted others to learn. However, I recently asked a cousin of mine from Milan to clean an artichoke for me and her method was not the authentic one, so the finished artichoke had inedible parts left on it. Here is the clever method of the Roman Jews:

Have a large bowl at hand, containing cold water and the juice of two lemons with the four halves of rind. Keep the artichokes in another bowl of cold water while you are working on them. Take one artichoke at a time, drain it, and pull off and discard the smallest outer leaves. Holding the artichoke with its bottom toward the little finger of your left hand, tilt the top away from you, and holding a small sharp knife tightly with your right hand, insert its tip, one leaf deep, into the tender, lighter part of the leaves. Keeping your right hand steady, slowly rotate the artichoke with your left hand so that the bottom moves in a clockwise direction, and cut upward in a spiral. The tough part of each leaf will fall off, while the tender, edible part remains attached. Peel the green layer off the bottom and stem and then drop the trimmed artichoke into the lemon water until you are ready to cook. This operation requires some practice; you will know if you have mastered it when the artichoke thus cleaned looks more or less like the one you started with, only smaller and whiter.

If you are not ready to use the artichokes immediately after you have cleaned them, try to keep them completely submerged in the lemon water. This is not easy. Artichokes are very buoyant and float to the surface, making it difficult to keep them covered. An inverted plate, just a bit smaller in diameter than the bowl, placed over the artichokes, will keep them below the surface. Another way is to crowd them inside a glass jar and cover them with the lemon water. If you plan to leave them at this stage for more than an hour or so, you must refrigerate them, but it is not advisable to keep artichokes this way for more than a few hours. Lemon is used to prevent discoloration; on the other hand, lemon will cause the artichokes to spoil very quickly.

If until now you have only eaten artichokes boiled, or at best marinated, like the commercial type you find in jars or cans in stores, I promise you a culinary adventure with the different dishes you will be able to prepare once you have learned to clean artichokes in the artistic style of the Roman Jews.

Artichokes Jewish Style

carciofi alla giudia

This is the most famous of all Italian Jewish foods. It originated with the Roman Jews, and owes its fame to having been served at a restaurant in the Roman ghetto where it was discovered and quickly adopted by connoisseurs of excellent food from all over Europe. Ultimately it found its way into many good Italian cookbooks. My mother, a Jewish woman who was born and raised in Rome, prepared especially delicious *Carciofi alla Giudia* (better than any you could find in any restaurant!). I watched her prepare them, and have prepared them myself, practically all my life. Here is my mother's technique in detail.

12 medium, fresh artichokes

2 lemons, juice and rinds

2 tablespoons salt

1 teaspoon freshly ground black pepper

3 cups olive oil

Trim the artichokes exactly as described on page 260 and keep them in the lemon water until you are ready to cook them.

Drain two artichokes and, holding one in each hand by the stem and bottom, gently hit the leafy parts against each other until the leaves of one artichoke open up a little. Place the opened artichoke, bottom up, on a board or a working surface.

Drain another artichoke from its bath and repeat what you did with the first two, and then line up the one that opens next to the first one. Continue until all the artichokes are opened up. The last one will have to be tapped against the board.

In a small bowl, combine the salt and pepper. Take one artichoke at a time and sprinkle all over, including between the leaves, with the salt and pepper mixture.

Heat the oil in a deep earthenware or similar saucepan. Cook as many artichokes at a time as fit in one layer over moderate heat for 20 to 25 minutes, or until the bottoms and the sides are well browned. During this cooking period, sprinkle some cold water over the artichokes to produce steam, so that the inside will be cooked, too. To do this the authentic way, have a bowl containing cold water near the range. Dip your closed fist in the water and then open it forcefully over the roasting artichokes. Repeat the sprinkling several times.

When all the artichokes are done, transfer them to a plate, bottom side down, to keep the moisture in. (Up to this point you may prepare the artichokes several hours ahead of time and keep them, bottom side down, so that they do not lose their moisture. Should they become too dry, sprinkle some cold water on them when reheating and press the leaves down against the bottom of the pan.) Pick them up at the bottom with a fork and dip them, one by one, in the hot oil again, pressing the leaves to the bottom of the pan. The artichokes will open up like roses and the leaves will become golden and crisp. Serve immediately.

NOTE: Although traditionally *Carciofi alla Giudia* are served piping hot, they are also delicious at room temperature.

serves 6

Golden Fried Artichokes

carciofi dorati e fritti

The reason why these fried artichokes are called *dorati* (gilded) is that they are dipped in a beaten egg before frying. Eggs from chickens raised on private farms have yolks of a much richer color than the eggs one finds in the market today, and food dipped in eggs acquire a golden color. (*Dorare*, when referring to baked products, means to brush with beaten egg.) The best artichokes for this dish are the very fresh and tender ones that have no choke at all and require only a very short cooking time.

12 small, tender artichokes
2 lemons, juice and rinds
1 cup flour
2 eggs
2 egg yolks
1 cup olive oil

Prepare the artichokes as described on page 260. Cut in half lengthwise and cut each half into 3 wedges; keep in the acidulated water for no longer than 15 minutes. Drain and pat dry with paper towels. Dredge with the flour and shake to remove the excess.

Beat the eggs and egg yolks together.

Heat the oil in a small frying pan. Dip the artichokes in the

Salt

1 lemon, cut lengthwise
into 6 wedges

beaten egg and fry, a few at a time, in moderately hot oil until lightly browned on all sides. Sprinkle with the salt, garnish with lemon wedges, and serve immediately.

serves 6

Parsley Artichokes

carciofi al prezzemolo

9 medium artichokes

2 lemons, juice and rinds

2 cups cold water

1½ teaspoons salt

¼ teaspoon freshly ground
black pepper

½ cup olive oil

1 clove garlic, minced fine

¼ cup freshly chopped
Italian parsley

½ cup coarse breadcrumbs
(page 311)

Prepare the artichokes as described on page 260. Cut lengthwise in half and keep in the acidulated water until you are ready to cook them. Drain and place in a large pan, where they can fit in a single layer, with the cut side up. Add the cold water. Sprinkle with the salt, pepper, and half the oil.

Combine the garlic and parsley and spread over the artichoke halves. Cook over moderate heat, covered, for 30 to 45 minutes, depending on the size and freshness of the artichokes. Remove from the heat. Sprinkle with the breadcrumbs and the remaining oil.

Just before serving, place under the broiler or in a 500°F oven for 3 minutes or until the tops begin to brown.

serves 6

Stewed Artichokes

carciofi stufati

12 medium artichokes

2 lemons, juice and rinds

1 cup water

2 cloves garlic, sliced

Clean and trim the artichokes and keep in the acidulated water until ready to cook.

Cut into 6 wedges each, remove any choke and place in a saucepan with all the other ingredients, including small amounts of salt and pepper.

2 tablespoons coarsely
chopped Italian parsley

6 tablespoons olive oil

Salt

Freshly ground black
pepper

Cook over moderate heat, covered, for 30 minutes, or until the bottom parts feel tender. Add a few tablespoons of water if necessary, but at the end uncover the pan and let the moisture evaporate so that the artichokes are left in a flavorful oil sauce. Taste for salt and pepper and correct.

serves 6

Artichokes Truffle Style

carciofi trifolati

 rifolato is an adjective often applied to certain vegetables, such as zucchini, mushrooms, and artichokes, to indicate that you cook them as you would *tartufi* or *trifola* (truffles). When truffles were plentiful and inexpensive, they were served, like any other vegetable, as a side dish. Since their natural aroma and taste are exquisite, only the simplest preparation was needed: sliced paper thin and quickly pan fried with a little oil, salt, and pepper.

12 medium artichokes

2 lemons, juice and rinds

½ cup olive oil

Salt

Freshly ground black
pepper

Prepare the artichokes as described on page 260. Cut in half lengthwise and keep under acidulated water.

Heat ¼ cup oil in a large skillet. Drain 6 artichokes very well. Cut into very thin slivers directly into the hot oil and fry, stirring frequently, for 10 minutes. Add salt and pepper to taste and continue to fry until the slices are golden brown and crisp.

Transfer to a hot serving dish and keep warm. Repeat with the remaining oil and artichokes.

serves 6

Stewed Green Beans

fagiolini in tegame

2 pounds green beans
1 medium onion, sliced thin
2 cups peeled tomatoes (fresh or canned) with juice
1 tablespoon shredded basil leaves
6 tablespoons olive oil
½ teaspoon salt
2 dashes freshly ground black pepper
1 cup cold water

Trim the beans at both ends, wash, and cut into 1½-inch pieces. Place in a saucepan with all the other ingredients, including 1 cup cold water, and cook covered for ¾ hour or until desired tenderness. Uncover and boil rapidly another 5 to 6 minutes or until the excess liquid has evaporated and the beans are in a thick and flavorful sauce.

serves 6

Stewed Broccoli

broccoli stufati

 Make sure to choose broccoli that are tight and of a bluish dark green color.

2 bunches fresh broccoli
4 tablespoons olive oil
1 teaspoon salt
¼ teaspoon freshly ground black pepper
2 large cloves garlic, sliced
½ cup cold water

Rinse the broccoli in cold water, holding by the stems. (Broccoli do not need much washing, but once in a while you will find a green worm clinging to one of the smaller stems and cold water will compel the intruder to let go.)

Remove and discard the large stems. Separate the big flowers into many florets and place in a saucepan with the oil, salt, pepper, and garlic. Add the cold water and bring to a rapid boil. Cook, covered, for 5 minutes. Uncover and cook another 2 minutes or until the broccoli are tender but still crisp and most of the liquid is gone. Serve immediately while still bright green.

serves 6 to 8

Brussels Sprouts

cavoletti di bruxelles

2 pints Brussels sprouts

4 tablespoons olive oil

½ teaspoon salt

⅛ teaspoon freshly ground black pepper

1 large clove garlic, minced

1 tablespoon freshly chopped Italian parsley

½ cup cold water

Discard the outer leaves from the sprouts and cut the bottoms flat. Wash thoroughly and place in a saucepan with the oil, salt, pepper, garlic, and parsley. Add the cold water and bring to a rapid boil. Loosely cover the pan and cook for 15 minutes or until the sprouts are tender and the excess moisture has evaporated.

Serves 6

Savoy Cabbage

cavolo cappuccio

2 pounds savoy cabbage

Salt

Ground red pepper

2 cloves garlic, sliced

2 tablespoons olive oil

2 medium ripe tomatoes, peeled, or 1 cup canned peeled tomatoes

½ cup water

Remove and discard the outer, tough leaves from the cabbage. Cut into 4 wedges and remove and discard the core and some of the larger ribs. Cut each wedge into three segments and wash thoroughly. Place in a casserole with small amounts of salt and pepper and the remaining ingredients.

Cook over moderately high heat, covered, for 15 to 20 minutes (cooking time depends on the freshness of the cabbage). Uncover and let some of the liquid evaporate. Taste for salt and pepper and correct if necessary.

serves 6

Stewed Carrots

carote stufate

1½ pounds carrots, peeled and sliced (about 5 cups)

3 tablespoons olive oil

1 tablespoon dehydrated minced onion

1 teaspoon salt

⅛ teaspoon freshly ground black pepper

¾ cup water

1 tablespoon freshly chopped Italian parsley

Place the sliced carrots in a skillet with the oil, onion, salt, and pepper. Add the water and bring to a boil. Lower the heat and simmer, covered, for 15 minutes.

Uncover and cook over high heat, stirring, 2 minutes longer or until most of the liquid is gone. Add the parsley, stir, and remove from the heat.

serves 6

Cauliflower with a Piquant Sauce

cavolfiore in salsa piccante

1 large white cauliflower

½ cup olive oil

8 anchovy fillets, cut up

2 cloves garlic, minced

2 tablespoons capers, drained and chopped fine

Salt

Freshly ground white pepper

¼ cup white wine vinegar

Remove and discard the outer leaves of the cauliflower. With a sharp knife separate the florets and cut the larger ones into halves or quarters. Boil or steam for 10 minutes or until fork tender, but not mushy. Drain and transfer to a warmed deep dish.

Meanwhile, lightly heat the oil in a saucepan; add the anchovies and garlic and stir until the anchovies are almost melted. Add the capers, small amounts of salt and pepper, and vinegar, and remove from the heat. Pour over the cauliflower and serve immediately.

serves 6

Eggplant Parmigiana
melanzane in tortino

2 pounds eggplant

Salt

1½ cups grated
Parmesan cheese

4 eggs

1 cup unbleached flour

1 cup olive oil

2 cups tomato sauce
(page 152)

Freshly ground black
pepper

Peel the eggplant and slice into ¼-inch slices. Lightly sprinkle with salt on both sides and place in a covered dish; set aside for ½ to 1 hour. Drain, rinse with cold water, and pat dry with paper towels.

Combine 4 tablespoons Parmesan cheese with 3 eggs and beat slightly. Dredge the eggplant slices with flour, dip in the cheese-egg mixture, and fry in moderately hot oil until golden on both sides.

In an ungreased ovenproof dish, arrange the slices in layers, sprinkling each layer with cheese and tomato sauce. Reserve 3 tablespoons cheese and 3 tablespoons sauce.

Beat the remaining egg with the reserved cheese and sauce. Season this mixture with salt and pepper to taste and pour over the eggplant layers. Bake in a 350°F oven for 40 minutes and serve hot.

serves 6

Eggplant Jewish Style
melanzane alla giudia

4 pounds medium, firm
eggplant

Salt

1 cup olive oil

2 large cloves garlic

¼ teaspoon freshly ground
black pepper

2 tablespoons freshly
chopped Italian parsley

Wash and trim the eggplant, but leave the peel on. Cut in half lengthwise, then cut each half into 3 to 4 wedges. With a sharp knife remove part of the pulp from each wedge (reserve this pulp for the recipe that follows), leaving the wedges ½-inch thick. Cut into 1-inch sections and place in a large bowl. Add 3 to 4 teaspoons salt, toss to distribute the salt evenly, then cover with an inverted dish slightly smaller than the bowl and leave in the refrigerator for at least 1 hour.

Rinse the eggplant in cold water, squeeze the liquid out, and blot dry with paper towels.

Place the oil and garlic in a large frying pan over high heat.

When the garlic is slightly golden, add the eggplant and stir-fry for 2 minutes.

Lower the heat and cook, covered, 5 to 6 minutes. Uncover, add the pepper and parsley, and cook another 7 to 10 minutes, stirring occasionally.

With a slotted spoon lift the eggplant and let most of the oil drain through before transferring the eggplant to a serving dish. Serve hot, cold, or at room temperature.

serves 6

Eggplant Croquettes
crocchette di melanzane

I always make these croquettes at the same time I make Eggplant Jewish Style, so that I can use the pulp from the preceding recipe. However, you can make this recipe by itself using whole eggplant, but make sure to remove and discard the peel.

3 cups diced pulp from eggplant

Salt

2 eggs, slightly beaten

Unseasoned breadcrumbs

½ cup grated Italian Parmesan cheese (optional)

2 tablespoons freshly chopped Italian parsley

2 cloves garlic, passed through a garlic press

Freshly ground black pepper

Olive oil for frying

Place the eggplant pulp in a saucepan with 1 teaspoon salt and cold water to cover. Bring to a boil and cook 5 minutes. Drain, let cool, then place in a piece of cheesecloth and squeeze the liquid out.

Place in a food processor with the eggs, ½ cup breadcrumbs, Parmesan cheese (if you opt for it), parsley, garlic, and salt and pepper to taste. Process a few seconds, or just until everything is mixed. Let rest for a while.

Have a dish or a piece of wax paper with a thick layer of breadcrumbs at hand.

Heat 1 cup oil in a medium frying pan. Drop the eggplant mixture by the rounded tablespoonful over the breadcrumbs and roll to coat. Fry a few croquettes at a time in the hot oil until golden brown on all sides. Serve hot.

serves 6

Cooked Escarole

scarola cotta

3 pounds escarole
½ cup cold water
1 medium onion, thinly sliced
4 tablespoons olive oil
¾ teaspoon salt
⅛ teaspoon freshly ground black pepper

Discard the outer, bruised leaves of the escarole. Cut each head in half, then each half into 3 wedges. Rinse in fresh water several times, drain, and pat dry with paper towels. Place in a saucepan with the cold water. Add the onion, oil, salt, and pepper and bring to a boil. Lower the heat and simmer, covered, for 20 to 30 minutes. Uncover, raise the heat, and cook until the excess liquid is gone. Let brown slightly in the oil before serving.

serves 6

Sautéed Kale

cavolo riccio in padella

2½ pounds fresh young kale
1 cup cold water
Salt
2 cloves garlic, minced
6 tablespoons olive oil
Freshly ground black pepper

Discard all the large stems and yellowed leaves, if there are any. Rinse the kale in cold water several times. Place in a large pot with 1 cup cold water and a pinch of salt. Cook over moderately high heat, covered, for 5 to 15 minutes or until tender. (Cooking time depends on the freshness of the kale.) Drain.

In a large skillet or iron frying pan, place the garlic, oil, and small amounts of salt and pepper. Sauté over moderate heat until the garlic is lightly golden. Add the kale and cook, stirring frequently, until the kale has lost much of its moisture and it is crisp and tasty.

serves 6

Fennel Jewish Style

finocchi alla giudia

12 medium round fennel knobs
2 cloves garlic
½ cup olive oil
Salt
Freshly ground white pepper
¾ cup water

Remove and discard all the bruised and tough parts of the fennel and cut into 4 to 6 wedges each. Wash thoroughly and blot dry.

Place the garlic and oil in a large skillet and sauté until the garlic is browned. Discard the garlic and add the fennel. Season with small amounts of salt and pepper and sauté for approximately 10 minutes, stirring frequently.

Add the water and cook over moderate heat, tightly covered, for 10 to 15 minutes or until tender. Uncover the skillet and let the liquid evaporate and the fennel acquire a nice golden tone. Serve hot or at room temperature.

serves 6

Creamed Fennel

finocchi colla besciamella

12 medium knobs fennel
Salt
½ cup butter
½ cup grated Parmesan cheese
2 cups dairy White Sauce (see following recipe)
¼ cup fine breadcrumbs (page 311)
White pepper

Use only the tender white core of the fennel. Cut the fennel cores into wedges and cook in salted water for 15 minutes or until fork tender. Drain and place in a small bowl. Dress with half the butter and all the Parmesan cheese and toss to mix. Place in a buttered baking dish; cover with the white sauce, sprinkle with breadcrumbs and white pepper to taste. Dot with the remaining butter and bake in a 400°F oven for 20 minutes or until the top begins to brown.

serves 6

White Sauce

salsa besciamella

4 tablespoons butter
4 tablespoons flour
2 cups hot milk

Melt the butter in a saucepan. Add the flour and cook, stirring, until the mixture acquires a light brown color. Add the milk all at once and stir vigorously to avoid lumps. Cook slowly for 5 minutes.

NOTE: For a thicker sauce, add 2 tablespoons butter and 2 tablespoons flour to the above quantities. For a thinner sauce, decrease the amount of butter and flour by 2 tablespoons each.

yields about 2 cups / serves 6

Spicy Mushrooms

funghi piccanti

2 pounds firm, small white mushrooms
4 tablespoons olive oil
1 clove garlic, minced
1 medium onion, sliced thin
3 large ripe, firm tomatoes
1 tablespoon shredded basil leaves
1 tablespoon freshly chopped Italian parsley
2 teaspoons salt
¼ teaspoon ground red pepper
¼ cup white wine vinegar
2 tablespoons tiny capers, drained

Trim, wash, and drain the mushrooms. Slice very thin. Place in a non-metallic saucepan with the oil, garlic, and onion and cook uncovered, over moderately high heat, for 5 minutes, stirring occasionally.

Wash and cube the tomatoes and add to the saucepan. Add the basil, parsley, salt, and pepper, and cook, uncovered, 10 to 15 minutes longer. Add the vinegar and capers, stir, and remove from the heat. Let cool. Serve at room temperature as an appetizer or reheat in a saucepan to serve as a side dish.

serves 6

Stewed Mushrooms

funghi in tegame

2½ pounds firm white mushrooms

½ ounce dried porcini mushrooms

½ cup warm water

6 tablespoons olive oil

2 tablespoons coarsely chopped Italian parsley

¼ teaspoon dried savory

3 large cloves garlic

Salt

Freshly ground black pepper

Trim, wash, and drain the mushrooms. Cut the larger ones into halves or into four pieces and leave the smaller ones whole.

Soak the dried mushrooms in the warm water for 5 to 10 minutes. Lift them from their bath with a fork, reserving the water. Remove and discard any parts that still have some dirt attached to them. Place in a non-metallic saucepan with the fresh mushrooms; add the oil, parsley, savory, garlic, and small amounts of salt and pepper.

Carefully pour in the reserved water from the soaked mushrooms, making sure that any sand remains at the bottom of the cup. Cook uncovered over low heat for 20 to 30 minutes, or until the liquid is reduced to a few tablespoons. Discard the garlic cloves and serve.

serves 6

Mushrooms Truffle Style

funghi trifolati

2 pounds firm white mushrooms

¼ ounce imported dried *porcini* mushrooms

¼ cup warm water

¾ cup olive oil

1½ teaspoons salt

¼ teaspoon freshly ground black pepper

Juice of 1 lemon

Trim and wash mushrooms, drain, and pat dry with paper towel. Cut into very thin slices.

Soak dried mushrooms in the warm water for 10 minutes. Lift them from their bath with a fork and cut into very small pieces. Reserve the water.

Heat the oil in a large skillet and add both kinds of mushrooms. Cook over high heat, stirring, 3 or 4 minutes. Add reserved water, taking care not to include any sand that might remain at the bottom of the cup. Cook over high heat, uncovered, another 8 or 10 minutes, stirring, or until moisture is gone. Add salt, pepper, and lemon juice and stir over high heat to combine with seasoning.

serves 6

Tomatoes Stuffed with Rice

pomodori ripieni di riso

8 round ripe tomatoes
(about 3 pounds)

¾ cup Italian rice

1 large clove garlic, minced

Extra virgin olive oil

Salt

Freshly ground black
pepper

½ teaspoon dried oregano

1 tablespoon freshly
chopped Italian parsley

1 tablespoon shredded basil
leaves

Wash the tomatoes, pat dry, and line on a working surface with stem side down. Slice the upper part almost through, but not quite, since you will use this as a lid.

With the help of a teaspoon, gently remove the pulp, juice, and seeds out of the tomatoes into a bowl. Arrange the tomato shells, standing with lids open, in an oiled baking dish.

Add the rice, garlic, 3 tablespoons oil, 2 teaspoons salt, ⅛ teaspoon pepper, oregano, parsley, and basil to the bowl with the tomato pulp and juice and mix well to combine.

Sprinkle the inside of the tomato shells with small amounts of salt, pepper, and oil, then fill with the rice mixture and close the lids as best you can.

Loosely cover with aluminum foil and bake in a 375°F oven for 1 hour. This is delicious hot or at room temperature.

serves 4

Baked Tomatoes

pomodori al forno

12 ripe round medium
tomatoes

Olive oil

1½ teaspoons salt

¼ teaspoon freshly ground
black pepper

1 clove garlic, minced

2 tablespoons freshly
chopped Italian parsley

2 large fresh basil leaves,
shredded, or 1 teaspoon
dried basil

½ teaspoon ground dried
savory

½ cup seasoned
breadcrumbs (page 311)

Wash the tomatoes and dry with paper towels. Cut in half and place in an oiled baking dish with the cut side up. Sprinkle with salt and pepper and set aside for a few minutes.

Combine the garlic, parsley, basil, and savory. Spread approximately ½ teaspoon of this mixture over each tomato half. Drizzle with oil, top with breadcrumbs, and sprinkle abundantly with oil. Bake uncovered in a 375°F oven for 45 minutes. Serve hot or at room temperature.

serves 6

Baked Potatoes and Tomatoes

patate e pomodori in forno

8 large baking potatoes

2 cloves garlic, minced fine

2 teaspoons salt

½ teaspoon freshly ground
black pepper

½ teaspoon dried
rosemary leaves

½ cup olive oil

6 large ripe tomatoes,
peeled (page 52)

1 tablespoon chopped
Italian parsley

Peel the potatoes and cut lengthwise into wedges. Place in a bowl with half the garlic, half the salt, half the pepper, and all the rosemary leaves. Add ¼ cup oil and toss to distribute the dressing evenly.

Cut each peeled tomato into 6 to 8 pieces and place in another bowl. Season with the remaining garlic, salt, pepper, and oil. Add the parsley and mix well.

Spread the potatoes in a large ungreased baking dish. Top with the tomatoes and bake uncovered in a 375°F oven for 1 hour.

serves 6

Stewed Peppers

peperonata

2 pounds green peppers
1 large yellow onion, sliced
4 large ripe tomatoes, peeled (page 52) and cut up
¼ cup olive oil
1 teaspoon salt
¼ cup dry white wine

Wash and core the peppers. Cut lengthwise into strips and place in a casserole with the onion, peeled tomatoes, oil, and salt. Cook over moderate heat for approximately ½ hour. (If the tomatoes are very juicy you will not need any additional water; otherwise, add a few tablespoons water when it becomes necessary.)

Add the wine and cook, uncovered, stirring occasionally, another 10 minutes or until most of the liquid has evaporated. Serve hot or at room temperature.

serves 6

Potato Croquettes

crocchette di patate

3 pounds boiling potatoes
Unsalted butter
4 tablespoons freshly grated Italian Parmesan cheese
1 egg
1 egg yolk
Salt
Freshly ground white pepper
2 dashes nutmeg
½ cup unbleached flour
Vegetable oil for frying

Boil the potatoes in lightly salted water until very tender. Peel and mash, or pass through a vegetable mill. Do not use a blender or processor.

Melt 4 tablespoons butter in a skillet; add the mashed potatoes and stir over low heat until the potatoes are dry and thick. Remove from the heat and let cool 5 minutes. Add the Parmesan cheese and mix well. Add the egg, egg yolk, salt and pepper to taste, and nutmeg, and mix very well to prevent bursting during frying.

Spread the flour on a working surface. Pour the potato mixture over the flour and quickly knead to incorporate some of the flour. Divide into 3 parts and shape each part into a rope about 1 inch thick. Cut into 2½-inch pieces and give each an elongated egg shape.

Heat the butter or oil or a mixture of the two in a skillet to a 1-inch thickness and fry the croquettes over moderately high heat, a few at a time, turning delicately, until golden on all sides.

serves 6

Cubed Fried Potatoes

patate fritte a tocchetti

 nce in a while everyone is entitled to indulge in "junk food." Fried potatoes, when eaten in fast-food joints, could be termed just that because we don't know what kind of fat is used, and above all we don't know how many times it is reused. The only fried potatoes we ate during my childhood and we eat now are the ones we prepare ourselves. This makes a world of difference not only in nutritional value but in taste as well.

2 pounds all-purpose potatoes
1 teaspoon minced garlic
Peppercorns in a mill
2 teaspoons rosemary leaves
1½ cups olive oil
Salt

Peel the potatoes, cut into ½-inch cubes, and place in a bowl with cold water to cover so that they get rid of some of the starch. Drain and pat dry, then season with garlic, a few turns of the mill with black pepper, 1 teaspoon rosemary leaves, and 1 tablespoon olive oil. Toss to distribute the seasoning evenly and set aside in a cool place for about 1 hour.

Heat the remaining oil in a medium saucepan. Add the potato cubes, making sure that any liquid that has formed remains in the bowl. Fry for 5 minutes, stirring occasionally, then turn the heat off.

With a slotted spoon, transfer the potatoes to a colander, and let the oil cool to room temperature.

Fifteen minutes before serving, reheat the oil, add the potato cubes, and fry for another 10 minutes, or until they are golden and make a dry sound when stirred. Transfer to a serving dish lined with paper towels.

Discard most of the oil, add the remaining rosemary leaves and small amounts of salt and pepper to the saucepan, and heat for a few seconds. Distribute over the potatoes and serve.

serves 4

Potato and Spinach Roll

rollata di patate e spinaci

2 pounds boiling potatoes
Salt
1 cup unbleached flour
2 eggs, slightly beaten
1 pound small-leaved bulk spinach
2 tablespoons olive oil
1 small onion, minced
⅛ teaspoon white pepper
2 quarts water
6 tablespoons unsalted butter, melted
½ cup freshly grated Italian Parmesan cheese

Cook the potatoes in lightly salted water until very soft. Peel, mash (do not use a blender or processor), and let cool for a while. Add 1 teaspoon salt, flour, and eggs and mix well until a smooth paste is formed. Spread over a piece of cheesecloth, making a 15 × 12-inch rectangle.

Wash and cook the spinach. Drain well and chop fine. Heat the oil in a skillet; add the onion and sauté for 2 minutes. Add the spinach, pepper, and ¼ teaspoon salt, and cook, stirring, for 5 minutes or until most of the moisture has evaporated. Spread over the potato paste, leaving a ½-inch margin all around.

Roll the short way as you would a jelly roll. Wrap the cheesecloth around the roll and fasten the two ends with a string.

Bring the water and 1 tablespoon salt to a boil in a fish poacher or a pot; add the roll. As soon as boiling resumes, lower the heat and simmer, covered, for 45 minutes to 1 hour.

Transfer the roll to a warm dish and let it rest for 10 minutes. Remove wrap, cut into 12 slices, and dress with all the melted butter and half the cheese. Serve immediately with the remaining Parmesan in a separate dish.

serves 4 to 6

Braised Red Radicchio

radicchio rosso brasato

6 large heads of red radicchio

2 large carrots, peeled and sliced

1 large onion, thinly sliced

6 tablespoons olive oil

1 tablespoon freshly chopped Italian parsley

Salt

Freshly ground black pepper

1½ cups water

Discard the outer, bruised leaves from the radicchio; cut into wedges and wash thoroughly.

In a large pot place the carrot slices, onion slices, and radicchio wedges, and pour the oil over all of it. Sprinkle with the parsley and small amounts of salt and pepper, then add all the water. Cook over moderate heat, covered, for 20 to 30 minutes. Uncover, raise the heat, and cook until the excess liquid is gone and the radicchio is lightly browned.

serves 6

Sautéed Garlic Spinach

spinaci saltati

3 pounds small-leaved bulk spinach

½ teaspoon salt

⅛ teaspoon freshly ground black pepper

2 cloves garlic, crushed

½ cup olive oil

Remove the stems and roots from the spinach and save for later use (see *Testine di Spinaci*). Rinse in cold water many times until any trace of sand is removed. Place in a large pot with ¼ teaspoon salt and no water other than the water the spinach retains from washing. Cook over moderately high heat, covered, for 5 to 6 minutes. Lift with a fork and transfer to a colander to drain.

In a large skillet, place the remaining salt, pepper, garlic, and oil. Cook, stirring, until the garlic becomes golden brown, but not burnt. Discard the garlic and add the spinach. Cook, uncovered, stirring frequently, until the spinach has lost most of the liquid and begins to get crisp.

NOTE: If you prefer, you can mince the garlic instead of crushing it and leave it in the spinach.

serves 6

Spinach Mold

sformato di spinaci

3 pounds small-leaved
bulk spinach

3 tablespoons olive oil

1 small onion, minced fine

1 teaspoon salt

Dash or two white pepper

Dash nutmeg

Butter

⅓ cup unbleached flour

1½ cups hot milk

6 eggs, beaten

4 tablespoons freshly
grated Parmesan cheese

Fine breadcrumbs
(page 311)

1 cup hot Funghi Trifolati
(page 274)

Trim, wash, and cook the spinach as described on page 280. Drain and chop fine.

Heat the oil in a skillet; add the onion and cook over moderately high heat for 1 minute. Add the spinach, salt, pepper, and nutmeg and cook over low heat for 3 to 4 minutes, until the spinach looks quite dry.

Make a white sauce with 3 tablespoons butter, the flour, and milk (see White Sauce recipes, page 245).

Combine the spinach with the sauce, add the eggs and Parmesan cheese, and mix well.

Butter a tube mold and sprinkle with breadcrumbs. Pour the spinach mixture into it and bake in a 350°F oven for 1 hour or until a knife blade plunged into it will come out clean. Remove to a cooling rack for 4 to 5 minutes.

Unmold onto a serving plate and fill the center hole with the mushrooms.

serves 6 to 8

Spinach Jewish Style

spinaci all'ebraica

3 pounds small-leaved bulk spinach

Salt

½ cup dark seedless raisins

1 cup lukewarm water

6 tablespoons olive oil

½ small onion, minced

¼ cup *pignoli* (pine nuts)

Freshly ground black pepper

Dash nutmeg

Remove the stems and roots from the spinach. Rinse in many changes of cold water until any trace of sand is removed. Place in a large pot with a pinch of salt and no water other than that retained from washing. Cook over moderately high heat, covered, for 5 minutes. Drain.

Soak the raisins in the lukewarm water for a couple of minutes, then drain.

Meanwhile, heat the oil in a large skillet, add the onion and sauté until the onion is soft and translucent; add the raisins, *pignoli*, and small amounts of salt and pepper. Sauté, stirring, 1 minute. Add the spinach and nutmeg and sauté, stirring frequently, until the spinach looks dry and crisp.

serves 6

Lemon Spinach

spinaci all'agro

3 pounds small-leaved bulk spinach

½ teaspoon salt

4 tablespoons olive oil

Juice of 1 lemon

Remove the stems and roots from the spinach. Rinse in cold water many times until any trace of sand is removed. Place in a large pot with ¼ teaspoon salt and no water other than that which clings to the spinach from washing. Cook over moderately high heat, covered, until desired tenderness. Transfer to a colander to cool.

Turn onto a cutting board and chop very fine. Do not use a food processor.

Place in a serving dish and flatten with a spatula. Sprinkle with the remaining salt and oil. Just before serving, sprinkle with lemon juice.

serves 6

Mashed Squash

zucca sfranta

This is an old recipe used primarily as part of the dinner at the end of Yom Kippur. Squash is very popular among the Italian Jews, and they prepare it in many ways.

3½ pounds large zucchini or butternut or other yellow squash

1 cup cold water

4 tablespoons olive oil

1 medium onion, cubed

4 large basil leaves, shredded, or 1 teaspoon dried basil

2 large sprigs Italian parsley, coarsely chopped

1 teaspoon salt

¼ teaspoon freshly ground black pepper

Wash, trim, and cube the zucchini. If you use yellow squash, trim and pare it. Cut open and scrape off all the seeds and fibers. Cut into 2-inch cubes and place in a saucepan with 1 cup water. Add all the remaining ingredients and place over moderate heat to cook, covered, for 20 to 30 minutes, stirring occasionally with a wooden spoon. If it becomes necessary, add a couple of tablespoons water and continue cooking until the squash is all mashed.

serves 6

Fried Squash Flowers

fiori di zucca fritti

24 squash flowers, washed

Olive or other vegetable oil for frying

Batter for Frying Vegetables (page 285)

Salt

Delicately remove all the pistils from inside the flowers, trying not to rip the corolla. Cut the stems so they are ½-inch long.

In a large skillet heat 1 to 1½ cups oil to 375°F on a deep-frying thermometer. Holding the flowers by the stem, dip one at a time in the batter and fry until golden and crisp on both sides. Remove to paper towels to drain, sprinkle with salt, and serve immediately.

serves 4 to 6

Stuffed Squash Flowers

fiori di zucca ripieni

18 squash flowers

8 ounces mozzarella cheese, shredded

White Sauce made with 6 tablespoons butter, 6 tablespoons flour, and 1½ cups milk (page 273)

Salt

Ground white pepper

Olive or other vegetable oil for frying

Batter for Frying Vegetables (page 285)

Remove the pistils, cut the stems, and wash the flowers as described on page 73.

Combine the cheese with the white sauce. Add salt and pepper to taste and stir to mix. Fill each flower with this mixture (one heaping tablespoon per flower).

In a medium-frying pan heat 1 to 1½ cups oil to 375°F on a deep-frying thermometer. Delicately dip each stuffed flower in the batter and fry until golden and crisp on both sides. Drain on paper towels and serve immediately.

serves 6

Batter for Frying Vegetables

pastella per fritti di verdura

1 cup unbleached flour
1 teaspoon baking powder
½ teaspoon salt
1 cup cold water
2 tablespoons olive oil
Ground white pepper

Sift together the three dry ingredients. Gradually add the cold water and oil, stirring just until a smooth batter is formed. Add pepper to taste and mix. Use as directed.

yields about 1½ cups

Swiss Chard Stems Venetian Style

coste di bietole alla veneziana

 or this dish you need to buy the type of Swiss chard with large, white stems. The green leafy part is not used here, but you needn't worry about wastefulness since with it you can prepare other delectable dishes.

4 pounds Swiss chard
½ cup olive oil
1 clove garlic, minced
1 tablespoon finely chopped Italian parsley
Salt
2 tablespoons white wine vinegar

Cut the stems from the leaves. Wash the stems and dice them. Place in a pot with cold water to cover and bring to a boil. Cook approximately 5 minutes, then ladle most of the water out and add the oil, garlic, parsley, and a small amount of salt.

Cook over moderate heat, covered, until quite tender. Uncover and let most of the moisture evaporate. Add the vinegar and keep uncovered until the vinegar also has evaporated and the stems are in a flavorful oil sauce.

serves 4 to 6

Fried Mixed Vegetables

fritto misto di verdura

½ recipe *Carciofi Dorati e Fritti (page 263)*

½ recipe *Fiori di Zucca Fritti (page 284)*

½ pound small white mushrooms

Olive or other vegetable oil for frying

½ cup unbleached flour

½ small cauliflower

Salt

½ pound small zucchini

Batter for Frying Vegetables (page 285)

1 large lemon, cut into 8 wedges

10 small sprigs Italian parsley

Freshly ground black pepper

Keep all the fried vegetables in a warm oven on a dish with paper towels.

Trim the mushroom stems and wipe clean. Cut the mushrooms in half or quarters, depending on the size. In a small frying pan, heat ¼ cup oil. Roll the mushrooms in the flour and shake to remove the excess. Fry in the hot oil, stirring, until the mushrooms are golden. Transfer to the dish in the oven.

With a sharp knife, separate the cauliflower flowers and boil for 5 minutes in salted water to cover.

Trim and cut the zucchini in half; cut each half lengthwise into many thin sticks about ¼-inch wide.

Heat 1 to 1½ cups oil in a large frying pan. Dip the vegetables in the batter and fry until golden and crisp. Drain on paper towels.

Arrange all the fried vegetables on a serving plate and garnish with lemon wedges and parsley sprigs. Sprinkle with small amounts of salt and pepper and serve immediately.

serves 8 to 12

Zucchini Pudding

sformato di zucchini

1 medium onion, minced

Olive oil

3½ pounds green or yellow zucchini

1 small carrot, peeled and grated or finely chopped

3 shredded fresh basil leaves or 1 teaspoon dried basil

1 tablespoon coarsely chopped Italian parsley

1 teaspoon salt

¼ teaspoon freshly ground black pepper

4 tablespoons freshly grated Parmesan cheese (optional)

2 large eggs, slightly beaten

½ cup fine breadcrumbs (page 311)

In a large pot, over low heat, cook the onion with 3 tablespoons oil.

Trim the zucchini at both ends and wash thoroughly. Dice and add to the onion. Add the carrot, basil, parsley, salt, and pepper; cook over low heat, covered, for 30 minutes to 1 hour, stirring occasionally. (Cooking time depends on the freshness of the zucchini.) If it becomes necessary, add a few tablespoons water and continue to cook until you have a puree. Uncover and cook, stirring, until the excess moisture has evaporated.

Remove from the heat, add the cheese if desired, and stir to combine. After the mixture has cooled a bit, add the eggs and stir vigorously. Pour into an oiled ovenproof dish sprinkled with breadcrumbs. Spread flat with a rubber spatula. Sprinkle with breadcrumbs and oil and bake in a 450°F oven for 20 to 30 minutes, or until the top is nice and brown.

serves 6 to 8

SALADS

insalate

he classic Italian salad is *insalata mista*, a mixture of two or more spring salad greens (which can include some red or brown) seasoned with only salt, olive oil, and a drizzle of vinegar. Whereas in many cultures this type of salad is served before the meal as a starter or antipasto, in Italy it is served exclusively at the end of the meal, just before the dessert.

Cooked salads such as *Insalata Tricolore* (page 294) are served as side dishes.

Other salads are used as main dishes: These are the ones that combine legumes (chickpeas, any kind of bean, green peas, and lentils) with cereals (rice, corn, wheat, or wheat products—pasta, bread, and such). These combinations result in complete (vegetarian) proteins.* One of my favorite among these is *Fagioli Conditi* (page 293) accompanied by a hearty chunk of garlic Tuscan bread.

The Jews, to obey their dietary laws (see introduction to Vegetables), make great use of these salads as main dishes in place of meat-laden or cheese-laden salads popular today, such as Caesar, which might not be kosher.

---

* It is interesting to note that long before it was scientifically confirmed, that legumes combined with cereals form a complete protein, Jews, and poor people in Italy, knew instinctively and used for their proteic nutrition in *risi e bisi*, rice and green peas, *pasta e fagioli*, pasta with beans, *pasta e ceci*, pasta with chickpeas, and others.

We were both Jewish and poor, so these vegetarian combination dishes often appeared on our table. Once an uncle from Rome came to visit and, seeing how eagerly we were eating, asked us, "You love your beans, don't you?"

"Yes," replied my brother Gino. "But if I had lamb chops, I would love them, too."

Beans

Fagioli

ntil a few years ago, beans in the shell and dried beans were greatly underrated in this country. There was a time when the only beans known to the average American housewife—or at least this was my impression—were frozen lima beans. This misconception, I presume, arose because the emphasis on protein intake was placed mainly, if not solely, on meat, fish, eggs, and milk products, while the protein value of vegetables was almost ignored.

When I was a child in Italy, only a handful of people could afford to eat meat every day. The rest of us had to rely on vegetable proteins. Beans were jokingly called "the steak of the poor." They were always eaten with grains and grain products for more complete protein value.

As with every vegetable, the best beans are the ones that are freshly picked during the harvest season and shelled just before cooking. In Tuscany *fagioli sgranati*, shelled fresh beans, are served in restaurants as a delicacy during the peak of the season and are, in fact, quite expensive.

The different varieties of beans are almost infinite, and the taste and texture change noticeably from type to type. I have never seen fresh beans in their shells sold here (except for lima and cranberry beans, which are excellent for soups and mixed with other vegetables) and we must rely on the dried ones. Dried beans are perfectly fine, except for the very old ones. To be as good as fresh beans, dried ones must be from the latest season's crop. With time—let's say over a year from when they were first picked—beans become somewhat spoiled. They acquire a sugary taste, require a much longer cooking time, and sometimes, as often happens with chickpeas and kidney beans, they never cook completely.

As a result, they are harder on the digestive system and thus undesirable.

It is not easy for the inexperienced cook to recognize fresh dried beans from stale ones, but if you make a conscious effort you can learn to make the distinction. Fresh beans are lighter in color than their stale counterpart. The majority are whole rather than split, and they are never pierced by larvae as beans that are not as fresh might be.

Another misconception surrounding dried beans is that they have to be soaked overnight before cooking, a practice that discourages many a cook from using them because it eliminates a spur-of-the-moment decision. Cooks, rejoice! Beans do *not* have to be soaked overnight (no amount of soaking can restore freshness to old beans), nor does cooking them take all day. Cooking time varies from place to place according to the alkalinity of the water and the altitude; it also varies according to the freshness of the beans and to the different types. On the average, though, cooking takes much less time than many recipes indicate.

When the hearth was not only a source of heat but also the only way to cook meals, a *pignatto* was used to cook beans. A *pignatto* was a tall earthenware pot with a very small bottom, a large belly, and a small opening on the top. It had only one handle. Beans were placed inside the pot with hot water; then the pot was placed at the edge of the hearth with a few red coals very close, under the belly, on the side opposite the handle. The beans cooked to a gentle, even simmering.

We can imitate this primitive method. First remove all stones and debris from the beans, then rinse them twice in warm water. Place in a large terra-cotta or enameled pot with enough hot water to quadruple their volume (for example, 1 quart water for each cup of dried beans, or 6 cups if you suspect that the beans are not quite fresh). Add 1 teaspoon salt for each quart of water and bring to a rapid boil. Reduce the heat to its lowest point and simmer beans, covered, for ½ hour. Add 1 fresh sage leaf (or ¼ teaspoon dried sage leaves—*not* powder) and ½ clove garlic, husk on, for each cup of beans and simmer ½ to 1 hour longer.

The beans I favor are the great Northern beans because their size and shape remind me of the beans I used to like best in my village. But I also use cannellini, navy, marrow, lima, kidney, and all the varieties I find in the market, and enjoy them all. I rarely have an important dinner without serving *fagioli* in one form or another, and my guests simply love them.

Bean Salad

fagioli conditi

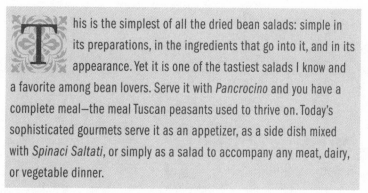

This is the simplest of all the dried bean salads: simple in its preparations, in the ingredients that go into it, and in its appearance. Yet it is one of the tastiest salads I know and a favorite among bean lovers. Serve it with *Pancrocino* and you have a complete meal—the meal Tuscan peasants used to thrive on. Today's sophisticated gourmets serve it as an appetizer, as a side dish mixed with *Spinaci Saltati*, or simply as a salad to accompany any meat, dairy, or vegetable dinner.

2 cups dried cannellini or great Northern beans

2 to 3 quarts hot water

Coarse table salt

1 large clove garlic, husk on

2 fresh or 1 teaspoon dried sage leaves

1 small white onion, sliced thin

Freshly ground (coarse) black pepper

¾ cup imported dark Italian olive oil

Pick and discard any stones or unhealthy looking beans. Rinse twice in warm water and place in a large pot with the hot water and 1 tablespoon salt. Bring to a rapid boil, then reduce the heat to minimum, and simmer, covered, for ½ hour. Add the garlic and sage and cook, covered, for another ½ hour or until the beans feel soft but not mushy.

Remove from the heat and let stand at room temperature until cool. Discard the garlic and sage. With a slotted spoon, transfer the beans to a serving bowl. (Save the water for a vegetable soup, if you wish.) Add the onion and salt and pepper to taste. Toss the bowl up and down in a gentle rotating motion toward you to distribute the seasoning evenly. If you use a spoon, be careful not to make a puree. Add the olive oil and wait until it has seeped through before serving.

serves 6 to 8

Green Bean Salad

fagiolini conditi

2½ pounds fresh green beans

2 cups cold water

Salt

Freshly ground black pepper

1 small clove garlic, minced fine

2 tablespoons freshly chopped Italian parsley

2 tablespoons wine vinegar

4 tablespoons olive oil

Trim the beans at both ends, wash them, and place in a saucepan with the cold water and 1 teaspoon salt. Bring to a boil and cook, covered, for 6 to 8 minutes, or until the beans are tender but crisp. (If you have a steamer rack by all means steam your green beans.) Drain and place in a salad bowl. Add salt and pepper to taste and all the other ingredients. Toss gently and serve at room temperature.

serves 6

Tricolor Salad

insalata tricolore

We used to call this salad "patriotic" because of its red, white, and green colors, which are those of the Italian flag. It was invariably served as part of the Rosh Hashana dinner when the three vegetables that compose it are at their youngest and tenderest.

1½ pounds tender, fresh string beans

12 small, new white potatoes

6 small beets, greens removed

Salt

Freshly ground black pepper

2 tablespoons red wine vinegar

⅓ cup olive oil

6 small sprigs Italian parsley

Trim the string beans at both ends. Cook each vegetable separately in a little salted water until tender but still firm (if you have a vegetable steamer, by all means steam your vegetables).

Peel the potatoes and beets. Slice both thin and arrange on a long serving plate with the potatoes at the center and the string beans and beets on either side. Season with salt and pepper to taste. Sprinkle with vinegar and oil and garnish with parsley sprigs.

serves 6

Artichoke, fennel, and Asparagus Salad

insalata di carciofi, finocchio, e asparagi

6 small, fresh artichokes

1 lemon, juice and rind

2 medium knobs fennel

1½ pounds small asparagus

1 scallion, cut up, with some green

Salt

Freshly ground black pepper

4 tablespoons extra virgin olive oil

2 tablespoons balsamic vinegar

1 medium head red radicchio

1 clove garlic

Trim the artichokes and keep in acidulated water until ready to use. Remove the outer leaves from the fennel; cut off and discard the long stems and most of the greens. Wash under running water and pat dry. Cut into small cubes (⅓ inch) and toss into a bowl.

Cut the tips of the asparagus 2 inches long (discard the rest) and cut again in half. Add to the bowl with the fennel.

Drain and pat the artichokes dry, cut in half, then into thin wedges, and place in the bowl. Add the scallion, and season with salt, pepper, oil, and vinegar. Gently toss.

Separate the radicchio leaves, wash, and pat dry. Rub the garlic on the inside of a serving plate, then discard. Line the plate with radicchio leaves, pour the salad over it, and serve.

serves 6

Chickpea Salad

ceci conditi

1 pound dried chickpeas
4 quarts warm water
Salt
1 small branch fresh
rosemary or 1 teaspoon
dried rosemary leaves,
wrapped in cheesecloth
1 clove garlic, husk on
Coarsely ground
black pepper
2 tablespoons chives or
scallion greens, chopped
Extra virgin olive oil

Distribute the chickpeas on a flat surface. Pick and remove stones and any debris. Rinse 2 to 3 times in warm water and place in a large pot. Add the warm water and 1 tablespoon salt, and bring to a boil. Lower the heat to minimum, add the rosemary and garlic, and simmer, covered, for 1 hour or until tender.

Remove and discard the rosemary and garlic.

With a slotted spoon, transfer to a bowl; add the chives or scallion greens, and season with salt and pepper to taste. Sprinkle with extra virgin olive oil and toss. Serve hot.

serves 6 to 10

Escarole Salad

scarola a insalata

The pleasant contrast in flavor and texture that results from combining bitter escarole with sweet, juicy oranges and crunchy almonds makes for a very interesting salad. Its simple preparation should provide an incentive to serve it often, for both family and company dinners.

3 large bunches of escarole
4 large, seedless oranges
Salt
Freshly ground black
pepper

Remove the outer green leaves and all the green parts of the inner leaves of the escarole and save for *Scarola Cotta*. Cut the whiter parts of each bunch into 1-inch pieces. Rinse many times in cold water, drain, and pat dry with paper towels.

Peel and cube the oranges.

⅓ cup olive oil

⅓ cup toasted slivered almonds

Combine the escarole and oranges in a large bowl. Sprinkle with salt and pepper to taste, add the oil, and toss well. Sprinkle with toasted almonds and serve.

NOTE: To toast the sliced almonds, spread them over a baking sheet and place the sheet under the broiler for 4 to 5 minutes, stirring a couple of times. Toasting enhances the flavor of nuts, but great care should be taken so that they do not burn.

serves 6

Couscous Salad

insalata di cuscussù

his salad can be served as a refreshing alternative to potato salad in summer dinners, or as an excellent hors d'oeuvre in any season. Couscous, pre-cooked and raw, can be found in most health food and specialty stores. I prefer to use the raw type.

1 cup raw couscous

6 tablespoons extra virgin olive oil

Salt

3½ cups cold water

¾ cup oil-cured black olives, pitted and cut up

½ large red pepper, cored and diced

½ yellow pepper, cored and diced

¼ cup freshly minced onion

2 tablespoons Italian parsley leaves

Freshly ground black pepper

Place the couscous in a large pan with 2 tablespoons oil and mix until all the grains are coated. Add 1 teaspoon salt and all the water and stir. Bring to a boil over high heat, stirring occasionally. Lower the heat and simmer, stirring frequently, ½ hour or until the couscous feels tender to the bite.

Let cool to room temperature, stirring from time to time to fluff it up, then add the chopped olives, peppers, onion, and parsley. Add salt and pepper to taste and the remaining oil. Mix to combine.

serves 6 to 8

Orange Salad
arance condite

Toward the end of World War II, after retaking possession of our home, which had been occupied by Fascists while we were in hiding, we heard a knock at our door early one morning. Before us stood a British officer, who politely introduced himself. He explained that he was in charge of buying wine for his company and needed to leave the money with a trustworthy family who knew English, and our family had been mentioned to him. After this flattering introduction, we let him in and without hesitation he emptied his knapsack into a cupboard, filling it with a mountain of one thousand-lire bills. Then he disappeared and we didn't see him until late that afternoon, quite loaded, in the company of the farmer who had sold him the wine. He begged my father to pay the man, pocketed the remaining bills, thanked us, and left. After that he came back once a month, and as a result we became close friends. To amuse us (as a civilian he had been a schoolteacher) he would recite the alphabet from A to Z and then in reverse in one breath. Often he would arrive when we were still in bed and, after my father had let him in, he would walk directly to the bedroom where my sister and I were still asleep and shout from the door, "Get up, lazies, it's almost 7 o'clock!" Then he would empty his sack and go about his business.

One afternoon he came back as we were about to eat our orange salad (in Italy salad is served at the end of the meal, not at the beginning), and my father offered him some. He looked puzzled and, frankly, quite revolted at the idea of coupling oranges with olive oil, but out of courtesy he tried the salad. He truly liked it, and it became his favorite snack when he came around. He swore he would introduce it in England, where his family ran a small restaurant business.

I never found out whether the British officer did introduce the orange salad in England, but I have introduced it in America quite successfully.

9 large seedless oranges

1 citron or 1 large lemon (optional), peeled and diced

Coarse salt

Coarsely crushed black pepper

Extra virgin olive oil

Peel the oranges with a sharp knife, leaving some of the white part of the peel attached to the fruit. Cut into ¼-inch slices and arrange them on a serving platter. Sprinkle with salt, pepper, and oil to taste. Serve with a crust of Tuscan or *Fruste* bread.

NOTE: We served our orange salad just as I have described it. However, some prefer to cut the sweetness of the oranges by adding a few pieces of citron or lemon to it.

serves 6

Fennel Salad

insalata di finocchi

The best knobs of fennel for this salad are the roundish ones, the light green tuft of which is fuzzy and firm. Avoid, when possible, flat, long, discolored fennel with dark and wilted tufts. It is not so bad for cooked dishes, but doesn't make a very good salad.

6 medium knobs of fennel

¼ cup olive oil

1 teaspoon salt

¼ teaspoon freshly ground black pepper

2 teaspoons wine vinegar (optional)

Remove and discard the bruised leaves from the fennel. Cut off and discard the long stems and most of the green. Wash under running cold water and pat dry. Cut into small cubes (⅓ inch) and place in a salad bowl. Add the remaining ingredients and toss to combine.

serves 6

Rice Salad

insalata di riso

1 cup chickpeas or navy beans

1 cup long-grain rice

3 cups water

3 tablespoons white wine vinegar

Salt

Freshly ground black pepper

Olive oil

1 cup shelled green peas

One 3-ounce can chunk tuna packed in oil, drained

3 ripe plum tomatoes, cut up

1 cup Artichoke Hearts in Oil (page 75)

1 tablespoon tiny capers, drained

1 sweet red pepper, cored and sliced

3 hard-boiled eggs, sliced

Cook the chickpeas or navy beans as described on pages 291–92.

Meanwhile, cook the rice in 3 cups lightly salted boiling water. Drain and spread over a plate to cool.

Drain the beans and add to the rice. Add the vinegar and lightly season with salt, pepper, and olive oil to taste.

If the green peas are young and tender leave them raw. Otherwise cook them, covered, in ½ cup salted boiling water for 6 to 7 minutes, drain, and add to the rice bowl.

Add the tuna, tomatoes, artichoke hearts, capers, red pepper, and eggs. Toss thoroughly.

serves 6 as a luncheon dish or 8 to 10 as a side dish

Roasted Pepper Salad

peperoni arrosto

3 pounds yellow, green, and red sweet peppers

3 teaspoons salt

¼ teaspoon freshly ground black pepper

3 tablespoons wine vinegar

⅓ cup olive oil

1 small piece lemon peel, minced fine

Wash the peppers and place them, still wet, in a large baking pan where they can fit in one layer. Bake in a 525°F oven for ½ hour or until the peel begins to blister and even burn at some spots. During baking, turn them once or twice.

When they look wilted and done, remove from the oven and drop into a basin filled with cold water. Peel, remove the stems and cores, and cut lengthwise into 10 to 12 strips each. Rinse in fresh, cold water and drain well. Place in a large bowl with the remaining ingredients and toss to combine. Serve at room temperature.

serves 6

Tomato Salad

pomodori conditi

What's so Italian Jewish about a tomato salad? I'll tell you: the fuss and care in preparing it. I was present once when two Italians, one a journalist from Bologna and the other a professor from Sicily, argued for hours over the relative merits of their respective ways of preparing a tomato salad. Each was convinced that his own method was the best. One insisted on lots of garlic, the other on oregano. Finally, the oregano party won. We were at the mountain lodge of the Bolognese in the Apennines, with no oregano in the pantry. So the loser had to drive a half-hour each way to the nearest village to buy a box of dried oregano! In my opinion each of their ways was good, but not as good as the way my mother prepared it. Here is her recipe for this simple, rustic, delightful delicacy.

12 leaves Boston, Bibb, or Salad Bowl lettuce

6 large round tomatoes, ripe but firm

1 large clove garlic

½ cup extra virgin olive oil

2 teaspoons salt

Black peppercorns in a mill

½ teaspoon dried oregano

1 tablespoon shredded fresh basil leaves

1 tablespoon freshly chopped Italian parsley

Rinse the lettuce leaves and pat dry with paper towels. Arrange on a large serving plate or, better, place 2 leaves on each of six individual salad dishes.

Wash and dry the tomatoes and place on a cutting board with the round side up. Rub the garlic on both sides of the sharp blade of a pairing knife and slice the tomatoes without cutting through. The slices should open like an accordion, remaining attached to one another at the bottom. Rub the garlic again on the blade of the knife for each tomato. Arrange all the accordions on the serving plate with the lettuce leaves, or place 1 over each individual salad dish.

Season in between the slices with half the oil and with salt, pepper, and oregano. Sprinkle the top with the remaining oil, and finally with basil and parsley.

serves 6

Tomato and Mozzarella Salad

pomodori e mozzarella

6 medium-to-large ripe tomatoes

1½ pounds *bocconcini* (fresh, bite-size mozzarella cheese)

A handful Italian parsley leaves, coarsely chopped

2 tablespoons shredded basil leaves

2 cloves garlic, minced

Salt

Freshly ground black pepper

Extra virgin olive oil

Balsamic vinegar (optional)

Remove some of the peel—that which comes off easily—from the tomatoes and dice them into a bowl. Add the *bocconcini* (the larger ones may be cut in half). Add the parsley, basil, garlic, and salt and pepper to taste. Gently toss. Sprinkle abundantly with olive oil and a small drizzle of vinegar if so desired.

NOTE: If you serve this salad as an appetizer, you may want to present it differently. Slice the tomatoes and place on a large plate, possibly on a single layer. Season with salt and pepper, and sprinkle abundantly with oil, but only a hint of vinegar if desired. Top with *bocconcini*, then sprinkle with herbs.

serves 6

Tuna and Fresh Bean Salad

tonno coi fagioli sgranati

I n late summer and early fall, there is virtually no restaurant in Florence (in fact, in all of Tuscany) that doesn't offer this simple but truly delectable salad. One of the genuine pleasures I reap from my annual return to Florence is to go to the farmers' market and get fresh beans in their shell and *cipolline novelle*, new onions, the bulbs of which have hardly begun to swell, for this salad. Here at home I have a minuscule herb garden that yields a few rows of white beans every year for my tuna and bean salad. Since not everyone can have access to fresh beans, dried beans can be substituted successfully.

3 cups freshly shelled white beans or 1½ cups dried beans such as cannellini, navy, or great Northern beans

1 clove garlic, husk on

2 fresh or 1 teaspoon dried sage leaves

2 small new white onions, sliced thin

Two 7-ounce cans solid tuna packed in oil

Salt

Freshly ground (coarse) black pepper

½ cup imported Italian olive oil

If you use fresh beans, cook in 1½ quarts water with 1 teaspoon salt for 20 minutes. For dried beans, follow the directions on page 292. Discard the garlic and sage from the beans; drain and place in a bowl with the onions.

Drain the tuna very well and add to the beans. Season with salt and coarsely ground pepper to taste and the olive oil. Toss to mix.

serves 6

Tuna and Potato Salad

insalata di tonno e patate

6 large all-purpose potatoes

Three 6½-ounce cans tuna
packed in olive oil

3 tablespoons chopped
scallions with greens

Salt

Freshly ground black
pepper

Extra virgin olive oil

Steam the potatoes until tender but not mushy. Peel, cut in chunks, and place in a bowl. Let cool a little. Drain the tuna and shred into the bowl with the potatoes.

Add the scallions, salt and pepper to taste, and a generous sprinkling of extra virgin olive oil. Toss gently and serve.

serves 6

BREADS, PIZZAS, AND BAGELS

pane, pizze, e ciambelle

he words "French bread" immediately summon up the image of a man rushing through a narrow street of Paris holding tight under his arm a long, unwrapped bread baguette, munching on morsels pulled from one extremity of the deliciously fragrant stick.

"Italian bread," on the other hand, does not evoke similarly strong imagery, because there is not such a thing as a "national" bread in Italy. Bread in Milan, for example, is quite different from bread in Florence or in Rome. It follows that the bread sold in America as "Italian bread" is misnamed. In fact, the variety of breads from region to region and from city to city that are sold in bakeries is quite impressive, and the habit of baking bread at home has long been abandoned by the average household. For the same reason, breads are seldom, if ever, listed in Italian cookbooks.

However, the Jews, to comply with the laws of kashruth and with tradition (challah bread for Shabbat, *Maritucci* for Sukkot, to cite two examples), have maintained the habit of bread baking at home. I have offered many types of breads, none of which could particularly be termed "Italian bread" in the American context. Nevertheless, they are indeed breads that are made in Italy, some only by Jews (*Bollo*), others by bakeries and Jews alike.

Simple Matza

azzima semplice

his matza is called "simple" to distinguish it from egg matza, wine matza, and so on. However, it really is not at all simple. It has only two ingredients: flour and water. But the finished product looks like a handmade doily, with festoons and embroidery. Passover wouldn't seem real to me if I didn't bake these primitive *matzòt* of my childhood. Unfortunately, Passover flour—the flour that is ground expressly for Passover—is not readily available to the consumer. The reason why, I am told, is that a drop of water, or even the atmospheric moisture, is enough to make it *chametz* (leavened or fermented) in a very short time (about 18 minutes) and therefore not suitable for Passover.

When I was growing up in Pitigliano, we made our own flour *kasher l' Pesach*, which means that it was watched from the harvesting of the grain through the grinding to the baking, to ensure that it was kosher for Passover. With that same flour we made a number of other Passover dishes, including *Minestra di Sfoglietti* and *Pan di Spagna*.

2½ cups cold water (spring water, if possible)

7 cups of the finest flour (if possible, kosher for Passover)

In a large cold bowl, quickly mix the water with enough flour to form a very stiff dough. Spread the remaining flour on a smooth working surface (preferably marble or glass) and turn the dough out over it. Knead with force for about 3 minutes. During this first phase of kneading, make a few cuts in the dough with a sharp knife, which will enable you to incorporate more flour into it. Continue to knead quickly until the dough is perfectly smooth.

Divide it into 12 equal portions (at this point, the more people who can help, the better). Have each of your helpers knead the little pieces of dough until they are elastic. With small rolling pins (I use a new wooden broomstick, cut into 18-inch sections), roll into 9 × 5-inch ovals or into disks 6½ inches in diameter.

To trim the edges: place your thumb at an angle at the edge of the disk and then pinch with the thumb and index finger to create a small bump. Repeat this motion at the same angle all around so the bumps are the same distance apart. Now for the holes: a quarter of an inch from the pinched border, attacking the disk from one side, pinch a piece of dough with the thumb and index finger, making two holes. Move the index finger into the hole made by the thumb (toward you) and pinch another hole. Repeat all around until the first loop of holes is completed. A quarter of an inch in from the first row, pinch the dough and make another loop of holes. Repeat until you have four concentric loops of holes. At this point your matza looks like a doily and it is almost ready to be baked.

With a metal comb (the metal comb we used was made for the purpose and looked like a segment of a saw. But commercially available metal combs are good enough.), prick many tiny holes all over your matza to prevent swelling and blistering during baking and bake in a 550°F oven (to be kosher, the oven should be from 600° to 800°F, and cooking time should not exceed 3 minutes to be acceptable by orthodox Jews) for 6 to 7 minutes, or until the *matẓòt* begin to have a pale color.

NOTE: This is a project for your entire family or a group of friends and can be a lot of fun. Though Simple Matza is not so simple to make, it is worth every bit of the effort.

yields 12 matzòt

Sweet Wine Matzòt

azzime dolci al vino

2½ cups Passover flour
(see page 106)
½ cup sugar
½ cup olive oil
½ cup dry white wine
2 teaspoons anise seeds
1 teaspoon salt

Combine all the ingredients in a bowl and form a dough. Turn out over an oiled surface and knead until smooth. Roll into a cylinder; then cut the cylinder into 6 equal slices. Roll each slice down to ¼-inch thickness. Pinch two concentric rows of holes (see preparation of Simple Matza) and arrange on a lightly oiled and well-floured baking sheet. Bake in a 450°F oven for 15 minutes. Serve as a wholesome snack or breakfast food.

yields 6 matzòt

Croutons

pane a dadini

Croutons are very useful in Italian Jewish cuisine and are very easy to prepare. You can make fried or toasted croutons. The former taste better; however, the latter can be prepared ahead of time, besides being more easily digestible than fried ones.

½ cup vegetable oil or
butter
Eight ⅓-inch slices White
Bread (see following
recipe), diced

Heat the fat in a large skillet until quite hot, but not smoky. Drop the diced bread into it and fry quickly, stirring, until golden brown, about 1 minute. Transfer to paper towels to drain the excess fat.

For toasted croutons, place the diced bread with no oil on a baking sheet. Toast under the broiler for approximately 2 minutes, shaking the baking sheet frequently. Remove from the heat and let cool thoroughly, stirring from time to time, before storing for later use.

For seasoned croutons, add ½ teaspoon Italian herb seasoning and 1 teaspoon garlic salt to fried croutons, or on toasted croutons while still hot.

NOTE: Fried croutons are generally used to supplement a clear or creamy soup and are served hot. Toasted croutons are used the same way, but can also be stored to be used for stuffings.

yields 4 cups

White Bread

pane in cassetta

his bread is rarely used in Italy except for toast and specialties such as *crostini, Mozzarella in Carrozza,* and so on. In Tuscany, where the word "bread" evokes sensations of crunchy and crusty textures, no *buongustaio* (gourmet) would ever be caught eating *Fagioli Conditi* with a slice of white bread. Nevertheless, do not assume that this bread is anything like the commercially available white bread. *Pane in Cassetta* is still a hearty, satisfying bread and so easy to make that it is worth having a good supply of it on hand in the freezer at all times. (*Pane in Cassetta,* like any bread, can be frozen wrapped in foil and enclosed in a plastic bag. Slice the loaves into ⅓-inch slices before storing in the freezer, so that one or more slices can be retrieved when needed, while the rest remain in the freezer.)

1 envelope active dry yeast
1 teaspoon sugar
2½ cups warm water
1 teaspoon salt
¼ cup vegetable oil
6 cups unbleached flour

Place the yeast and sugar in a bowl with the warm water and let stand 5 minutes. Add the salt and oil and ½ cup flour at a time while mixing, until a soft dough is formed. Turn onto a floured working surface and knead 3 minutes. Divide into two equal parts; knead each 2 minutes, cover with a clean kitchen towel, and let rest 5 minutes.

Pull and fold each piece of dough and roll down to a rectangle of approximately 8 × 4½ inches. Place in two oiled 8 × 4½ × 2½-inch loaf pans and set aside in a warm place to rise for 45 minutes to 1 hour, or until doubled in bulk.

Preheat the oven to 375°F and bake the loaves for 35 to 40 minutes.

yields two 1-pound loaves

Breadcrumbs

pangrattato

Make your own breadcrumbs with leftover homemade bread. Not only will they be cheaper and more nutritious but you will be sure that they are kosher.

For fine breadcrumbs, let the bread scraps become quite hard and dry before crumbling them in a blender or food processor.

For coarse breadcrumbs, process the bread while it is still soft, then dry the crumbs in an oven at low heat for several hours.

For seasoned breadcrumbs, add 1 teaspoon Italian herb seasoning and 1 teaspoon garlic salt to each cup of coarse breadcrumbs and mix thoroughly.

Let the crumbs cool completely before storing them in a glass jar in the refrigerator.

A Hearty Garlic Bread

pancrocino

ancrocino, also called *Bruschetta* in Rome and *fettunta* in Florence, is, I am sure, the original of the various garlic breads of today. The authentic *Pancrocino* was made with olive oil freshly milled and you cannot duplicate that. But you can still make a very good *Pancrocino*, and it is always a success with family and friends.

1 loaf stale Tuscan bread

4 large cloves garlic

Coarse table salt

Freshly ground (coarse) black pepper

1 cup imported dark Italian olive oil

Divide the loaf in half. Cut each half in half again. Then, cutting horizontally, split each piece in half, thus obtaining 8 split pieces. Toast these pieces on both sides under the broiler until dark brown.

Rub the garlic over the split sides of each piece, then sprinkle with salt and pepper to taste.

Cut the pieces in half again and arrange on a large serving dish in one layer. Pour all the oil over the bread and let it seep through before serving.

serves 6

Challah Bread

pane del sabato

2 envelopes active
dry yeast
2 tablespoons sugar
1¾ cups warm water
3 eggs
1 tablespoon salt
¼ cup warm vegetable oil
7 cups unbleached flour
1 egg yolk

Have all the ingredients at room temperature except the oil and water, which should be warm. Dissolve the yeast and a pinch of sugar in ½ cup warm water.

Lightly beat the eggs with the salt in a large bowl. Add the yeast mixture, the remaining sugar, oil, and 1¼ cups warm water.

Gradually add 5½ cups flour, mixing with a fork at first, then with your hands (or beaters if you have an electric dough-maker) until the dough easily leaves the sides of the bowl.

Spread the remaining flour on a working surface and turn the dough out on it. Knead with force, incorporating as much flour as needed to make a rather stiff dough. Shape into a ball and place on a floured board. Lightly brush the top with oil, cover with a clean towel, and let rise in a warm place for 2 hours or until its bulk has increased from three to four times.

Punch down and divide into 2 equal parts. Divide each part into 3 equal parts and roll each into a 13-inch rope, bulging at the center and tapering at the ends. Fasten 3 ropes at one end and make a braid; fasten at the other end. Repeat with the other 3 ropes.

Place on a lightly oiled and generously floured baking sheet, far apart. Cover with a towel and set in a warm place to rise for 1 hour or until more than doubled in bulk. Brush the tops with the egg yolk beaten with 1 teaspoon water.

Place the baking sheet on the middle rack of a cold oven, and a shallow pan of cold water on the bottom rack. Set the temperature at 400°F and let the oven warm up with the bread inside. After 15 minutes, lower the heat to 350°F and bake the bread for another 30 minutes, or until the crust is deep brown. Remove to a cooling rack.

yields two 1½-pound loaves

Rosh Hashanah Challah Bread

challa di rosh hashanà

2 envelopes active dry
yeast
2 tablespoons sugar
¼ cup honey
1 tablespoon salt
1½ cups warm water
7 cups unbleached flour
¼ cup warm olive oil
3 eggs, slightly beaten
1 egg yolk, beaten with
1 teaspoon of water

Place the yeast, sugar, honey, salt, and water in the large bowl of a mixer and beat for 1 minute. Add 2 cups of flour and beat for another minute. Cover with a clean towel and set aside in a draft-free place for 1 hour or until the batter begins to bubble.

Replace the beaters with the dough hook. Add the oil, beaten eggs, and enough flour to make a rather stiff dough. Knead until the dough is satiny and easily parts from the sides of the bowl. Shape into a ball and place in a lightly oiled bowl; turn it once, cover with a towel, and set aside until it has more than tripled in bulk.

Turn onto a lightly floured working table, punch down and divide into 2 parts. Shape each part into a long rope and roll the rope in a spiral, first flat on the table, then over itself, until you have a pyramid-like loaf. Repeat with the second rope. Place the loaves over a lightly oiled and floured baking sheet, well apart. Cover loosely with a towel and set aside for 1 hour or until more than doubled in bulk.

Brush the tops with the egg-yolk-and-water mixture and bake in a 400°F oven for 30 minutes or until the crust is deep brown. Remove to cooling rack.

yields two 1½-pound loaves

Sourdough Challah Bread

pane del sabato con lievito casalingo

1 cup Sourdough Starter
(see following recipe)

1½ cups warm water

7 cups unbleached flour

3 tablespoons sugar

¼ cup warm olive oil

1 tablespoon salt

3 eggs, slightly beaten

1 egg yolk, mixed with
1 teaspoon water

Have all the ingredients at room temperature. (In winter you might have to take the starter out of the refrigerator the night before baking.) Place the sourdough starter in the large bowl of a mixer. Add ½ cup of warm water and 1 cup of flour and beat very well. Cover the bowl with plastic wrap and let rest in a draft-free place for several hours until doubled in bulk. Add the sugar, oil, salt, eggs, and 1 cup warm water, and beat to homogeneity. Replace the beaters with the dough hook. Gradually add 5½ cups of flour and beat until the dough easily leaves the sides of the bowl. Spread the remaining flour on a working surface and turn the dough onto it. Knead while incorporating enough flour to make a rather stiff dough. Shape into a ball and place in an oiled bowl, turning once. Cover with plastic wrap and set aside for 2 hours, or until more than tripled in bulk.

Turn on the working surface and punch down. Divide into two equal parts. Divide each part into three equal parts and roll each into a 13-inch rope bulging at the center and tapering at the ends. Fasten 3 ropes at one end and make a braid; fasten the other end. Repeat with the remaining 3 ropes.

Place on a lightly oiled and generously floured baking sheet and set aside for 1 more hour, or until doubled.

Brush the tops with the egg-yolk-and-water mixture and bake in a preheated 400°F oven for 15 minutes. Lower the temperature to 350°F and bake for another 30 minutes, or until the crust is deep brown.

yields two 1½-pound loaves

Sourdough Starter

il lievito casalingo

To start this starter, simply mix 1½ cups of unbleached flour and 1 teaspoon of active dry yeast with 1½ cups of warm water in a glass, ceramic, or plastic container. Cover with plastic wrap and leave at room temperature until the batter grows and bubbles (this may take several hours to happen, especially in winter). Place in the refrigerator until you are ready to use it.

The day you wish to make bread, take the container out of the refrigerator and leave it at room temperature for a few hours. Use 1 cup of batter, and replenish the starter by adding 1¼ cups of unbleached flour and 1 cup of warm water to the container. Mix just a little (lumps will dissolve by themselves) and leave at room temperature a few hours, then return to the refrigerator until next time.

If a long time elapses between bread makings, you may find that your sourdough starter looks different. There might be either a dry crust or a greyish liquid at the top, and even some mold. Do not use as it is, of course, but do not throw it away either. Remove the crust or the liquid and any parts that look spoiled. Transfer the remaining batter into a clean container, add 1¼ cups of unbleached flour and 1 cup of warm water, mix a little, and let stand at room temperature for a couple of hours; your starter will be fresh and ready to use again.

NOTE: In winter you may want to use sourdough in conjunction with a teaspoon of active dry yeast to speed up the rising process.

Yom Kippur Bread

il bollo

5½ cups unbleached flour

2 envelopes active dry yeast

1 teaspoon sugar

1 cup warm water

3 eggs

1¼ cups sugar

½ cup olive oil

2 tablespoons anise seeds

2 teaspoons vanilla extract

2 teaspoons salt

1 teaspoon grated lemon rind (optional)

1 egg yolk

Have all the ingredients at room temperature. Combine 1½ cups flour with the dry yeast, 1 teaspoon sugar, and the warm water in a large bowl. Beat until you have a very smooth soft dough. Lightly sprinkle the top with flour, cover with a clean kitchen towel, and set aside in a warm place for about 2 hours or until more than doubled in bulk.

Add the eggs and 1¼ cups sugar and begin to beat. Scald the oil with the anise seeds and add to the bowl, while beating. Add the vanilla extract, salt, and grated lemon rind, if desired. Gradually add enough flour to make a soft dough.

Spread the remaining flour on a working surface. Turn the contents of the bowl over it, and knead, gathering the flour, until you have a dough that is stiff enough to hold its shape. Divide into two equal parts, knead 2 minutes, and let rest 5 minutes. Shape each part into a 12-inch oval loaf and place on a lightly oiled and generously floured baking sheet.

Cover with a towel and let rise in a warm place for 1 to 2 hours or until doubled. Brush the tops with the egg yolk beaten with 1 teaspoon water and place in a preheated 450°F oven. Immediately lower the heat to 350°F and bake 30 minutes or until dark brown.

yields two 1-pound loaves

Sourdough Tuscan Bread

pane toscano col lievito casalingo

When I came to this country, I began to make my own Tuscan bread with the commercial active dry yeast and it was satisfactory, but not quite authentic. In time, however, I began to make it with *Lievito Casalingo*, and was finally able to recapture the taste and texture of the bread of my childhood.

1 *Lievito Casalingo*
(page 316)
8 cups unbleached flour
2 cups warm water

The day before you want to bake, free the hardened sourdough sponge from all the old flour (and any dust that may have settled on it, since it was not covered), and soak it, from 3 to 12 hours, in a bowl with cold water to cover and an inverted dish to keep it from floating.

At night, carefully pour all the water out, trying not to disturb the sediment at the bottom. Add 1 cup flour and 1 cup warm water and stir to mix. Loosely cover the bowl with wax paper and leave in a warm place overnight.

The next day, add 1 cup warm water and stir to dissolve the batter. Add enough flour to make a rather stiff dough. Turn out on a floured working surface and knead for 5 to 10 minutes. Divide into 2 equal parts; knead each a couple of minutes, then cover with a towel and let rest 5 minutes.

Shape each piece of dough into an oval loaf and place on a lightly oiled and generously floured baking sheet as far apart as possible. With a sharp knife cut 3 slashes widthwise, ¼-inch deep, on the top of each loaf.

Cover with a towel and let rise in a warm place for 1½ to 2 hours, or until more than doubled in bulk. If you see that the loaves don't seem to leaven and expand quickly enough, put the sheet on the middle rack of a cold oven. Place a shallow pan with cold water on the rack below it; set the thermostat at 400°F and the timer at 15 minutes. When the timer goes off, lower the temperature to 375°F and bake 30 minutes longer or until the crust is uniformly light brown. While the oven gets hot, the bread has a chance to leaven some more.

If, on the other hand, the loaves are well expanded (it takes a bit of practice to recognize the ideal leavening point) it is better to bake them in a preheated 450°F oven for 10 minutes, then lower the heat to 375°F and proceed as above. This way the already leavened bread gets cooked quickly and does not become overleavened.

Remove to a wire rack for at least 1 hour before serving.

NOTE: Any yeast bread, batter, or dessert can be made with a sourdough starter. But remember that it takes longer to rise.

yields two 1½-pound loaves

Rosemary Bread

pan di ramerino

2 envelopes active dry yeast
2 cups warm water
1 tablespoon salt
⅓ cup warm olive oil
7 cups unbleached flour
½ cup Malaga or Muscatel raisins
1 tablespoon rosemary leaves
1 egg yolk, beaten with 1 teaspoon water

Dissolve the yeast in ½ cup warm water and let rest for 10 minutes. Add 1½ cups warm water, salt, oil, and enough flour to make a not-too-stiff dough. Manipulate with your hands or the dough hook of an electric beater until the dough easily leaves the sides of the bowl. Turn onto an unfloured working table and knead 2 minutes. Spread the raisins over the table and knead until the dough has incorporated all of them. Divide into 6 parts, knead each 2 minutes, then cover with a towel and let rest for 10 minutes.

Shape into oval little loaves and place on a well-floured baking sheet. Gash the tops diagonally in both directions forming a crisscross pattern. Sprinkle with rosemary and press down with your fingers to anchor the rosemary leaves into the dough. Cover with a towel and set aside for 1 to 2 hours, or until doubled in bulk.

Brush the tops with the egg yolk-and-water mixture, taking care not to disturb the rosemary, and bake in a preheated 350°F oven for 30 minutes, or until the crusts are nicely browned.

yields six ⅓-pound loaves

Flat Bread with Oil and Salt

schiacciatina all'olio

 ust as the Roman children used to grab a *pizza e ricotta* on their way to school, Florentine kids did the same (and still do) with *Schiacciatina*. Housewives know better than to go to the bakery between 7 and 8 o'clock. They do their shopping for baked goods very early in the morning or after all the children are in school, since they know that the bakers wouldn't even look at them during the hour that they are busy serving and chatting with a garrulous flock of children.

3 cups unbleached flour

1 envelope active dry yeast

1 teaspoon salt

Olive oil

1 cup warm water

1½ teaspoons coarse table salt

Combine the flour, dry yeast, and salt in a bowl. Gradually add ¼ cup oil and the warm water, mixing to make a rather stiff dough.

Turn onto a floured working surface and knead for 3 or 4 minutes. Shape into a ball, place on an oiled baking sheet, and set aside in a warm place, covered with a kitchen towel, to rise for about 1 hour.

Roll down to a rectangle of approximately 13 × 15 inches. With your fingers, make dimples all over the surface. Sprinkle with coarse salt and with 2 or 3 tablespoons olive oil. Let rest ½ hour. Meanwhile heat your oven to 375°F, then bake the *schiacciatina* for ½ hour.

serves 6 to 8

Cornmeal Bread

pane colla farina gialla

3 cups unbleached flour

1 cup whole grain cornmeal

1½ teaspoons salt

2 tablespoons sugar

1 teaspoon active dry yeast

1½ cups warm water

1 cup Sourdough Starter (page 316)

Mix 1 cup unbleached flour with the cornmeal, salt, sugar, and dry yeast in a large bowl. Add the warm water and sourdough starter and mix thoroughly. Cover with a kitchen towel and let stand in a warm place for 30 minutes.

Spread the remaining 2 cups flour on a working surface. Pour the mixture over it and work with your hands until you have incorporated enough flour to make a very stiff dough.

Knead for another 5 minutes. Shape into a ball and place on a baking sheet previously sprinkled with cornmeal. Cover with a kitchen towel and leave in a warm, draft-free place for 1 hour or until more than doubled in bulk.

Bake in a preheated 425°F oven for 30 minutes or until a nice dark crust is formed. Transfer to a rack until thoroughly cooled, then wrap in a kitchen towel. Reheat in a 425°F oven for 15 minutes before serving.

yields one 2-pound loaf

Calzone Jewish Style

calzone ebraico

 riginally this calzone was conceived with *bottarga* (the roe of fine fish salted and dried in its own sack) grated over mozzarella. Here *bottarga* is still a rarity, and I have used anchovies, which make calzone even tastier, if less delicate.

1 envelope active dry yeast

1 teaspoon salt

1½ cups warm water

3½ cups bread flour

12 ounces mozzarella, shredded

12 anchovy fillets

6 rounded tablespoons ricotta, drained

Peppercorns in a mill

6 tablespoons unsalted butter, melted

Place the yeast and salt in a bowl with the warm water, stir, and let rest for 5 minutes. Add enough flour and mix to make a rather stiff dough. Turn out onto a floured working surface and knead for 1 minute. Cover with a clean kitchen towel and let rest in a warm, draft-free place for 1 hour, or until more than doubled in bulk.

Divide into 6 parts, shape each into a ball, and flatten each ball into a disk approximately 6 inches in diameter.

Spread 2 ounces mozzarella over each disk and place two anchovy fillets over the cheese. Cover the anchovies with 1 tablespoon ricotta, sprinkle with pepper, and drizzle with butter. Fold the disks and close the edges tightly. Cut slots on the top of the calzones to let the expanding hot air out. Brush with the remaining butter and bake in a preheated 450°F oven for 15 minutes or until the edges are quite browned.

serves 6

Sukkot Bread

maritucci

The aroma that comes from the oven when I bake this bread invariably takes me back, as if in a dream, under the leafy bough roof of the Sukka—lavishly decorated with luscious pears, apples, pomegranates, Chinese dates, and all sorts of dried fruits and nuts, which we used to build every year on the temple terrace (see Sukkot).

At the closing of the service, my father would bless the bread and wine; this was one of the rare occasions when the children could bring some wine to their lips.

At the end of the eighth day, we were finally allowed to eat the fruits that were hanging from above, and we suddenly turned into little monkeys to reach the goodies that we had coveted for a week.

Many Jews in other parts of Italy use this bread in place of a challah on a Shabbat, but in Pitigliano it was baked only during the festival of the harvest.

2 envelopes active dry yeast
2 cups warm water
6 cups unbleached flour
1 tablespoon salt
1 tablespoon anise seeds
½ cup warm olive oil
1 egg yolk

Dissolve the yeast in ½ cup warm water. Combine the flour, salt, and anise seeds in a large bowl. Gradually add the yeast solution, oil, and 1½ cups warm water while working the flour in with a fork. Turn onto a floured working surface and knead well for 10 minutes. Divide into 2 equal parts and knead each for 2 minutes. Cover with a kitchen towel and let rest 10 minutes.

Shape each piece of dough into an oval loaf and place on a well-floured baking sheet as far apart as possible. Gash the tops diagonally 1 inch apart in both directions, forming a crisscross pattern. Cover and set aside in a warm place until doubled in bulk, about 1¼ hours.

Brush the tops with the egg yolk beaten with 1 teaspoon water. Bake in a preheated 375°F oven for 30 to 45 minutes.

yields two 1-pound loaves

Sfilatini Bread

sfilatini

filatini is probably the most widely used bread in Italy. It is not regional (as is Tuscan bread, for example), although it may be called by different names in different places. It is incredibly easy to make, and it keeps almost indefinitely in the freezer, when tightly wrapped in aluminum foil and placed in a plastic bag. It is used as an ingredient in many Italian Jewish recipes, and it makes a very delicious garlic bread.

1 envelope active dry yeast

2 cups warm water

6 cups unbleached flour

3 tablespoons vegetable oil

2 teaspoons salt

Cornmeal

1 egg white

Dissolve the yeast with ¼ cup warm water in a large bowl. Add enough flour (approximately ½ cup) to make a soft dough. Cover the bowl with a clean kitchen towel and set it aside in a warm place for about 2 hours.

Add 1¾ cups warm water and mix to dissolve the leavened dough. Add the oil, salt, and enough of the remaining flour to make a rather stiff dough. Turn onto a floured working surface and knead 5 minutes. Divide into 4 equal parts; knead each 2 minutes, then cover and let rest 5 minutes.

Shape each piece of dough into a 13-inch roll, bulging at the center and tapering at the ends. Place on a lightly oiled baking sheet sprinkled with cornmeal. Gash the tops diagonally ¼ inch deep. Cover and let rise in a warm place for 45 minutes or until doubled in bulk.

Preheat the oven to 400°F. Place the sheet in the oven; after 5 minutes, lower the heat to 375°F and bake for 15 minutes. Remove from the oven and brush with the egg white beaten with 1 tablespoon water. Return to the oven and bake 15 minutes longer.

yields four ½-pound loaves

flat Leavened Bread

pizza

It has often been suggested that pizza is one of the many foods Jews have brought to Italy from the Middle East. Nothing seems more plausible, since not only does pizza in its many forms resemble *pita*, the Middle Eastern leavened flat bread, but the name itself might very well be a variation on the original one. In fact, this type of flat leavened bread is called pizza in Rome, and south of it, where—according to historical records—a large number of Jews lived prior to the coming of the Common Era. As we go north, it is no longer called pizza but, more commonly, *stiacciata* or *schiacciata*, which literally means "flattened," or *focaccia*, from *foco* or *fuoco* (fire, combustion, hearth).

I have another reason for believing that pizza was brought to Italy by the Jews. The practice of throwing a piece of flattened dough into the oven before putting in the bread goes back to biblical times. One of the precepts in the Torah is that a piece of dough be taken from the unbaked batch and given to the priests. After the Temple was destroyed, the Jews continued to fulfill this commandment by throwing a piece of dough into the oven and letting it burn. This served as a symbol of the offering to the priests. I myself remember this ritual being performed in the matza bakery each day before the baking of the *matzòt*. The little piece of dough was called *challah* which, literally, means "dough."

When I was growing up, *focaccia* was used in the public bakeries to test the oven temperature. A piece of flat bread dough was thrown into the stone oven, in a corner far away from the hot coals, before the bread was put inside. If *focaccia* rose quickly, forming a hollow pocket and burning, it meant that the oven was too hot for the bread. Ashes were then placed over the red embers, and the mouth of the oven was left open to cool it off a bit. If, on the other hand, *focaccia* did not rise at all and it took a few minutes to barely turn golden, the fire had to be rekindled by adding twigs and firewood. The ideal temperature was one that allowed *focaccia* to puff up and brown in 8 to 10 minutes.

Basic Pizza Dough

pasta per pizze

3 cups unbleached flour
1 envelope active dry yeast
1 teaspoon salt
1 cup warm water
Vegetable oil

Combine 2½ cups flour with the dry yeast and salt in a large bowl. Gradually add the warm water and 1½ tablespoons oil and mix into a soft dough.

Spread the remaining flour over a working surface. Turn the dough onto it and knead until the dough is smooth and elastic. Shape into a ball and place in a large oiled bowl; lightly brush the top with oil. Cover with a clean kitchen towel and let rise in a warm place for 2 hours or until tripled in bulk.

Punch down and let rest for 1 hour longer or until ready to use.

yields enough dough to make two 12-inch pizzas or
six 5½-inch individual pizzas / serves 4 to 6

Pizza Neapolitan Style

pizza alla napoletana

1½ pounds ripe firm
tomatoes, peeled (page 52)
6 tablespoons olive oil
2 fresh or ¼ teaspoon
dried basil leaves
Salt
1 recipe Pizza Dough
(see above)
1 pound whole milk
mozzarella, shredded
8 anchovy fillets, cut up
2 teaspoons dried oregano
Freshly ground black pepper

Cut up the peeled tomatoes and place them in a colander for a few minutes to lose some of the liquid. Place in a skillet with 3 tablespoons oil, basil, and ½ teaspoon salt. Cook over moderately high heat for 5 to 6 minutes, stirring frequently.

Place the pizza dough on a floured working surface. Divide into two equal parts and shape each into a ball. Flatten the balls first with the palms of your hands, rotating and turning the piece of dough from one side to the other. When the disk is about 8 inches in diameter, lift it by one side with your fingers and quickly begin to rotate it, holding the border so that the weight of the dough will perform the thinning. The disk should measure about 12 inches, be paper thin, but have a rim high enough to contain the filling.

Place each pizza on a lightly oiled and generously floured

baking sheet. Coat the tops with a light film of oil. Spread half the tomatoes on each. Top with the mozzarella and anchovies. Sprinkle with the oregano, salt, and pepper to taste and the remaining oil. Bake in a preheated 450°F oven for 15 to 20 minutes.

NOTE: If you find it difficult to thin the dough using only your hands, use a rolling pin, but be sure to leave a raised edge all around.

yields two 12-inch pizzas / serves 4 to 6

Flat Onion Bread

focaccia colla cipolla

1 envelope dry active yeast
1½ cups warm water
4 cups unbleached flour
1 teaspoon salt
4 tablespoons olive oil
1 cup chopped onion
1 cup water
1½ teaspoons coarse table salt
Freshly ground black pepper

Dissolve the yeast in ½ cup warm water and let rest for 5 minutes. Place the flour and 1 teaspoon salt in a large bowl. Add the dissolved yeast, 2 tablespoons oil, and 1 cup warm water while mixing.

Turn out onto a floured working surface and knead for 5 to 10 minutes. Shape into a ball and place on a well-floured board to rise, covered, for 1 to 2 hours or until more than doubled in bulk. Punch down and divide into 8 equal parts.

Shape each part into a little ball and allow to rest 5 minutes. With the palms of your hands, flatten the balls to ¼-inch thickness.

Place the chopped onion in a saucepan with 1 cup water. Bring to a boil and cook for 2 to 3 minutes. Drain well and spread 2 tablespoons of the onion over each *focaccia*. Sprinkle with coarse salt, pepper, and the remaining oil.

Preheat the oven to 500°F. Place 4 *focacce* on each of 2 well-floured baking sheets and bake for 8 to 10 minutes.

serves 6 to 8

Whips

fruste

1 envelope active dry yeast

2 cups warm water

6 cups bread flour

2 tablespoons olive oil

1 teaspoon salt

Dissolve the yeast with ¼ cup warm water in a large bowl. Add enough flour (approximately ½ cup) to make a soft dough. Cover the bowl with a clean kitchen towel and leave in a warm place for about 1½ hours.

Add 1¾ cups warm water and work with your hands, or the dough hook of an electric mixer, to dissolve the leavened dough. Add the oil, salt, and enough flour to make a rather stiff dough. Turn onto a floured working surface and knead 2 minutes. Divide into 6 equal parts; knead a couple of minutes each, then cover and let rest for 5 minutes.

Roll each piece of dough into a long stick about 1 inch in diameter. Dredge with flour and place on a well-floured baking sheet. Loosely cover with a towel and let rise in a warm place for 1 hour or until doubled in bulk.

Bake in a preheated 375°F oven for 20 minutes or until the *fruste* have acquired a lovely hazelnut color. Eat the same day, or freeze well wrapped in aluminum foil or plastic wrap and eat as soon as defrosted.

yields six 5-ounce whips

Bagels
ciambelle

1 envelope active dry yeast

Sugar

1¼ cups warm water

4 cups unbleached flour

1½ teaspoons salt

1½ tablespoons dehydrated minced onion

2 tablespoons olive oil

4 quarts water

Dissolve the yeast and ½ teaspoon sugar in 1¼ cups warm water and let rest for 5 minutes.

Combine 3½ cups flour with the salt and half the onion in a bowl. Add the yeast mixture and the oil, and mix while gathering enough flour to make a rather stiff dough. Place the remaining flour on a working surface; turn the dough onto the flour and knead for 3 minutes. Cover with a towel and let rest for 10 minutes.

Divide into 24 equal parts. Take one piece of dough at a time and shape into a ball. With thumbs and forefingers punch a hole in the center of each ball and set aside on a floured board.

Starting from the first, gently lift each bagel and stretch it to make the hole larger. Cover with a towel and set aside to rise in a warm, draft-free place for 20 minutes.

Bring 4 quarts of water with 2 tablespoons of sugar to a boil in a large pot. Lower the heat to a gentle simmer. Drop 4 bagels at a time into the simmering water and cook 3 minutes on each side, turning only once.

Place on an ungreased baking sheet and sprinkle with the remaining minced onion. Bake in preheated 375°F oven for 30 minutes.

NOTE: For garlic, sesame, or other flavorings, substitute the ones you like for onion. For plain bagels omit the onion.

yields 24 bagels

Turin Bread Sticks

grissini torinesi all'olio

1 teaspoon dry active yeast

1 teaspoon salt

¼ cup olive oil

½ cup warm water

2 cups unbleached or bread flour

In a small bowl place the yeast, salt, oil, and water. Stir a little, then add enough flour to make a rather stiff dough. Knead 2 to 3 minutes, then form into a ball. Cover the bowl with a damp towel and set aside in a warm place to rise until doubled in bulk.

Turn out onto a working surface, punch down, and divide into 32 small pieces. Roll the pieces of dough into sticks, as thin as you can make them (they should measure about 10 inches in length), and arrange on an ungreased baking sheet 1 inch apart. Cover and set aside to rest for ½ hour.

Place the baking sheet in a preheated 400°F oven, place a shallow pan with cold water on the lower rack, and bake 10 minutes or until the bread sticks are lightly browned.

NOTE: If you have a gas stove, you don't need the addition of water in the oven.

yields 32 sticks

Sourdough Crackers

gallette col lievito casalingo

4 cups unbleached flour

2 teaspoons salt

1 teaspoon poultry seasoning

½ teaspoon black pepper

1 cup Sourdough Starter at room temperature

½ cup warm olive oil

Sift together all the dry ingredients except for the cornmeal. Add sourdough starter, warm oil, and enough warm water to make a rather stiff dough. Knead for a few minutes, then set aside to rest for 20 minutes.

Oil a baking sheet and sprinkle it with coarse cornmeal. With a heavy rolling pin, roll ¼ of the dough at a time very thin, and spread it over the prepared baking sheet. Score it with a pizza or pastry cutter into small squares or rectangles, brush with oil, and sprinkle with cornmeal.

½ cup warm water

Oil

Coarse cornmeal

Bake in preheated 450°F oven for 10 minutes. Break into crackers, let cool thoroughly, then store in a jar.

yields several dozen crackers

Passover Crackers

gallette per pesach

or these crackers to be used on Passover, you must buy Passover flour, and all the other ingredients should be, of course, *kasher l' Pesach*. On the other hand, since they are so tasty and always a big success, you may want to serve these crackers all year round substituting unbleached flour for Passover flour.

1 cup cold water

½ cup olive oil

1 tablespoon salt

1 tablespoon freshly minced garlic

¼ teaspoon powdered red pepper

5 cups Passover flour

Mix together the first 5 ingredients. Add enough flour to form a rather stiff dough. Knead a few minutes on a lightly floured working surface. Roll thin with a heavy rolling pin or, better, with a metal, hand-operated pasta machine, with the rollers at the next-to-the-thinnest notch. Spread over a lightly oiled baking sheet and score with a dented pastry cutter into 2 × 6-inch rectangles.

With a metal comb, prick all over in a crisscross pattern to prevent swelling and blistering during baking, and bake in a 550°F oven for 5 to 6 minutes. Break into crackers and cool thoroughly before storing inside a clean white cotton sack. (A new, washed pillowcase used only for this purpose would be perfect.) Do not store in the refrigerator.

yields approximately 6 dozen crackers

DESSERTS

dolci

t is said that sweets numb our taste buds, stopping us from craving more food. I don't know how scientifically proven this is, but it is a fact that in our civilization we have chosen to put *dulcis in fundo*, the sweet at the end of the meal.

Sweets at the end of a meal—whether presented as a simple dish of fresh fruits or as an elaborate, rich, sugary dessert—have become standard in the cuisines of most cultures (even though I am aware that many people use some form of sweet in soups, main dishes, vegetables, salads, and even straight at the beginning of a meal). The cuisine of the Jews is no exception.

Jews, more than most people of other cultures, have traditionally prepared their own desserts, even when—as is the case in Italy—the store-bought ones can be, and often are, not only better presented visually but also better tasting than anything that is made at home. There are two reasons why Jews have always prepared their own desserts. The first and foremost is—at least for those who strictly adhere to it—the observance of their dietary laws. The multimillion-dollar kosher food industry of today is a relatively young business. However, before this kosher food boom—and certainly outside of the United States where until recently there was no obligation to list the ingredients—Jews who observe kashrut were not at liberty to buy their desserts. Whereas other people could choose to make *or* to buy their desserts, observant Jews had no such choice—if they wanted to be sure that no non-kosher ingredients were included in their preparations—but to make their own.

The second reason gives Jewish desserts a unique and folkloristic dimension. Having been chosen by the rest of humanity as the target against which to satisfy its need for aggressiveness and destructiveness, Jews have experienced, throughout their history, more than their share of persecutions from their fellow humans. This unconscionable reality has brought about much pain and misery, needless to say. In order to counteract, and, in some superstitious minds, to ward off such obnoxious and unwarranted behavior toward them, the Jews have resorted to preparing their own special desserts to sweeten up a little of their otherwise embittered and miserable existences. Even in times of relative tranquillity, desserts that symbolize their past tribulations are prepared and served on special occasions, but only when there is a happy ending to the historical event. For example, the mortar the Jews of antiquity were forced to toil with to build Pharaoh's pyramids became the sweet charoset used for the Passover Seder and throughout the remaining eight days of this celebration of freedom. Hamantashen, at Purim, mimic the tripointed hat supposedly worn by their vicious persecutor Haman of biblical notoriety. Latkes, or pancakes fried in oil, traditionally eaten during the eight days of Chanukah, remind us of the victory over the Syrian army of Antiochus Epiphanes by the Maccabee brothers, and the miracle of the oil. Chanukah lasts eight days to celebrate this miracle, in which one day's worth of consecrated and undefiled oil, used to feed the eternal light inside the sanctuary, lasted eight days, the time needed to prepare and consecrate a new supply of oil.

Jewish women have always vied with one another in preparing more and more diverse types of desserts. Keep in mind that for everyday meals fruit in season and a piece of cheese is a delectable dessert in itself. But for special occasions and holiday dinners, here are some of our traditional favorites. Next to each recipe I have indicated whether the dessert is to be used only a dairy meal (D), or whether it can be used with both a dairy or a meat-based meal (P), pareve. You will know from the index under which category a dessert falls.

Preparing desserts is a very satisfying endeavor. Parents should get into the habit of encouraging children to help make desserts. Not only are a few extra pairs of helping hands really needed to speed up operations but also the process gives the very young children a feeling of self-worth, and the not-so-young ones less time to get into trouble.

Almond Torte (D or P)

crostata con pasta di mandorle

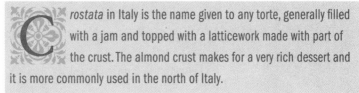

Crostata in Italy is the name given to any torte, generally filled with a jam and topped with a latticework made with part of the crust. The almond crust makes for a very rich dessert and it is more commonly used in the north of Italy.

1 cup shelled almonds
1 cup sugar
1 cup unbleached flour
1 teaspoon powdered cinnamon
¼ pound butter or non-dairy margarine, chilled
1 egg
2 egg yolks
1½ cups orange, peach, or strawberry preserves

Place the almonds in a food processor fitted with the metal blade and process 10 seconds. Add the sugar, flour, cinnamon, and butter and process just enough to obtain a coarse meal. Do *not* overprocess.

Add the egg and egg yolks and mix until all is moist. With two-thirds of the mixture line a 10-inch pie plate. Reserve a few pieces of preserve and spread the rest over the crust.

With the remaining crust mixture, make strips and form a lattice over the preserve. Garnish with the reserved pieces of preserve and bake in a preheated 350°F oven for 45 minutes.

serves 12

Mamma's Anisettes for Passover (P)

biscotti della mamma per pesach

1⅓ cups sugar
½ teaspoon salt
⅓ cup olive oil
3 eggs
2 tablespoons anise seeds
¼ cup anisette liquor
1 teaspoon vanilla extract
3½ cups Passover cake flour

Cream together the sugar, salt, and oil. Add the eggs, one at a time, beating after each addition. Add the anise seeds, anisette liquor, and vanilla extract. Add enough flour to make a rather soft but manageable dough.

Turn out over an oiled working surface, and divide into three parts. Oil your hands and shape into 3 cylinders 15 inches long. Place on a lightly oiled and floured baking sheet and bake in a 350°F oven for 25 minutes or until the tops are golden.

Remove from the oven (move the rack to the top shelf and

raise the oven temperature to 450°F) and cut diagonally to make approximately 60 slices, ½- to ¾-inch thick. Line up on the baking sheet resting on a cut side and bake on the top rack for 10 minutes or until nicely toasted on both sides.

Cool thoroughly on the cooling rack before storing.

yields 4 to 5 dozen biscotti

English Soup (D)
Zuppa Inglese

hen I was a little child, Mother would take me with her to visit the homebound and the sick on Sabbath afternoons. During one of these visits, bored and restless, I climbed a few steps and leaned on a little window that opened into a dark pantry. The window was not fastened and I fell three or four feet on my back. I did not hurt myself, but I was frightened and began to cry. In order to calm me down, the young lady in the house gave me a serving of her divine *Zuppa Inglese*. To this day it remains one of my favorite desserts.

1 cup Alchermes or any bright-red liqueur

30 *Savoiardi* or ladyfingers

Crema Pasticcera

¾ cup strong coffee

2 tablespoons brandy

1 pint heavy cream

¼ cup confectioners sugar

1 teaspoon vanilla extract

Soak 14 of the ladyfingers in red liquor and line the bottom and sides of a straight-sided glass serving bowl. Pour half the cream into the lined bowl.

Combine the coffee and brandy; quickly dip 8 ladyfingers in this mixture and cover the cream with them. Pour the remaining cream over the ladyfingers, then top it with the last 8 ladyfingers soaked in the coffee-brandy mixture.

Whip the heavy cream until soft peaks form; add confectioners sugar and vanilla extract and mix gently. Top the bowl with mounds of whipped cream. Refrigerate before serving.

yields 12

Cinnamon Turnovers (P)

borricche alla cannella

> he authentic *borricche* we used to make for Purim was prepared with homemade flaky dough. Now I can buy kosher phyllo dough practically in any supermarket, and the preparation of *borriche* is no longer the lengthy process it used to be. Phyllo dough is much more delicate than homemade flaky dough, and now I like *borricche* even better than the original.

¾ cup sugar

1½ tablespoons powdered cinnamon

2 tablespoons brandy

Eight 12 × 18-inch sheets of phyllo dough, defrosted according to manufacturer's directions

¼ cup olive oil

1 egg, beaten with pinch salt

Sift together the sugar and cinnamon in a small bowl. Add the brandy and mix with a spoon until most of the mixture is slightly moist.

Delicately unfold the phyllo dough over a clean surface. Brush a thin film of oil over each sheet, stacking the sheet back together. With a sharp knife or pizza cutter, divide across the length into two, and make two cuts widthwise to form 6 squares.

Spread one sixth of the sugar mixture over each square, covering only one triangle, and leaving 1 inch free along the edges. Starting from the corner of the triangle with the mixture, roll each *borricca* and close it tightly by moistening with water (using a clean brush, not the oily one) the openings and pressing firmly with your fingers. With a sharp pointy knife, poke a few slots on the tops to allow the steam to escape while baking.

Brush the tops with the beaten egg, line up on an ungreased baking sheet, and place in a preheated 425°F oven for 7 minutes.

yields 6 pastries

Aunt Delia's Purim Doughnuts (P)

ciambelline della zia delia per purim

Aunt Delia, like most housewives in Italy before World War II, did not have an oven in her kitchen in Pisa, where she lived with her husband, the *chazàn* of that community and her son, Rabbi Attilio Orvieto. Nor did she have easy access to a public oven, as we did in Pitigliano. Because of this, most of her specialties were fried. I have successfully converted many of her fried dishes into baked ones. For these delicious doughnuts, however, I give the authentic recipe as it was passed on to me.

2½ cups unbleached flour

1 cup sugar

½ cup unsweetened cocoa

1 teaspoon baking soda

½ teaspoon salt

¼ cup olive oil

4 eggs

½ cup finely chopped toasted almonds

1 teaspoon vanilla extract

Oil for frying

Vanilla-Flavored Sugar (see following recipe)

Sift 1½ cups flour with the sugar, cocoa, baking soda, and salt in a large bowl. Add the olive oil, eggs, almonds, and vanilla extract and beat at medium speed just until you have a homogeneous batter. Add enough of the remaining flour to form a soft dough. Turn out onto an oiled surface and quickly knead for a minute or so.

Divide into 24 or 30 pieces and shape each piece into a ball. With your thumb and forefinger make a hole through the center of each ball, stretching it and shaping it into a ring.

Heat enough oil in a small saucepan to be 3 inches deep. Fry one doughnut at a time for 1 minute on each side, turning only once. Transfer to paper towels. Add oil to the pan as necessary. When all the doughnuts are done, roll them in vanilla-flavored sugar. Let cool thoroughly before serving.

yields 2 to 2½ dozen doughnuts

Vanilla-flavored Confectioners' Sugar (P)

zucchero vanigliato

Whenever a recipe calls for vanilla-flavored sugar, it is always intended to be confectioners' sugar rather than granulated sugar. Here is how you can easily make your own. But be careful that you don't lose it as once happened to me!

In one of my cooking classes, I demonstrated how easy it was to prepare vanilla-flavored sugar, then I put the jar in the pantry for use in the next class. When the time came, though, the jar was nowhere to be found. I inquired around, but nobody had even seen it. The mystery was revealed when the director of the school came to tell me to be more careful when I closed the jars: she had found the sugar jar full of bugs and had to throw the whole thing away. The little pieces of precious vanilla beans had appeared to her myopic eyes as dead bugs!

2 cups confectioners' sugar
2 whole vanilla beans, cut into 1-inch sections

Place the confectioners' sugar and vanilla beans into an airtight glass jar and set aside at room temperature for at least 2 weeks before using.

Sift just the quantity of sugar you need, then replenish the jar with equal amounts of new sugar. Return any pieces of beans that you might find in the sifter into the jar, cover tightly, and put aside until next time.

Replace the beans with new ones every 3 to 4 months.

yields 2 cups

Doughnuts to Break the Yom Kippur Fast (P)

dictinobis di kippur

hereas in Pitigliano we used *Bollo* to break the fast, in some parts of Italy *Dictinobis* are used. They are an excellent holiday breakfast or midday snack.

2 envelopes active dry yeast

¼ cup warm water

Sugar

¼ cup warm olive oil

2 teaspoons vanilla extract

1 jumbo egg

½ cup confectioners' sugar

1½ cups unbleached flour

Oil for frying

Have all the ingredients at room temperature, except the water and olive oil which should be warm.

In a small bowl, dissolve the yeast in the warm water with 2 teaspoons sugar. When it begins to foam, add the warm oil, vanilla extract, egg, and confectioners' sugar and beat for 1 to 2 minutes. Gradually add 1 cup flour while mixing with a spatula.

Spread the remaining flour over a working surface and turn out the mixture over it. Knead, gathering enough flour to form a very soft dough. Divide into 12 equal parts, cover with a kitchen towel, and let rest for 5 minutes.

Roll each piece of dough into an 8-inch rope, then fasten the two ends to form a ring. Place the rings on a floured board, cover with a kitchen towel, and let rise in a warm place for 1 hour, or until the rings are doubled in bulk.

Heat the oil in a small frying pan to 375°F on a deep-frying thermometer and fry one ring at a time until golden on both sides, turning only once. Place on paper towels to drain, then roll in granulated sugar. Serve hot or at room temperature.

NOTE: When stoves with ovens were a rarity in private homes, most baked goods were done at a public oven, and many of the smaller desserts were fried at home. I have tried *dictinobis* baked in a 375°F oven for 20 minutes, and although the texture and even the flavor are less desirable, they have the advantage of containing less fat.

yields 12 doughnuts

Chanukah Fritters (P)

frittelle di chanukà

This ancient recipe was a specialty of my father's oldest sister, Aunt Argia. During the eight days of Chanukah, Aunt Argia would get up at the crack of dawn to make *frittelle* for the extended family. Punctually, at mealtime, she would show up at our door with a large plate of fragrant hot *frittelle*. This is the original recipe, which I slightly modified to make it simpler.

3 cups unbleached flour
2 envelopes active dry yeast
1 teaspoon salt
2 teaspoons anise seeds
1 cup dark, seedless raisins
1 cup warm water
Olive oil
1½ cups honey

Combine 2½ cups flour with the yeast, salt, anise seeds, and raisins in a mixing bowl. Gradually add the warm water and 2 tablespoons olive oil, mixing until a consistent dough is formed. Turn out onto a floured surface and knead for 5 minutes or until the dough is smooth and elastic.

Shape into a ball, place on a floured cutting board, and cover with a clean kitchen towel. Let rise in a warm place for 1 hour or until it has more than doubled in bulk.

With the palms of your hands flatten down to about a ½-inch thickness. With the sharp, oiled blade of a long knife, cut into 36 diamonds. Let rest, uncovered, 15 to 20 minutes.

Heat enough oil in a saucepan to stand 1½ inches deep. The oil is at the right temperature when a small piece of dough dropped into it comes sizzling to the surface right away. Fry a few diamonds at a time, until they are golden on both sides, turning each once. Transfer to paper towels to drain.

Heat the honey in a saucepan and let it boil for just 3 minutes. Arrange the *frittelle* on a serving plate and pour the hot honey over them. Serve immediately.

yields 3 dozen fritters

festive fruit Cake (P)

panforte

¾ cup sugar

⅓ cup honey

½ teaspoon cinnamon

½ teaspoon cloves

1 teaspoon vanilla extract

2 cups whole almonds, unblanched

½ cup diced candied citron peel

⅔ cup unbleached flour

Vanilla-Flavored Sugar (page 341)

In a large skillet, place the sugar, honey, cinnamon, cloves, and vanilla extract. Bring to a boil and cook 3 minutes, stirring occasionally. Add the almonds, citron peel, and flour and remove from the heat. Stir for a minute or so until all is well amalgamated.

Lightly oil and sprinkle with flour a 9-inch springform cake pan. Pour the mixture into it and flatten down with a spatula. Bake in a preheated 350°F oven for 5 minutes. Remove from the heat and let cool at room temperature, then transfer to a serving dish and sprinkle abundantly with vanilla-flavored confectioners' sugar.

serves 6 to 8

Haman's Ears (P)

orecchi di aman

For the Italian Jews *orecchi di Aman* are as synonymous with the festival of Purim as *Hamantashen* are for the Ashkenazim. There are perhaps as many versions of this sweet as there are Jewish families in Italy. I regard this recipe as the finest. From this basic recipe you can create variations limited only by your own imagination.

2 eggs

2 egg yolks

¼ cup sugar

½ teaspoon salt

1 teaspoon freshly grated lemon rind

2 tablespoons olive oil

1 teaspoon vanilla extract

2 tablespoons rum or brandy

2½ cups unbleached flour

1 cup olive or other vegetable oil for frying

Vanilla-Flavored Sugar (page 341)

In a small bowl, beat the eggs and egg yolks with the sugar, salt, lemon rind, 2 tablespoons olive oil, vanilla extract, and rum. Gradually add enough flour to form a rather soft dough. Turn out onto a floured surface and knead for a minute. Roll very thin. With a pastry cutter, a pizza cutter, or a very sharp knife, cut into strips 1 inch by 4 to 7 inches.

Slowly heat the oil in a small saucepan. Oil is at the right temperature when a small piece of dough dropped into it floats to the surface and begins to sizzle. Fry a few strips at a time, twirling them to give them odd shapes, until lightly golden. Drain and place on paper towels.

When all the ears are done, mound on a large serving plate, sprinkling each layer abundantly with vanilla-flavored confectioners' sugar.

yields 3 to 4 dozen pastries

Honey and Nut Sticks (P)

sfratti

> The etymology of *Sfratti* goes back to when the law that prevailed was the "law of the stick." When landlords could not collect from poor tenants, they would evict them with the persuasive aid of a stick. The same applied to Jews of any status when they no longer were wanted in a community. In Italy the word *sfratto,* in fact, means eviction, and this marvelously tasting dessert looks just like the sticks used by those heartless landlords and by the enemies of the Jews.

3 cups unbleached flour
1¼ cups sugar
¼ teaspoon salt
⅔ cup dry white wine
⅓ cup vegetable oil
1 cup honey
½ teaspoon cinnamon
½ teaspoon ground cloves
¼ teaspoon black pepper
Dash ground nutmeg
Freshly grated rind of
1 orange
15 ounces walnut meats,
chopped

Place the flour, sugar, and salt in a large bowl. Add the wine and oil and quickly mix with your fingers or with a fork. Form into a ball, wrap in wax paper, and set aside in the refrigerator.

In a large skillet, over high heat, bring the honey to a boil and cook for 3 minutes. Add the spices, orange rind, and nuts and cook another 5 minutes, stirring constantly. Remove the skillet from the heat and continue to stir until the mixture is cool enough to handle. Turn over onto a floured working surface and divide into 6 equal parts. Using your hands, roll each part into a cylindrical stick about 13 inches long. Then push it away from you.

Take the pastry dough from the refrigerator and divide it into 6 equal parts. With a small rolling pin, roll out each piece to form 4 × 14-inch strips. Place one stick of filling on each strip and wrap the dough around the filling, covering it completely. Pinch the ends closed. Place on a well-floured baking sheet, seam side down.

Bake in a preheated 375°F oven for 20 minutes. Remove from the baking sheet still warm, and wrap individually in aluminum foil. Leave at room temperature where *sfratti* keep fresh for several weeks. They actually taste better after they have been allowed to age for a few days. Just before serving, unwrap and cut slantwise into 1½-inch sections.

yields 6 sticks; 48 diamonds

Honey Cake (P)

dolce di miele

I n Italy we call this cake *dolce*, sweet, instead of *torta*, cake, because the word torta presumes something roundly shaped and somewhat fancy. Honey cake can be baked in a round, square, or any other shape of pan, and it never looks very elegant. Conversely, in spite of its appearance, it is a favorite among food connoisseurs.

½ cup olive oil

½ teaspoon salt

¼ cup sugar

4 eggs

1 cup honey

½ cup espresso coffee

3 tablespoons brandy

3 cups unbleached flour

2 teaspoons baking powder

1 teaspoon baking soda

1 teaspoon cinnamon

¼ teaspoon black pepper

¼ teaspoon ground cloves

1 teaspoon grated orange rind

½ cup walnut meats, coarsely chopped

½ cup dark, seedless raisins

½ cup diced dates

¼ cup diced candied orange peel

¼ cup *pignoli* (Italian pine nuts)

10 to 12 healthy walnut or pecan halves

Cream together the oil, salt, and sugar. Add the eggs, one at a time, beating constantly. Mix the honey, coffee, and brandy in a 2-cup measuring cup with a spout, and sift together the flour, baking powder, baking soda, cinnamon, pepper, and cloves on a piece of wax paper.

Alternatively add the honey and flour mixtures to the bowl. Stir in the orange rind, chopped walnut meats, raisins, dates, candied orange peel, and pine nuts.

Pour into a greased loose-bottom tube cake pan. Top with the walnut or pecan halves, and bake in a 375°F oven for 45 minutes to 1 hour, or until a skewer inserted into the highest part of the cake comes out dry.

Remove to a cooling rack for 15 minutes, then invert the whole pan standing on its feet over a piece of aluminum foil; let cool thoroughly before unmolding and placing up side up on a cake dish.

serves 12 to 20

Ines's Cake (D)

torta di ines

A slice of this simple and delicious cake, a dollop of home-made vanilla ice cream, and a small glass of sweet vermouth were the only refreshments served on the day of my Bat Mitzvah, June 5, 1938 (Shavuot 5698).

¾ cup granulated sugar

6 tablespoons soft butter

3 eggs

½ teaspoon vanilla extract

Grated rind of 1 lemon

1½ cups cake flour

1 teaspoon baking soda

3 teaspoons cream of tartar

½ cup milk

Milk chocolate curls (page 367) or

Vanilla-Flavored Sugar (page 341)

Cream together the sugar and butter. Add the eggs, one at a time, beating after each addition. While beating, add the vanilla extract and lemon rind. Gradually add the flour and beat just enough for the batter to be smooth.

Combine the baking soda and cream of tartar in a cup and stir, adding the milk while stirring. The mixture will foam and expand. When it is about to overflow from the cup, pour into the bowl with the batter, and quickly stir until the batter is smooth again.

Pour into a buttered and lightly floured 9-inch cake pan and bake in a preheated 350°F oven for 35 to 40 minutes, or until a straw inserted at the center of the cake comes out dry. Remove from the oven and let cool on a wire rack for ½ hour. Turn upside down on a cake dish and cover with milk chocolate curls or sprinkle with vanilla-flavored confectioners' sugar.

serves 8 or more

King's Cake (P or D)

torta del re

I gave this cake the name "King's Cake" because according to a family story it came from the secret recipe files of the pastry chef of the king of Italy, Vittorio Emanuele III.

As a young woman my mother's aunt, Flora, was the tutor of the child of Senator Mosconi of Vicenza, whose wife was bedridden. In addition to tutoring the child, the young woman was also apparently consoling the senator, because one day she found herself pregnant. Since this could not be tolerated in her family, she jumped from the window of her third-floor apartment (which in Italy is pretty high) with the intent of taking her own life. But she didn't die, and while she was recovering from a few broken bones, the senator's wife died and the senator married my great-aunt, thus saving her honor.

My mother, as a young lady, was often invited to this aunt's house for dinner when this cake was served, and she heard over and over again from the mouth of Donna Flora herself, that the recipe for it had been given to the senator's chef by his friend, the king's chef. Eventually, as an adult, my mother was able to obtain the recipe, which she made for her family on very special occasions.

This is a true story, and not only did I choose to call it King's Cake for the reason I mentioned but also because it is "fit for a king" and it is my pièce de résistance for important dinners and at Passover.

2 tablespoons pareve
(Passover) margarine
or butter
2 tablespoons breadcrumbs
or matza meal
5 eggs, separated
Pinch salt
1¼ cups sugar

Grease with margarine or butter and sprinkle with breadcrumbs or matza meal a 10-inch springform cake pan and set aside.

Beat the eggs whites with salt until stiff and dry.

In a larger bowl, beat the egg yolks with the sugar until lemon colored. Gradually add the chopped almonds, then the two extracts and lemon rind. You should have a very hard paste. Mix one third of the beaten egg white with the almond mixture to make it softer. Delicately fold in the remaining egg white and pour into the prepared cake pan.

2½ cups (10 ounces)
blanched almonds,
chopped fine
1 teaspoon vanilla extract
1 teaspoon almond extract
Grated rind of 1 lemon
Vanilla-Flavored Sugar
(page 341)
Sliced almonds, toasted

Place in the center of a middle rack in a preheated 325°F oven and bake for 1 hour without ever opening the oven door. After the hour is over, turn the heat off and leave the oven door ajar for 10 to 15 minutes; then remove the pan from the oven and invert on a cooling rack. When the cake is thoroughly cool, remove it from the pan and place it upside down on a cake dish. Top with vanilla-flavored confectioners' sugar, using a sifter, and sprinkle with toasted sliced almonds.

serves 12

Almond Macaroons (P)

moscardini di pesach

1½ cups ground toasted
almonds
1 cup sugar
Small pinch salt
¼ cup unsweetened cocoa
¼ cup matza meal
Grated rind of 1 orange
½ teaspoon almond extract
1 egg, slightly beaten
1 egg yolk
Oil and matza meal for
baking sheet

Combine the first 9 ingredients in a small bowl and mix well. Drop the mixture with a small scoop on a baking sheet previously oiled and dusted with matza meal 1½ inches apart.

Bake in a preheated 350°F oven for 12 minutes, then transfer to a cooling rack.

yields approximately 2½ dozen cookies

Mascarpone Cheesecake (D)

torta al mascarpone

3 eggs, separated
9 tablespoons sugar
1 pound Mascarpone cheese, at room temperature
2 tablespoons rum
¾ cup cold strong coffee
40 *Biscottini di Rona* (page 371), or vanilla cookies
¼ cup sugar-toasted chopped almonds

Beat the eggs whites until stiff peaks form. Gradually add half the sugar and beat until the mixture has the consistency of marshmallow.

In another bowl, beat the egg yolks with the remaining sugar until frothy and lemon colored. Reduce the speed, add the cheese, and beat until well mixed. Add the whites and mix well.

Mix together the rum and coffee. In a serving bowl, make alternate layers of the cheese mixture and cookies quickly dipped in the coffee mixture, ending with the cheese.

Sprinkle the top with toasted almonds and chill at least 1 hour before serving.

NOTE: To make sugar-coated toasted almonds, place the chopped almonds in a small skillet with 2 tablespoons sugar, 2 tablespoons water, and 1 teaspoon almond extract. Bring to a boil and cook, stirring, for 2 to 3 minutes, or until the almonds are dry and light brown. Remove from the heat and stir until cool.

This is exactly the way we made *Torta al Mascarpone*. If you don't think you can trust raw eggs, however, you'd be better off making the Tiramisù on page 365, which is a variation of the above.

serves 6 or more

Tuscan Matza Cake (P)

dolce toscano di azzime

2 regular *matzòt*

Water

½ cup sugar

1 tablespoon cinnamon

4 eggs, separated

1 teaspoon grated
lemon rind

Vanilla-Flavored Sugar
(page 341)

Soak the *matzòt* in water until soft. Place the sugar with 1 tablespoon water and cinnamon in a small pan and boil until the sugar is dissolved.

Drain the matza, squeeze the water out with your hands, and place in a bowl. Add the egg yolks, the sugar-cinnamon syrup, and the lemon rind and mix well.

Beat the egg whites until stiff and dry, and fold into the matza batter. Spoon into a greased 8-inch springform baking pan and bake in a preheated 300°F oven for 45 minutes or until a skewer inserted at the center comes out clean.

Unmold upside down and let cool to room temperature before sprinkling it with vanilla confectioners' sugar.

serves 6 to 8

Matza Omelet (P)

matza coperta

It is customary for Catholics in Italy to go for a picnic on the Monday following Easter Sunday. When we were children our Catholic friends would invite us to join in the feast. We would gladly go, but would bring our own kosher foods. Our typical basket contained hard-boiled eggs, a few slices of homemade cold cuts, *Carciofi Trifolati* (slivered artichokes sautéed in olive oil), and *Matza Coperta*.

6 regular *matzòt*

12 eggs, slightly beaten

½ teaspoon salt

½ cup dark, seedless raisins

Soak the *matzòt* in cold water until they are soft. Drain and squeeze the water out, but do not leave the *matzòt* too dry. Combine with the eggs, salt, raisins, nuts, and lemon rind.

Heat 3 tablespoons oil in a large, heavy skillet. Add the matza mixture and flatten down with a rubber spatula. Fry gently on

¼ cup *pignoli*
(Italian pine nuts)

Freshly grated rind of
1 lemon

6 tablespoons olive oil

Cinnamon sugar

very low heat, shaking the skillet from time to time, until a light crust is formed at the bottom. Invert onto a large dish.

Return the skillet over the low heat, add the remaining 3 tablespoons oil and slide the omelet into it. Fry gently until a crust is formed also on the other side. The omelet is done when it is firm all the way through.

Place on a serving plate and pat dry with paper towels. Top the omelet with cinnamon sugar and serve.

serves 8 to 12

Matza Pancakes with Honey (P)

pizzarelle col miele

8 regular *matzòt*

5 eggs, slightly beaten

½ teaspoon salt

2 tablespoons shredded
lemon rind

2 tablespoons brandy

½ cup chopped
walnut meats

¾ cup dark, seedless raisins

Olive oil

¾ cup honey

3 tablespoons water

1 tablespoon lemon juice

Soak the *matzòt* in cold water for ½ hour or until softened through. Squeeze the water out. You should have 4 cups of firmly packed soaked matza. Combine with the eggs, salt, lemon rind, brandy, nuts, and raisins.

Heat ⅓ cup oil in a large skillet. Drop the matza mixture by the tablespoonful into it and fry over moderate heat, turning, until golden on both sides. Drain on paper towels. Continue to fry until you have used up all the mixture, adding oil to the pan as it becomes necessary.

Combine the honey, water, and lemon juice in a small saucepan. Bring to a boil and cook for 5 minutes. Arrange the pancakes on a serving plate and pour the honey syrup over them. Serve immediately.

serves 6 to 8

Passover Almond Biscotti (P)

biscotti alla mandorla per pesach

The word "biscotti" in Italy has come to designate all sorts of hard cookies. But in reality this word was originally coined for what nowadays, in America, is appropriately called "biscotti." In fact "bis" derives from Latin and means "once more, twice," and "cotti" is the Italian word for cooked, baked. Therefore, biscotti are called thus because they are cooked twice.

Although the classic, the typical, the "authentic" biscotti Mamma prepared for the eight days of Pesach were the anisettes of the recipe on page 337, occasionally almond biscotti were also made for Passover. They differ in taste and texture, but they were both winners in my parents' household in Italy as they are in my American home.

1⅓ cups sugar
½ teaspoon salt
⅓ cup olive oil
3 eggs
1 cup whole unblanched almonds
2 teaspoons almond extract
1 teaspoon vanilla extract
3½ cups Passover cake flour

Cream together the sugar, salt, and oil. Add the eggs, one at a time, beating after each addition. Add the almonds, almond extract, and vanilla extract. Add enough flour to make a rather soft but manageable dough.

Pour over an oiled working surface and divide into three parts. Oil your hands and shape into 3 cylinders 15 inches long. Place on a lightly oiled and floured baking sheet and bake in a 350°F oven for 30 minutes or until the tops are golden.

Remove from the oven (move the rack to the top shelf and raise the temperature to 450°F) and as soon as can be handled, cut diagonally to obtain approximately 60 slices, ½- to ¾-inch thick. Line up on the baking sheet resting on a cut side and bake on the top rack for 10 minutes, or until toasted on both sides.

Cool thoroughly on the cooling rack before storing. I would suggest not to store them in an airtight bag or jar, or in the refrigerator, but, as my mother did—and I still do—place them in a clean pillowcase at room temperature and they will remain crisp for the eight days of Passover.

yields approximately 5 dozen biscotti

Passover Chocolate Cake (P)

torta di cioccolata per pesach

6 tablespoons Passover pareve margarine

2 tablespoons fine matza meal

4 ounces unsweetened baking chocolate, coarsely chopped

1 tablespoon instant dark coffee powder

5 eggs, separated

Pinch salt

1 cup sugar

1¼ cups finely ground toasted almonds

1 teaspoon vanilla extract

Freshly grated rind of 1 orange

¾ cup toasted and coarsely chopped hazelnuts

4 ounces non-dairy semisweet chocolate chips

3 tablespoons unsweetened cocoa

Grease a 9-inch springform cake pan with 2 tablespoons margarine, sprinkle with matza meal, and invert to remove excess.

Melt the unsweetened chocolate with the remaining 4 tablespoons margarine in a heavy saucepan over low heat. Add the dry instant coffee and stir until all is well amalgamated.

Beat the egg whites with salt in a small bowl until stiff and dry. In a larger bowl, beat the egg yolks with sugar until thick and lemon colored. Decrease the speed and gradually add the melted chocolate, almonds, vanilla extract, orange rind, and one third of the beaten egg whites. Add the hazelnuts and chocolate chips and mix to combine.

Delicately fold in the remaining egg whites and pour into the prepared cake pan. Bake in a preheated 325°F oven for 45 minutes, then turn the heat off, open the door ajar, and allow the cake to cool inside for 10 minutes. Remove from the oven and let cool thoroughly on a wire rack before inverting the cake over a serving dish. Brush off the loose matza meal and sprinkle with cocoa.

serves 12

Passover Fruit and Nut Balls (P)

charoset edda

Charoset, the mortar-like paste used as a dip during the Passover Seder, comes in many versions and it is prepared as elaborately as people's imagination suggests. Mine is a favorite among family and friends not only as a dip but also as a dessert.

½ pound pitted dates

½ pound walnut meats

3 large apples, cored and peeled

1 large whole seedless orange, unpeeled, washed

3 ripe large bananas

⅓ cup sweet Malaga wine

½ teaspoon cinnamon

⅛ teaspoon ground cloves

1 tablespoon lemon juice

Matza meal, as needed

¼ cup unsweetened cocoa

¼ cup Vanilla-Flavored Sugar (page 341)

Chop the dates, walnuts, apples, and whole orange very fine and place in a bowl. Peel and mash the bananas and add to the bowl. Add the wine, cinnamon, cloves, and lemon juice and mix well. Add enough matza meal to make a mortar-like paste.

Mix together the cocoa and confectioners' sugar. Make little balls out of the paste and roll in the cocoa/sugar mixture.

serves 12 to 20

Passover Cookies (P)

apere di pesach

Bruno D'Angeli, a dear old friend from Venice, gave me this recipe for cookies that are traditionally made for Passover. They are so light and delightful that you will want to have them at hand any time of the year.

5 eggs
1½ cups sugar
1 teaspoon anise extract
1 teaspoon freshly grated lemon rind
2 cups Passover cake flour

Beat the eggs with the sugar, anise extract, and lemon rind. Gradually add enough flour to form a not too loose batter.

Spoon over a nonstick baking sheet, holding the spoon vertically to obtain round medallions. Bake in a preheated 300°F oven for 10 minutes, or until the cookies are lightly golden. Let cool on the baking sheet at room temperature before storing in a clean white pillowcase.

yields approximately 48 cookies

Passover Walnut Cake (p)

torta di noci per pesach

2 tablespoons Passover pareve margarine
3 tablespoons matza meal
6 eggs, separated
⅛ teaspoon salt
1½ cups granulated sugar
2½ cups (10 ounces) choice walnut meats
Grated rind of 1 orange
1 teaspoon honey
½ teaspoon vanilla extract
½ teaspoon cinnamon
¼ teaspoon ground cloves
Vanilla-Flavored Sugar (page 341)

Grease a 10-inch springform cake pan with margarine, sprinkle with matza meal, and invert to remove excess. Place the walnut meats in the work bowl of a processor fitted with the metal blade, and process until chopped fine, 10 to 13 seconds.

Beat the egg whites with salt until stiff and dry. In a large bowl beat the egg yolks with sugar until thick and lemon colored. Gradually add the finely ground walnut meats and one-quarter of the beaten egg whites. Add the orange rind, honey, vanilla extract, cinnamon, and cloves and mix to combine.

Delicately fold in the remaining egg whites, then spoon into the prepared cake pan. Place at the center of the middle rack in a preheated 325°F oven and bake for 1 hour without opening the oven door. When the hour is over, test with a skewer at the center, and if it comes out dry the cake is done; otherwise bake for another 10 to 15 minutes. Remove from the oven and invert over a cooling rack. Allow to cool thoroughly before unmolding upside down over a cake dish. Using a sifter, lightly sprinkle with vanilla-flavored confectioners' sugar.

serves 12 or more

Purim Manicotti (P)

manicotti di purim

> This is one of those recipes one should watch while it is being prepared, because the actual preparation is much less complicated than its description. The aid of a manual pasta machine would be helpful, but not indispensable.

2 eggs

⅛ teaspoon salt

1½ cups unbleached flour

1 cup olive oil or other vegetable oil for frying

1½ cups honey

Lightly beat the eggs and salt together. Gradually add 1¼ to 1½ cups flour and mix until a rather soft dough is formed. Turn over onto a floured surface and knead for 1 minute or so, then roll down as thin as you can. With a very sharp knife or pizza cutter, make 24 strips, approximately 2 × 8 inches.

Heat the oil in a small frying pan. Holding one strip of dough at one end with your hand, plunge the other end into the hot oil 1 inch deep. At once insert the frying part of the strip between the prongs of a fork held with your other hand, and roll the fork while letting the rest of the strip slide into the oil. The strip will fry while it is rolling around the fork.

When the *manicotto* is golden, remove from the oil and gently place on paper towels. Repeat until all the manicotti are done.

Heat half the honey in a small saucepan. As it starts to boil, drop 2 or 3 manicotti in it for a few seconds to be coated with honey, then transfer to a serving dish. Lower the heat and continue to dip the manicotti, gradually adding more honey, until all have been coated. Cool thoroughly before serving.

yields 24 pastries

Purim Nut Cookies (P)

marroncini

The name *Marroncini* derives from the Hebrew *maror*, bitter. These cookies were given their name because the Jews in Pitigliano used the almonds of peach pits to make them, and those almonds are bitter indeed! I recall that after drying the pits in the sun, they were saved in old pillowcases throughout the entire peach season. We were aware that they contained prussic acid, which is poisonous, but we also knew that our ancestors, who had been eating *marroncini* all their lives, had enjoyed good health and many reached ripe old ages. At any rate, the so-called almond extract one buys on the American markets today *is* made from peach-pit almonds! I have seen *marroncini* made (and make them myself) with hazelnuts or sweet almonds and almond extract, and they are simply delicious.

1½ cups coarsely chopped hazelnuts or almonds, toasted

3 cups unbleached flour

½ teaspoon ammonium bicarbonate or 1 teaspoon baking powder

Grated rind of 1 lemon

1½ cups sugar

2 cups cold water

1½ teaspoons almond extract

Combine the nuts, flour, baking powder, and lemon rind and mix well. Mound on a working surface or in a large bowl and make a well in the center.

Place the sugar and the cold water in a saucepan and bring to a boil. When the solution reaches full boil, start stirring with a wooden spoon. After 3 minutes, begin to test for the right cooking point of the syrup, which comes when a drop held between the thumb and forefinger, in an opening and closing motion, forms a thread at the fourth opening.

Add the almond extract, stir, and pour into the center of the well. Quickly mix in the dry ingredients and, also quickly, knead for a minute or so.

Divide the dough into 4 parts, and roll each part into a cylinder 1½ inches in diameter. Cut each cylinder into 1-inch-thick disks. With your thumb, make a depression at the center of each disk. Coat with the flour mixture that has remained on the working surface or bowl.

Place in a well-floured baking sheet and bake in a preheated

400°F oven for 15 to 20 minutes. The cookies are done when the bottom is golden brown.

NOTE: To toast the nuts, place them in a single layer on a baking sheet and place the sheet under the broiler for 4 to 5 minutes, shaking the sheet a couple of times. Allow to cool at least 10 minutes before chopping.

Ammonium bicarbonate can be purchased from pharmacies. It is *not* the same as sodium bicarbonate (baking soda) available in supermarkets.

yields about 50 cookies

Purim Moscardini (P)

moscardini di purim

1¼ cups ground toasted almonds

1¼ cups sugar

¼ cup unsweetened cocoa

¼ cup unbleached flour

½ teaspoon ground cinnamon

1 egg, slightly beaten

1 egg yolk

Combine all the dry ingredients in a small bowl. Add the egg and egg yolk and mix well. Shape the mixture with your hands, a teaspoonful at a time, into 3-inch oval balls. Place on an oiled and floured baking sheet 2½ inches apart and flatten down with a fork.

Bake in a preheated 350°F oven for 10 minutes, then transfer to a cooling rack.

yields about 2½ dozen cookies

Drunken Ricotta (D)

ricotta ubriaca

icotta Ubriaca was one of my father's favorite desserts. It was made with finely ground real coffee beans and Cognac, and because of these two ingredients we children were not allowed to have it. A version without coffee and brandy was what we had instead.

As an adult I tasted the original version and liked it very much, and I make it also with instant coffee powder.

---

1 pound whole milk ricotta

½ cup sugar

2 teaspoons finely ground espresso coffee beans or instant espresso

4 tablespoons brandy

2 tablespoons *pignoli* (Italian pine nuts)

Place the ricotta in a colander over a container and let it drain in the refrigerator at least 24 hours. Transfer to a bowl, add the sugar, and mix with a wooden spoon until fluffy and smooth. Add the coffee, stir a little (you don't want to stir too much if you use instant coffee), and place in the refrigerator uncovered.

Moments before serving, remove from the refrigerator, add the brandy, and stir to combine. Spoon into small bowls or ramekins. Sprinkle with *pignoli* and serve.

serves 6

Taiglach (P)
ceciarchiata

eciarchiata is one of the many sweets used for Purim and Rosh Hashanah. It owes its name to the tiny pieces of dough in it, which resemble *ceci*, chickpeas. I first discovered after I had come to America that Jews of different backgrounds from mine also make it with slight variations. This is the authentic ancient recipe I learned to make as a child in Leghorn from my mother's aristocratic sister, Aunt Letizia.

3 eggs, slightly beaten

2 cups unbleached flour

½ teaspoon salt

1 cup olive oil (optional)

1 cup honey

1 cup hazelnuts

1 tablespoon lemon juice

2 teaspoons grated lemon rind

1 cup coarsely chopped toasted almonds

Combine the eggs, flour, and salt in a small bowl and mix to make a rather soft dough. Turn out on a floured surface and knead a minute or two. Shape into a ball, flatten down with your hands, then roll down to a ¼-inch thickness with a rolling pin, sprinkling with flour. With a sharp knife or pizza cutter, cut into ¼-inch strips and dredge with flour. Cut a few strips at a time into pea-size bits, and again dredge with flour to prevent them from clumping together. Use a large sifter to remove excess flour.

If using the oil, heat it in a small saucepan and fry a handful of pasta bits at a time until golden. Drain on paper towels.

If you prefer to avoid fried food, forget the oil, and bake the bits, one third at a time, on an ungreased baking sheet in a 400°F oven for 7 minutes.

Bring the honey to a boil and cook over moderately high heat 3 minutes. Add the "chickpeas," hazelnuts, lemon juice, and zest and cook over lower heat 7 minutes longer, stirring constantly.

Spread the toasted almonds over an oiled round dish and pour the hot mixture on it. Let settle for a few minutes. When the mixture is cool enough to handle, shape into a ring using your moistened hands and the help of a spoon. Let cool thoroughly at room temperature, then cut into 2-inch segments.

serves 8 to 12

Edda's Rice Pudding (D)

budino di riso edda

Although I like rice in any form or shape, none of the various rice puddings I had tasted were good enough for my palate. And as I mentioned time and again, when a food is not satisfying, one tends to eat more of it in the vain search for gratification. So I made up my own version of this pudding, a small amount of which is sufficient to make me happy.

4 tablespoons unsalted butter

1 cup Italian or short-grain rice

3 cups milk

½ teaspoon salt

2 tablespoons flour

1 cup sugar

½ cup raisins

2 teaspoons vanilla extract

1 egg, slightly beaten

2 tablespoons rum

2 teaspoons freshly grated lemon rind

Whipped cream (optional)

Place 2 tablespoons butter in a saucepan over moderately high heat with the rice, and stir until the rice is all coated. Add 2½ cups milk and salt and bring to a gentle simmer. Reduce the heat to a minimum, cover the pan, and let cook for 20 to 25 minutes, stirring occasionally. Remove from the heat.

In a large skillet melt 2 tablespoons butter with 2 tablespoons flour. Add the remaining ½ cup milk and stir constantly over moderate heat until thickened and smooth. Add the sugar, raisins, vanilla extract, and beaten egg and cook, stirring, 5 more minutes. Remove from the heat, add the rice, and stir to combine. Let cool for a while, then add the rum and lemon rind and mix. Spoon into flute glasses and refrigerate until ready to serve. Serve as is or topped by whipped cream.

serves 12

Chocolate Salami (P)

salame di cioccolata

1 cup sugar

⅓ cup water

8 ounces semisweet baking chocolate, cut into chunks

3 tablespoons Alchermes (brightly colored red liquor)

10 ounces unpeeled almonds or hazelnuts, toasted and finely powdered

¼ cup diced candied citron peel

¼ cup *pignoli* (Italian pine nuts)

½ cup unsweetened cocoa

1 tablespoon Vanilla-Flavored Sugar (page 341)

Dissolve the sugar with water in a heavy-bottomed pan over high heat. When the mixture appears transparent (after 2 minutes or so), add the semisweet chocolate chunks, lower the heat, and stir until the chocolate is melted, approximately 5 minutes. Remove from the heat, add the liquor, toasted nut powder, citron peel, and pine nuts and mix well.

Wait until the mixture has reached room temperature, to shape, with the help of a sheet of plastic wrap, into a 10-inch-long cylinder to resemble a salami. Let rest several hours until quite firm. Spread the cocoa and then the confectioners' sugar (without mixing) over a piece of wax paper, and roll the salami over it coating all sides. Store unwrapped in the refrigerator for several hours, then wrap it tightly. When almost ready to use leave for 30 minutes at room temperature, then cut slantwise into thin slices.

serves 8

Sponge Cake (P)

pan di spagna

Pan di Spagna (bread of Spain) is a typical Jewish dessert. Its name derives probably from the fact that it was brought to other parts of Europe and to the Middle East by refugees at the time of the Spanish Inquisition. It is a delicate dessert in its own right; however, it is also very useful in the preparation of *dolci al cucchiaio*, desserts that must be eaten with a spoon, such as *Zuppa Inglese*. Tightly wrapped in plastic, it can be frozen for a long time, so that it is at hand when needed.

| 6 eggs, separated |
| ½ teaspoon cream of tartar |
| ¾ cup sugar |
| 1 teaspoon vanilla extract |
| ½ cup cake flour |

Beat the egg whites with the cream of tartar until stiff peaks form. In a separate bowl beat the egg yolks with the sugar until fluffy and lemon colored. Add the vanilla extract and one quarter of the beaten egg whites. Mix well, then fold in the remaining egg whites.

Line a bread loaf pan with wax paper. Spoon the batter into it and bake in a 350°F oven for 45 minutes. Remove to a cooling rack and wait until completely cool to unmold.

serves 8

Tiramisù (D)

irami sù means, literally, "pull me up." And, in fact, this rich, delicious, yet delicate dessert was once used to give convalescent people a new strength. Many, many years ago (I was a child of seven), while Mother was recovering from an illness, our maid made *tirami sù* every day and that's when I learned to love it.

In recent years *tiramisù* (now spelled as one word) has made a triumphal comeback and has become a household name both in Italy and America, and a favorite at fine restaurants.

1 pound mascarpone cheese
¼ cup Vanilla-Flavored Sugar (page 341)
Crema Pasticcera (see following recipe)
36 ladyfingers
¼ cup rum or other liqueur
¼ cup espresso coffee
4 ounces milk chocolate, melted
⅔ cup milk chocolate curls (page 367) or
⅓ cup unsweetened cocoa

Have all the ingredients at room temperature. Gently mix the mascarpone and sugar with a rubber spatula. Add the *crema pasticcera* a little at a time and keep on stirring by hand until all is amalgamated.

Place 12 ladyfingers at the bottom of a square or rectangular oven-to-table dish. Mix the liqueur and coffee and drizzle the cookies with one third the mixture, cover with one third the mascarpone mixture, and sprinkle with half the melted chocolate.

Repeat the layering in the same order, covering the top with chocolate curls or unsweetened cocoa. Place in the refrigerator until ready to serve.

serves 8 or more

Custard Filling (D)

crema pasticcera

 This type of custard is called *pasticcera* because it is used exclusively for pastry filling, or as part of a creamy dessert, such as Tiramisù and *zuppa inglese*.

4 eggs yolks
⅔ cup sugar
Small pinch salt
¼ cup cake flour
2½ cups hot milk
Two 2 × ½-inch strips lemon peel
1 tablespoon unsalted butter

Beat the egg yolks, sugar, and salt together until frothy and lemon colored. Gradually beat in the flour. Add the milk slowly and mix well. Pour into a heavy-bottomed saucepan; add the lemon peel and place over moderately high heat. Bring to a gentle boil while stirring constantly. Lower the heat and simmer for 3 to 4 minutes, stirring occasionally.

Remove from the heat, discard the lemon peel, add the butter, and stir. Cool for 1 to 2 hours, stirring from time to time to prevent a film from forming on the surface. If you don't use it right away, pour into a bowl and cover with a piece of wax paper, letting the paper touch the cream, then store in the refrigerator.

NOTE: If you wish to use *crema pasticcera* for a Passover dessert, substitute Passover cake flour for regular cake flour.

yields 2 to 2½ cups

English Custard (D)

crema inglese

In olden times in Italy all that was delicate and elegant was referred to as "English." (My mother used to call my older daughter *Inglesina*, little Englishwoman, because of her refined looks and manners.) This custard is called English as opposed to any other custard made with flour or other thickeners.

6 egg yolks
¾ cup sugar
2 cups hot milk
1 teaspoon vanilla extract
Vanilla cookies or
ladyfingers

Beat the egg yolks with the sugar until frothy and lemon colored. Add the hot milk a little at a time, beating constantly.

Pour into a double boiler or a heavy-bottomed saucepan and place over moderate heat. Cook, stirring constantly, with a wooden spoon until the cream coats the spoon evenly. (Be careful not to allow the cream to reach the boiling point.) Add the vanilla extract, remove from the heat, and stir.

Cool to room temperature, stirring from time to time, then pour into individual custard cups and refrigerate. Serve with vanilla cookies or ladyfingers.

serves 6

Chocolate Curls (P or D)

ricci di cioccolata

This is the simplest way of making chocolate decorations, and simple were indeed most desserts of the Italian Jews. Simple, however, applies only to the preparations and looks, because tastewise, their desserts are unsurpassable. If you want your curls to be pareve, you must use semisweet chocolate. For dairy desserts, I recommend milk chocolate, which is more malleable.

½ pound block chocolate
Vegetable slicer or peeler

Keep the chocolate at room temperature, if your working room is 80°F. If, on the other hand, the room temperature is at 68 or 70 degrees, you must keep the block a few seconds in a warm oven, or zap it for 3 seconds in the microwave oven. If the block is too hard, instead of curls you will get shavings; if it is too warm, it will not make curls but blobs.

When your block is at the ideal point (you will have to make a few trials before you reach the desired consistency) begin to pass the vegetable slicer or peeler over it, and let the curls drop on a piece of wax paper.

Store in airtight glass jars at room temperature until ready to use. Handle with care so as not to lose the shape. Use as directed.

Hard Cookies of the Jews (P)

torzetti dell'abbrei

orzetti and *Marroncini* were specialties of Pitigliano made for holidays as well as for family celebrations. When as a married woman living in the United States I went to Pitigliano to learn from my old aunt how to make them, she regretfully told me that she didn't remember because she had not made them in decades. No written recipes had ever existed; both were handed down from generation to generation by word of mouth and observation. I never had seen them made, because Mother, being from Rome, preferred to have her sisters-in-law make the Pitigliano specialties for our family and to reciprocate with her Roman ones. However, my aunt told me, one of the public bakers was making them much like the originals. I went to interview the baker—an intelligent young Christian woman—and I found out to my amusement that she had bestowed on them the attribute *dell'abbrei*, the way of saying "of the Jews" in the Pitiglianese dialect.

I asked her how she knew about *torzetti* and she told me this interesting story: she had learned to make them from *La Bafifa*, the old woman who had been our baker for over half a century. The old woman was so jealous of the treasured recipes she had learned from the Jews that she was very reluctant to share them with anyone. Only after a lot of pressure from the young apprentice had she finally agreed to show her how to make *torzetti*. However, she withheld one detail. When the moment came to test the sugar, the old woman held her large apron high, as a screen to block the other's view. It took a lot of begging to win the old woman's heart, but at last the young baker gained the skill that would otherwise have been lost. (None of my cousins remembered how to make *Torzetti* or *Marroncini*, although I stirred up a world of beautiful memories when I mentioned them.)

The young baker kindly invited us to watch her while she made them. So, while I paid careful attention, and my husband stood ready with paper and pen, we recorded two of the oldest Italian Jewish dessert recipes. Typical of the generosity of the Pitiglianesi and their long-standing friendship with the Jews, after the cookies were baked, the young woman insisted that we take all of them as a gift. Since in Pitigliano there are no Jews left, she bakes them for her Christian customers only around Christmas, she said. These were made—in the middle of the summer—expressly for me and my family!

3 cups unbleached flour
½ teaspoon ammonium bicarbonate *or* 1 teaspoon baking powder
1 teaspoon ground cloves
Grated rind of 1 orange
Grated rind of 1 lemon
1¼ cups sugar
1 cup cold water

Combine the flour, baking powder, cloves, and orange and lemon rinds. Mound on a working surface (or in a large bowl) and make a well in the center.

Place the sugar with the cold water in a saucepan and bring to a boil. When the solution begins to reach full boil, start stirring with a wooden spoon. After 3 minutes, begin to test for the ideal cooking point of the syrup, which comes when a drop held between thumb and forefinger, in an opening and closing motion, forms a thread at the fourth opening.

Pour all the hot syrup at the center of the well. Quickly mix in the flour mixture and knead while the dough that forms is still hot. With a rolling pin roll down to a ½-inch thickness. Cut into 2-inch-tall diamonds with a sharp knife; then coat the diamonds all over with the leftover flour mixture.

Place on a well-floured baking sheet and bake in a preheated 400°F oven for 10 to 12 minutes. If everything went well, the *torzetti* should be slightly less white and each should have formed a bubble of air at the center.

NOTE: Ammonium bicarbonate can be purchased from pharmacies. It is *not* the same as sodium bicarbonate (baking soda) available in supermarkets.

yields about 50 cookies

Sweet Shavuot Tortelli (D)

tortelli dolci di shavuot

1½ cups ricotta

2 egg yolks

Sugar

2 tablespoons minced candied citron peel

2 tablespoons *pignoli* (Italian pine nuts)

½ teaspoon vanilla extract

2 cups unbleached flour

½ teaspoon salt

2 eggs

3 tablespoons vegetable oil

2 tablespoons rum or brandy

½ teaspoon freshly grated lemon rind

Vanilla-Flavored Sugar (page 341)

In a large skillet heat the ricotta and stir until most of the moisture has evaporated. Let cool a little, then combine with 1 egg yolk, 3 tablespoons sugar, citron peel, *pignoli*, and vanilla extract; mix well and set aside in the refrigerator.

Make a soft dough with the flour, salt, eggs, the remaining egg yolk, ¼ cup sugar, oil, rum, and lemon rind. Knead for 3 minutes, then cover with a clean towel and let rest for 5 minutes. With a manual pasta machine or rolling pin roll the pastry thin. Cut into disks with a round cookie cutter or wineglass about 3 inches in diameter.

Place 1 teaspoonful ricotta mixture off center on each disk. Fold over in half and press the round edge with the prongs of a fork to seal. Poke a few holes on the tops, place the *tortelli* on an ungreased baking sheet, and bake in a preheated 350°F oven for 25 minutes. Sprinkle with vanilla-flavored confectioners' sugar and serve.

yields about 3 dozen tortelli

Rona's Vanilla Cookies (P)

biscottini di rona

Biscotti or biscottini, when they are small, specify in Italy any kind of hard cookies. These cookies were devised by my daughter Rona when she was a little child: she told me what ingredients should go into making them and I took care of the amounts and measurements of those ingredients. She not only liked them for herself but also and above all to offer them to her little friends when they took a break from their play at teatime.

¾ cup firmly packed raw sugar
½ cup olive oil
¼ teaspoon salt
2 eggs
2 teaspoons vanilla extract
1¼ cups unbleached flour

In a small bowl, cream together the sugar, oil, and salt. Add one egg at a time, beating after each addition. Add the vanilla and beat again. Gradually add the flour and continue to beat until you have a smooth batter.

Drop by the teaspoonful (holding the spoon perpendicular to the sheet to obtain rounder cookies) on a lightly oiled baking sheet, dusted with flour, 2 inches apart. Bake in a preheated 375°F oven for 7 minutes or until the cookies are slightly browned. Cool thoroughly before storing in cookie jars.

yields about 3 dozen cookies

HOLIDAY MENUS

i menu delle feste

he world holiday, generally speaking, means a day that has been set apart to completely halt, or at least to modify, the course of routine activities in order to celebrate or commemorate an important event, or to rest and engage in spiritual acts. Three kinds of holidays are universally recognized by Western civilization: family, national, and religious holidays. All three offer the opportunity for the people involved to get together and share in the festivities.

At the time when I was growing up, Catholicism was the state religion in Italy. This meant that state funds were used to celebrate a Catholic religious holiday publicly, with great pomp. This also meant that the Jews, as a minority, were excluded from the celebrations, and Jewish children were often vilified or even physically abused by their peers on such occasions. The words *festa religiosa*, religious holiday, therefore, had come to mean something that was alien or even frightening to us. We used the Hebrew word *mo'adim* when referring to *our* religious holidays.

Our *mo'adim* were very intimate and celebrated privately, without showiness. Yet we were not meek or underhanded about them. On the contrary, during our holidays a sense of community, of true belonging, of shared interests prevailed. Brotherhood, justice, and caring were not abstract concepts for us, but principles that we practiced in our everyday life. The holidays provided special moments for togetherness and the opportunity to show our regard for each other. For me, being the target of injustice gave inner strength, and the certitude that I would never identify with the oppressor; it gave me the desire to preserve and pass on my beautiful heritage.

Sabbath

shabbàt

abbath is the holiest of the Holy Days. It is the only holiday that is mentioned in the Ten Commandments: "Remember the sabbath day and keep it holy. . . . You shall not do any work."

For us it was a day of true rest and togetherness. The heavy working week culminated with a busy Friday. At daybreak my father would get up and after *Shachrìt*, the morning prayer, would go and meet the farmers to bring home *le primiʒie*, the first fruits of the season, the fresh taste of which was unsurpassable: *mandorlini* (fresh almonds at the stage when the husk is still green and everything is edible, including the part that later in the season becomes the woody shell); tiny peas; artichokes so fresh and tender they had no choke at all; *ovuli* (egg-like mushrooms, particularly suitable for eating raw); *mespilus* fruits (exotic little apples good after frost and when almost rotten, brownish in color and with a tart afterflavor); cherries, wild strawberries, and dozens of other *primiʒie;* and, on rare occasions, a bunch of wild asparagus. He would bless each *primiʒia* and distribute one to each child before storing the rest away to be used for the Sabbath meals. We would close our eyes and make a wish while savoring the tasty new fruit.

After enjoying our delight in tasting the fresh new fruits, my father would rush to temple where, with the help of the *Shamàsh* (the temple caretaker and assistant), he would prepare about two hundred oil lamps that were to be lit just before *Arvìt,* the evening prayer. The amount of oil was measured to last from one sundown to the next so that the lights would begin to go out soon after the *Havdalà* (literally, separation, in

Hebrew), the ceremony at the end of Sabbath. These oil lamps, in the shiny bronze chandeliers, projected a warm, golden light, which created an intimate, festive, indescribably rich atmosphere.

At home, Mother was busy tidying up the house and preparing for the special Sabbath meals, while the boys ironed their pants, polished their shoes, and practiced their assigned *Tefillòt* (prayers) and *Piẓmonim* (solo chants that each male in the community contributed to the liturgy of the festivities).

For us girls the excitement of the Sabbath started on Friday afternoon when we raced to finish the dress, blouse, skirt, or whatever we had started that week so that we could wear it at temple. The garment completed, we cleaned, oiled, and closed the sewing machine. Those items that could not be finished were neatly folded away in a closet with our embroidering and knitting baskets, and nothing would be touched again until Sunday, because the saying went that even after sundown on Saturday one was not allowed to work, except to sew shrouds for the dead, and who wanted to meddle with that!

The tradition of wearing something new every Friday night began because every girl was considered to be the bridesmaid for the beautiful bride, the Sabbath. But our intentions were less pious: we simply wanted to be pretty and show off our talents and accomplishments to the boys. Of course, during services, we were relegated to the *matroneó*—the dark upstairs gallery with a carved wooden baroque grate painted in gold leaf, which was reserved for women—and the boys could not see us. But as soon as the Thirteen Articles of Faith, or *Yigdàl,* a song that was sung at the end of the service, was over, we ran down to the *piaẓetta* where we giggled and squirmed and shook hands and wished *Shabbàt Shalom* (a peaceful and wholesome Sabbath) to one another before going home for dinner.

On Saturday morning, after the service, during the months of good weather—which in Pitigliano lasted from February to November—my mother would pick up at the newsstand a copy of *Il Corriere dei Piccoli,* a weekly children's paper (which father would pay for the following day, since money could not be handled on Sabbath), and read it to the children. My mother had a marvelous imagination and a unique flair for storytelling and was not content to just read the captions; she embellished the stories with her own inventiveness, which made them infinitely more interesting. She would sit on one of the benches that surrounded the monument to the dead of World War I, and around her many children would gather, sitting on the sidewalk, standing near her, behind her, trying to get as close to her as possible. She really looked like the brood hen with her flock of chicks. We, her own children, were not jealous of our cousins and friends; we were actually very proud of her.

It was customary in Pitigliano to spend the Sabbath afternoon visiting the old and sick. Strange as it might seem to some of today's youth, we children looked forward to these visits. We would bring our freshness and gaiety into their lives and they would delight us with stories of their own childhood. It was during one of these Saturday afternoons that I learned of the interminable discussions that had taken place among our notable ancestors on how to address the Grand Duke of Tuscany during his first visit to our temple. "How about calling him 'Our Master and Lord'?" "It would lower our dignity." "Then we'll call him 'Mister Grand Duke.' " "We'll make fools of ourselves." And so on in an untranslated old Judeo dialect that would make us double with laughter. (I never did find out how they finally addressed him and I'm still curious.) Or we would be told of the times when, during the Good Friday procession, the Jews had to lock themselves up in their homes; otherwise, they would have been stoned on sight.

I believe that it was in the sitting rooms or at the bedsides of these people that my strong sentiments about my Jewish heritage, formed first at home, were further strengthened and forever fixed. I realized now what a wealth of good feelings we gave one another regardless of age and state of health.

Our Sabbath meals varied greatly according to the season, but fish was never missing from the festive table, and when fresh fish was not available, it was either *baccalà* (dried salted cod) or salted anchovies, or *bottarga*, which my mother had shipped to her from Rome. Bottarga is one of those delicacies for which I have preserved a nostalgic craving, since I have not so far been able to find it here. It is the roe of the mullet, salted and dried in its own skin, and pressed. It is served as an appetizer, sliced very thin, with a sprinkle of olive oil on it.

The following are examples of our Sabbath menus.

FRIDAY EVENING

Fish and Chicory Casserole
Pesce e Indivia

Roast Chicken for Sabbath
Pollo Arrosto per Shabbàt

Sautéed Garlic Spinach
Spinaci Saltati

Challah Bread, Rona's Vanilla Cookies, Fruit in Season
Pane del Sabato, Biscottini di Rona, Frutta Fresca

SATURDAY LUNCH

Marinated Artichoke Hearts
Carciofi Marinati

Flat Onion Bread
Focaccia colla Cipolla

Sabbath Saffron Rice
Riso del Sabato

Fillets of Sole with Lemon
Filetti di Sogliole al Limone

Escarole Salad
Scarola a Insalata

Fruit in Season
Frutta Fresca

The New Year

rosh hashanah

osh Hashanah, the Jewish New Year, may occur any time from early September to early October, according to the Hebrew calendar. In preparation for it, our house was given a thorough cleaning, including the laundering of curtains, the changing of drapes and bedspreads, the replacing of carpets and rugs that had been stored away during the hot months.

My father would carefully inspect his three *shofròt* (*shofàr*, singular: natural wind instruments made of emptied ram horns) to make sure that moths had not attacked them and made any holes, since even the tiniest hole would make a *shofàr pasùl* (unkosher). He used the wing feather of a huge bird (I now believe it was that of a turkey, but then I thought it belonged to an eagle) dipped in wine vinegar to clean the inside walls. Apparently this operation did something to maintain or improve the sound of the primitive instrument. My father was such a powerful *shofàr* blower that when the blasts—especially the prolonged ones—came out of his instrument, even the Christians in the fields could hear them.

The Rosh Hashanah Seder was almost as important as the Pesach Seder. The table was set with our most magnificent hand-embroidered tablecloth, best crystal, gold-rimmed porcelain dishes, and baroque silverware of my mother's wedding dowry. At one end of the table, near where my father sat, all the special dishes were neatly gathered to be blessed. Closest to him were the wine and *Kiddùsh cup* (a silver goblet reserved especially for the blessing of the wine) and the beautiful Challah breads; in a semicircle around them various dishes were arranged: one with a boiled rooster's head, comb and all; another with fish (usually fillets of salted anchovies well washed and sprinkled with olive oil, but occasionally also *bottarga*); another with boiled, peeled, and sliced beets; and lots of seasonal fruits. Fresh figs were always present as was the exotic pomegranate—delight of the children and irritation to Mother because on opening it the crowded seeds would snap out and jump all over the place, creating red stains that were hard to remove. There was a fruit called *giuggiole*, meaning "things of little value," but to the children they were very valuable. Unfortunately, I haven't seen them in the New York area, perhaps because here too they are considered of little value. But I wish, for the children's sake, that they would begin to sell them. Their botanical name is *joojooba*, but in English they are also called "Chinese dates." They have the shape and appearance of fresh olives, except that when they are very ripe they turn from pale green to a rich rust color. They are sweet and aromatic and have a dry, snappy texture.

At the center of the table there was a dish with a round cake of dried sourdough, or leavening, on which the palm and fingers of our father's right hand had been previously impressed, and with a bunch of fennel weed, complete with stems and seeds, standing in the center. At each side of the leavening stood dishes with growing green blades that resembled grass. They were prepared about a week in advance this way: the bottoms of two fancy fruit dishes were loosely covered—one with grains of wheat, the other with corn kernels. Water was added to cover and then the dishes were left on top of the mantelpiece until the night of the Seder. During this period the seeds were kept very moist until they began to root. Thereafter, a light sprinkling twice a day was all the rooted grains needed. Soon each grain would sprout a little blade, the wheat darker and thinner, the corn paler and fatter, and by the night of the Seder the wheat would be three to four inches and the corn two to three inches high. The sprouting of the grains was a project we children were responsible for, and we were fascinated by the transformation and growth occurring under our eyes.

The Rosh Hashanah Seder was not established to remember or celebrate any historical event. Rather it revolved about the themes of growth, prosperity, and sweetness for the year to come. Each of the foods gathered on the table was blessed, and each blessing ended with the refrain, "Grow and multiply like the fish in the ocean; grow and multiply like the seeds of the pomegranate; grow and multiply like the leavening, like the grain, like the fennel," and so on. Sweetness was symbolized by the beets and the sweetest fruits, and by desserts made with honey.

Among the desserts the most characteristic was *Sfratti*, the interesting origin of which I have already described. But there were many others, some of which, I later discovered, also belong to the tradition of Eastern European Jews, such as *Taiglach*, which is called, in its Italian version, *Ceciarchiata*, for the size and shape of the bits of dough that resemble ceci (chickpeas), and it is also served on Purim. After the Seder our typical Rosh Hashanah menu was as follows:

Jellied Striped Bass
Muggine in Bianco

Tricolor Salad
Insalata Tricolore

Chicken Galantine
Pollo in Galantina

Zucchini Pudding
Sformato di Zucchini

Taiglach, Honey and Nut Sticks
Ceciarchiata, Sfratti

Apples, Fresh Figs, Dates
Mele, Fichi Freschi, Datteri

The Day of Atonement

yom kippur

om Kippur, the Day of Atonement or Forgiveness, is the culmination of the ten-day High Holy Day period, which starts with Rosh Hashanah. The Jewish children in Pitigliano were very much aware of the solemnity of Yom Kippur. Esther's fast before the joyous festival of Purim, or the fast of the 9th of *Av*, commemorating the two destructions of the Temple of Jerusalem, were observed by only a few. But the fast on the Day of Atonement or Forgiveness was observed by everyone, including the nonreligious, so the children took it very seriously. They began to practice fasting at about ten years of age to make sure that by the time they celebrated their Bar or Bat Mitzvah they would hold up as well as the grown-ups. This practice consisted of fasting for as long as one could stand it without getting sick, but most of us capitulated at about two o'clock in the afternoon.

The night of the 9th of *Tishrì* (the eve of Yom Kippur) we had dinner before sundown and even though we were allowed to eat as much as we wanted, we refrained from having desserts or any frivolous foods.

The temple was decorated in white to symbolize the purity of conscience, and in addition to the usual Shabbat lights of the chandeliers and the *Tamìd* (perennial light in front of the Ark of the Torah scrolls, which was kept alive by adding oil to it every morning before *Shachrìt*), there was one oil lamp flickering for each member of the community who had passed "to a better life" in the past few decades. The Renaissance wood panels of the western wall of the temple had a built-in shelf that ran the width of the wall, which was crowded with these oil lamps, each representing one name. During the *Kol Nedarìm* (literally "all vows"; it is the plural of *Kol Nidrè*, the prayer that opens the Yom Kippur services) the names were mentioned one by one, noting their relationship to the living members. All the services in Pitigliano were conducted entirely in Hebrew, including the reading of those names.

After services we took walks on the outskirts of town—with a waxing moon as the only means of illumination—to enjoy the last bit of warmth of the dying summer, and to engage in talmudic discussions. If we were very young, our discussions centered on whether or not we were allowed to brush our teeth, since the fast was so strict that not even a drop of water should be ingested. If we were a trifle more mature, the discussion would revolve about the value of fasting not only as a means of atonement but also as an exercise in self-control.

On the morning of Yom Kippur my father would leave the house very early, and we children all climbed into bed with Mamma to loaf for a while, it being the only day of the year when she did not have to start her work at daybreak. When the competition for getting to be closest to her became a little too rough, she would get up, get dressed, and go to temple remaining there with my father until after sunset, when the last blows of the *shofàr* marked the end of the fasting.

When we were little children, we were left in the care of a neighbor because our housekeeper, though Christian, was not allowed to work or cook on that day. The only things she did, when she heard the final sound of the *shofàr*, was to set the tables and heat up the foods that Mother had prepared the previous day. We lived near the temple in the house provided for the rabbi by the community but the powerful sound of my father's *shofàr* could also be heard far away.

When I grew a little older and we had no help in the house, it was I who left the temple a few moments before the end of the service to go home and set the large table for dinner, and a smaller one with *Bollo* and vermouth for all the Jews who came to break the fast before going to their own homes for their dinner. I would slice the pickled tongue (my favorite among the homemade cold cuts, the aroma of which was enough to tempt even the most devout person), cook the soup, and heat up the main dishes, without giving in to the temptation of putting bits of food into my mouth, in order to exercise my willpower.

The High Holy Days drew back to their native village many of the Pitiglianesi who had left to seek higher education and better opportunities in larger towns or cities. Often they had no temple and no Jewish life where they had moved, but they would come also from such cities as Milan, Florence, and Rome, where there were large and active Jewish communities, for the opportunity of spending the holiday with relatives and friends who had remained in Pitigliano. Above all they returned to take part in the services that included the familiar and well-loved liturgy of their ancestors.

A tradition that began before I was born was that our family would be host to one such family from Grosseto, chief town of the province, who came to celebrate the holiday with us. The wife of the family had been my mother's best friend since their grade school days; both came from Rome and both married a Servi from Pitigliano.

My mother and her friend were both excellent and imaginative cooks, and between the two of them they prepared and cooked fabulous meals. If the ten days between Rosh Hashanah and Yom Kippur were days of penance, they were more than compensated for by the meal that followed the great fasting.

The following menu serves as an example:

Yom Kippur Bread
Il Bollo

Soup with Tiny Pasta Squares
Quadrucci in Brodo

Red Snapper Jewish Style
Triglie all' Ebraica

Fennel Jewish Style
Finocchi alla Giudia

Cold Thin Egg Noodles with Brusco Sauce
Taglierini col Brodo Brusco

Chicken Breast Patties with Celery Fingers
Pizzette di Petto di Pollo coi Sedani

Challah Bread
Pane del Sabato

Cinnamon Turnovers
Borricche alla Cannella

Fresh Figs, Pears, Grapes
Fichi Freschi, Pere, Uva

Festival of the Harvest

sukkot

ncluding HOSHANÀ RABBÀ, the Great Hosanna;
SHEMINÌ ATZERET, Festival of the Rain;
SIMCHAT TORAH, Rejoicing in the Torah.

Sukkot, the festival of the harvest, also called the
Festival of the Tabernacles, encompasses on its seventh day *Hoshanà Rabbà* (the Great Hosanna), which is a half holiday.
Special services are said, but work is permitted when the services are
over. The celebrants carry the palm and citron seven times around the
temple, while chanting special prayers (*Hoshanòt*). The eighth day of the
Sukkot is *Sheminì Atzeret*, which is marked by the prayer for rain. *Simchat Torah*, the rejoicing with the Torah, occurs the following day and
marks the beginning of the Torah reading cycle and the conclusion of
the High Holiday season that had started with the first day of *Tishrì*,
Rosh Hashanah.

Sukkot, in Pitigliano, not only meant a great deal to us but to our
Christian neighbors as well. For the Jews it was the only festival that was
closely related to the real life of our surroundings, since Pitigliano
depended for its survival almost entirely on its meager agricultural
resources; for the Christians it represented the manner by which God
would show his divine benevolence or wrath. It was a belief among Gentile peasants that if it rained at least once during the eight days of
Sukkot, it was a sign that God had forgiven the Jews their sins and would
grant a plentiful harvest that year. Today, with warehouses, refrigeration, fast transportation, and a more efficient system of food production
and distribution, no particular place suffers if its harvest is poor. But in
our village—and I suppose in all rural areas of that era—local produce

was the main source of sustenance and it went directly from the farmers to the consumers. If drought killed or even reduced the crops, everyone was immediately and disastrously affected by the scarcity, and the Jews—as usual—were blamed. Fortunately for us, during that period of the year, almost every day rain-laden clouds sprinkled the earth as they pass over Pitigliano's region.

For seven days during the morning prayers the following ritual took place: the bunch was held with both hands—the *lulav* on the right, the *etrog* on the left, and the myrtle in the middle—and shaken in all directions to symbolize the omnipresence of God, and indeed the snapping of the bladelike palm leaves against each other produced an awesome sound.

For seven nights we gathered under the bough for the Kiddush and the *Hamotzì*, the blessings of the wine and bread. The special wine used for Sukkot was *Moscatello*, a sweet white wine my father made from the delicious local grapes, and *Maritucci* was the special bread Mother baked for this festival. *Ciambelle*, our version of the Ashkenazic bagels, were also used during Sukkot, especially for breakfast, either dry or with ricotta and a cup of black, sweetened coffee or *grané*, a coffee substitute made from roasted wheat grains.

The end of Sukkot was marked by Simchat Torah, a very colorful festival in which all the beautiful and precious *sepharim*, the Torah scrolls—covered with magnificently embroidered silk or velveteen cloths and decorated with *remonim* (elaborately embossed silver crowns, placards, and ringing bells)—were taken out of the ark and carried in a procession all around the temple. Men took turns carrying the scrolls so that everyone would have a chance, and sang choral or solo songs during the seven rounds of the procession.

One of the highlights of Simchat Torah was the election of two male members of the community to become *Chatàn Toràh*, bridegroom of the law, and *Chatàn B'reshìt*, the groom of the beginning or the Genesis, for the year.

The procedure was an elaborate one. All the names of the candidates for *Chatàn Toràh* were written in beautiful Hebrew calligraphy on a 6 × 6-centimeter piece of parchment; the little parchments were then rolled like cigarettes and inserted through the holes of ballots (wooden balls five centimeters long resembling pitted olives). All these wooden ballots with the rolled parchments inside, with about half a centimeter showing at each end, were placed inside a rolling glass urn with a crank. A child was called to turn the crank to mix up all the ballots and then to pick one up and hand it to the outgoing *Chatàn Toràh*, who would ceremoniously slide the little parchment scroll out of the ballot and read aloud the Hebrew name on it. The chosen one's face would light up and everyone looked toward the lucky man beaming with wide smiles. The whole ritual was repeated for the election of the *Chatàn B'reshìt*. A number of ceremonial songs were sung in celebration and in honor of the two newly elected men. Finally, at the end of the service, everyone was invited to the reception that was held in the library at the other end of the *piazzetta* across from the sanctuary. The traditional refreshments consisted of a variety of cakes and cookies served with sweet vermouth, and *confetti*, the sugar-coated almonds used at every wedding.

Altogether it was a very pleasant and joyous occasion and I really believed that the election of the two men was left to chance, as I described it. Only recently have I learned that the two men to be elected were chosen ahead of time by a committee who would make sure that everyone (among the wealthy and educated!) got his turn at holding those distinctions. Every ballot placed in the urn had the name of the already designated winner on it, so that only he could win. The ceremony was carried out merely for the sake of tradition and for the benefit of the children.

I now believe that this innocent deception was a great idea because for those who were unaware of it as well as for those who knew the mechanism behind the "casting of the lots," the ritual was very exciting and memorable.

This is a traditional Sukkot menu:

Vegetable Cream Soup
Passato di Verdura

Veal Scaloppine with Madeira or Marsala Wine
Scaloppine al Madera / Marsala

Fried Mixed Vegetables
Fritto Misto di Verdura

Stuffed Cabbage
Cavoli Ripieni

Sukkot Bread, Bagels
Maritucci, Ciambelle

Pomegranates, Grapes
Melagrane, Uva

AS A MIDNIGHT SNACK

Festive Pasta Rolls with Parmesan and Cinnamon
Masconod

The Festival of Lights

chanukah (dedication)

good many years ago, when my oldest daughter was not quite five years old, she was taking ballet lessons for the first time. Her teacher, a Russian-born retired ballerina, asked her just before Christmas vacation what she expected Papa Noël to bring her. To my astonishment my tiny daughter replied with a clear voice in front of all the other students and their parents, "We don't celebrate Christmas, we celebrate Chanukah." My feelings about her response were mixed. On the one hand, I felt pleased and proud that the terror of letting someone know I was Jewish, still carried with me as a result of my painful experiences in Europe, was not shared by my children. On the other hand, I felt a bit uneasy that my child had so readily made a connection between Christmas and Chanukah. Was she like one of those Jewish American children for whom Chanukah is nothing but a "substitute" for Christmas? But I was wrong. The only connection she had made was that Christian children in America receive presents for Christmas and Jewish children for Chanukah.

When I was a child this connection between Christmas and Chanukah could not have been made. Christmas trees and reindeer, which are Nordic legends and traditions, were not known in Italy. Furthermore, Christian children did not receive presents on Christmas but on January 6 as a remembrance of the gifts of incense, gold, and myrrh brought by the Magi to the infant Jesus. And it was not Papa Noël who brought those presents on a sled pulled by reindeer, but a witch riding on a broom. And the Jewish children did not receive presents on Chanukah, but on Purim, which occurs two and a half months later.

For my children, the celebration of Chanukah is a unique experience, due in part to the fact that I carry on the tradition of my ancestors, which is somewhat different from the tradition of other Jewish groups. We do not light a Menorah (candelabrum with seven or nine candlesticks), for example, but an ancient oil *Chanukiya* that had belonged to my grandfather and perhaps to his grandfather. It is not a free-standing lamp, but hangs from a hook on the wall with a panel containing the Chanukah prayer in Hebrew letters behind it. It is made of sculptured bronze in a somewhat triangular shape, with the eight lamps looking like square basins with a long spout hanging in a row at the bottom of the triangle. The *shamàsh* (literally, the beadle, the ninth lamp or candle on the *Chanukiya* that is used to light the other lamps or candles) is another square basin like the others, situated halfway up on the left side of the sculptured sheet. All these basins are filled with oil, and a cotton wick a few centimeters long is placed in each basin, with one end coming out and hanging through the spout; this is the part that is lit.

The use of oil for Chanukah was not limited to the lighting of the lamps; it was also used for cooking, especially for frying. During Chanukah we ate all sorts of fried foods: fried chicken, fried vegetables, fried fruits, and fried desserts. We made pancakes and fritters with potatoes, apples, rice, and so on. But in Pitigliano the words *Frittelle di Chanukà* (Chanukah fritters) were used to mean only diamond-shaped pieces of bread dough with anise seeds and raisins inside, which, after frying, were coated with hot honey. A meal of all these fried foods eaten in the summer would be hard to digest, but at the beginning of the cold season, when we needed more calories to burn, it was both digestible and delicious.

Here is a typical Chanukah menu:

Rice with Raisins
Riso coll'Uvetta

Fish-Filled Pastry
Pasticcini de Pesce

Fried Chicken for Chanukah
Pollo Fritto per Chanukà

Eggplant Jewish Style
Melanzane alla Guidia

Chanukah Fritters
Frittelle di Chanukà

The New Year of the Trees

rosh hashanà leilanòt

oday this holiday is called *Tu B'Shevàt*, the 15th of *Shevàt*, which is simply the date that has been set aside to celebrate the first warmth of spring. We called it *Rosh Hashanà Leilanòt*, the New Year of the Trees. In fact, this is the time of the year—generally toward the middle of February—when, in warm climates like Israel's, new saplings are planted.

We did not plant trees on *Rosh Hashanà Leilanòt*, but we did participate in the festival in a very real way. Every Jewish home in Pitigliano had a *bossolo* hanging on a wall, a blue tin box with the map of what was then Palestine printed on its face. It had a little door at the bottom, the key to which was kept by the coordinator, a woman who would come around once a year to collect the money we had put into this bank. That money, mostly small coins given by children and housewives who could ill afford them, went to buy trees to plant in the desert areas of Palestine. There was a slot at the top of the *bossolo* through which to drop coins. The slot had two metal meshes hanging on the inside. If a child, after generously contributing his penny, tried to get the coin back (or if anyone else tried to get that money) by turning the box upside down and shaking it, the two meshes would cover up the slot, making it impossible for the coin to roll out. Any other kind of coin bank, made of clay or plaster, could be easily broken or, with a little patience, emptied through the slot. But the *bossolo* was constructed to make sure that no one would be tempted to "borrow" the money, not even for an emergency.

During my childhood the coordinator for Pitigliano was Jenny Lattes, sister of Dante Lattes, both my grandmother's cousins. She was a learned, pious, sweet woman, totally dedicated to the cause of Zionism. When she came to Pitigliano to collect the coins, it was an occasion of great joy. She would tell us beautiful stories of other children like us in a faraway land, *Eretz Israel*, transforming the desert into an oasis by planting new saplings bought with our savings. We were spellbound and felt very proud to participate, in our small way, in this act of creation.

Besides Jenny's stories, *Rosh Hashanà Leilanòt* was marked by a festival in which all the children took part. We played games, and sang songs, and danced in circles holding hands, as we had heard the children in Israel did after each planting of a new tree. No candies or other sweets were served. To celebrate the New Year of the Trees, we were given small bags of dried fruits and nuts. My memory of this time still stirs feelings of great fulfillment and joy.

Often *Rosh Hashanà Leilanòt* fell on my birthday, and this made me feel very important. On our birthdays we did not have parties or receive presents. The only event that marked that day as special was breakfast in bed for the birthday child, brought by Mother, who also granted the privilege of choosing the menu for the day. The breakfast itself was special and it would be the same for all members of the family. Our everyday breakfast consisted of a great big cup of *grané* with milk and sugar, filled to capacity with bits of hard bread. On these special birthday mornings, the *grané* contained one egg yolk beaten with sugar, and the bread was toasted, and occasionally spread with ricotta.

The roasting of the wheat grains was done at home, on the balcony. We had a device, *il bruschino*, which was built by the tinker for this purpose. It consisted of a cylinder twelve inches long and five inches in diameter. It had a sliding door in the side, through which the wheat was put in and taken out. At one end it had a long, thin rod; at the other a crank with a wooden handle. The rod and the crank rested on a holder so that the cylinder could be turned. Under the holder burned a fire of twigs. As the cylinder of the *bruschino*, black with soot, was turned, the grains inside made a rustling noise that became less and less acute as they got evenly toasted. The aroma of roasting wheat grains is not as tempting as that of roasting coffee, but to us it was the real thing and very pleasant. In fact, this was the only "coffee" that ever entered our household (both our parents believed in wholesome foods and coffee was not in this category), and to this day I prefer the mild taste of a grain drink to real coffee. Here is a typical menu:

Humus and Tahina
Crema di Ceci e Sesamo

Squash Ravioli with Sage Oil
Tortelli di Zucca alla Salvia

Veal Scaloppine with Madeira or Marsala Wine
Scaloppine al Madeira / Marsala

Orange Salad
Arance Condite

Bagels, Turin Bread Sticks
Ciambelle, Grissini Torinesi all'Olio

Hard Cookies of the Jews
Torzetti dell'Abbrei

The Feast of Lots

purim

*allegrete macomme che e purimme,"* the Roman Jews used to say to each other on Purim. This ironical saying, "Rejoice O toilet, because it's Purim," was an exhortation to everyone in the Jewish household to celebrate this day with boundless joy. Purim, the Hebrew word for "lots," reminds us of the only time in Jewish history when a prospective massacre (plotted by the wicked Haman who had it planned to the last detail except for the date of execution, which had to be established by drawing lots) was converted into a feast because the tyrant, by interference of the good Queen Esther, was eliminated.

The above-mentioned funny saying was brought to Pitigliano by my mother from her native Rome. At the time when my father married her and brought her back to his village, the Jewish women in Pitigliano must have been rather homely, and the Gentiles ignorant of the legendary beauty of Queen Esther. My mother was extremely beautiful, witty, and elegant. When the Christian Pitiglianesi saw her for the first time, they began to comment: "How could the son of Salomone Servi and Debora Lattes marry a Gentile?" So my father, to dispel this rumor and convince his Christian friends that his bride was indeed Jewish in spite of her stunning beauty, told them the story of Queen Esther and how she had conquered the heart of the Syrian king with her loveliness. He also tried to convince them that perhaps there had been a few other beautiful Jewish women in between!

Purim was the only festivity without the least bit of austerity and solemnity. It was a day for feasting on sweets and wines, and for dancing, masquerading, and comedy. It was a day when even the scholarly acted silly and teachers dressed up in gay costumes, which made them seem less awesome and forbidding.

For the children it was a dream day. Those who had talent displayed it in playacting, singing, or dancing. But even those who didn't receive the reward of the applause got presents and *ma'ot* (money), much as American children receive presents and *gelt* on Chanukah. In fact, Purim was the only occasion when children were given presents. For this reason, the children truly cherished their gifts, which were generally interesting and sturdy, so that they remained in good condition for years.

The main feature staged on Purim was based on the story of Esther who persuaded her husband, the foolish King Ahasuerus, to save all the Jews, her people, and let Haman perish instead. This was broadly played, as a comedy, and there were also other comedies on various subjects, although most of them were Purim related. I vividly recall one in which three children, left alone one night while their parents had gone to the theater, had decided to stay up until midnight instead of going to bed at their regular hour. But midnight was a long wait, and after a series of funny dialogues and bets on who would stay up longer, they began to get bored. Just to pass the time, they raided the pantry and ate all the sweets their mother had prepared for the coming festivity of Purim. With their bellies full, they became groggy and one by one slid into a deep sleep, including the twelve-year-old who had solemnly pledged to himself that he would resist sleep at any cost. During the rehearsals of this sketch, the "sweets" consisted of some dried fruits, but on the day of the performance, our mothers had prepared several trays full of real Purim sweets. There were *Orecchi di Aman*, *castagnole*, *Manicotti*, *ricciarelli*, *Moscardini*, and so on. That night, after the bows and curtain calls, all the children in the audience were invited on stage to share the delicious Purim sweets.

A typical Purim dinner would include the following:

Purim Ravioli
Ravioli di Purim

Lamb Loaves
Polpettoni d'Agnello

Artichokes Truffle Style
Carciofi Trifolati

Haman's Ears, Purim Manicotti, Purim Moscardini
Orecchi di Aman, Manicotti di Purim, Moscardini di Purim

Passover

pesach

n the weeks immediately preceding Passover much
went on, and the days were very busy in our house.

Toward the end of February or at the beginning of
March, our parents would hire the masons and house
painters who would invade our house with their rat-
tling wooden trestles, their paper cones full of powdered pigments of all
colors, their brushes of various dimensions and shapes. A smell of lime,
varnish, cleanliness filled the air while each room was freshly
whitewashed and given pale new pastel colors, always different from
those of the preceding year.

The few, loose-jointed antiques that furnished our rooms were emptied of their contents in order to be washed, scraped, glued, and
polished. Drawers and cabinets were lined with new sheets of tissue
paper cut up to resemble embroidered doilies. The shelves were also
lined with new paper carefully trimmed to look like lace on the side that
hung over the front of each shelf.

Children shared in the excitement and helped with the chores. Polish-
ing the brass handles was our specific job, and we competed with each
other to achieve the greatest shine on an assigned piece. The older children were allowed to do the windowpanes and the mirrors, too, while the
women made the glassware, dishes, and utensils sparkle. Everything
smelled of spring, which entered sweetly through the windows that were
kept open so the plaster would dry faster.

The dressmaker was hired by the day. She would come early in the
morning and spend several days near the window of the dining room

making little pants and jackets out of father's old suits, and little dresses, petticoats, and underwear from mother's cast-off garments.

I'll never forget the continuous tinkling of her wedding ring on the crank of the wheel of the hand-operated sewing machine, which she knew how to wield with agility and elegance. Using only a nimble movement of her wrist, she seemed barely to skim over it without really touching it.

When she was not talking with my mother about her newborn, red-headed baby girl, she sang songs. Songs were my passion. The radio had not yet become part of the household; only public places, such as cafés and clubs, had them. But the dressmaker knew all the songs, latest hits and oldies, and she sang and sang until I learned them all. By then, she would have finished her work and would not come back again until the next year.

But there were more new and exciting events: new shoes to be bought at the market stalls, new socks, new satin and taffeta ribbons for our hair. And, most important of all, there was the opening of the matza bakery.

Great comings and goings down and up those dark, slimy steps—an adventure to instill terror. But then came the light, the marble tables, the crackling of the twigs in the oven, the smell of the freshly ground flour. We were fascinated as we watched the long, heavy wooden kneading pole, rattling under the strong hands of the *shamàsh*. It emanated screeches made by a rusty hinge, alternating with a cry that was almost a wail, produced by the bending wood. And all the women, whose capable hands refined the dough, giving it a perfect oval shape, adding eyelets and festoons to each little piece that was to become a matza—a matza uniquely different from the modern *matzòt* we find in supermarkets today. Made and shaped entirely by hand, the *matzòt* of my childhood were either round or oval, much thicker than the commercial ones, and had a more substantial texture. Finely detailed, they could be made to look like pieces of art.

Toward evening the men came to share in the joys of this almost mystical ritual with their mothers, sisters, wives, friends.

When the big wicker baskets were filled to capacity with fresh and fragrant *matzòt* and sweets, each family brought home their own, hiding the contents inside those cabinets and shelves that had been previously emptied and cleaned for the purpose, not to be touched until the great night—the night of the first Seder—arrived.

Bedikàt Chamètz, the ritual searching for the leavened bread, took place on the night preceding the Seder. During the day our mother helped us to place a piece of bread on one corner of every surface in the house. At night we followed our father, who lit a candle after a brief prayer, turned all the lights off, and silently went around in search of the *chamètz*. Silently we helped him find the pieces of bread, and he, with a long feather, brushed each one, and its crumbs, into a heavy paper cone. When the last piece of *chamètz* was collected, he would throw the feather into the paper cone and close this tightly. The next morning the cone and its contents were burned (*Biur Chamètz*). In this way, the house was purified from all the *chamètz* and was ready for Passover.

On the evening of the Seder, after temple services, all the Jews in our village came to our house for the reading of the Haggadah (the text for the Seder), and the blessings. This was done before the dinner that each family held afterward at their own homes.

What emotion, what joy to see all those people gathered around our immaculate table to celebrate the festival of freedom from bondage with all those beautiful rituals! Father recited the prayers and blessed and distributed the foods and wines, while the women busied themselves with washing basins and towels for the ritual washing of hands. When it came to the recitation of the ten plagues of Egypt, which was accompanied by the pouring of a drop of wine into a basin for each plague, the windows were thrown open, and at the mention of the last plague, the glass went into the basin with the last drop of wine. Eventually, the glass was disposed of together with the wine to exorcise—or so I believed—the possibility that the plagues might hit our home. The main door was kept open during the whole Seder to invite hungry and needy Gentiles to come in and share in the festivity and satisfy their needs.

While the blessings went on, we children, all dressed up in our recycled dresses and the new shoes that hurt our feet, were excited and mischievous. If we became too loud or impatient, our father reprimanded us, and we lowered our eyes, letting them wander over the table now sprinkled with crushed eggshells and matza crumbs.

By the time dinner started, we were no longer hungry, but the menu invariably included a dish of artichokes, and for those we could always find a little room in our stomachs.

MENU FOR THE FIRST NIGHT

Passover Chicken Soup with Rice
Minestra di Riso per Pesach

Jellied Striped Bass
Muggine in Bianco

Sautéed Garlic Spinach
Spinaci Saltati

Baby Goat for Passover
Capretto per Pesach

Artichokes Jewish Style
Carciofi alla Giudia

Matza Omelet
Matza Coperta

Passover Almond Biscotti
Biscotti alla Mandorla per Pesach

Passover Sfoglietti Soup
Minestra di Sfoglietti per Pesach

Baked Fish
Spigola Arrosto

Stuffed Artichokes
Carciofi Ripieni

Matza Pancakes with Honey
Pizzarelle col Miele

King's Cake
Torta del Re

The Festival of Weeks

shavuot

Shavuot, the Festival of Weeks, thus called because it occurs seven weeks after Passover, brings back many wonderful memories. My own Bat Mitzvà took place on Shavuot 5698–June 5, 1938.

In Pitigliano, in addition to the dairy dishes, a typical Shavuot menu would include *Matza Coperta*, a Passover dish repeated on this occasion because Shavuot comes exactly seven weeks after Passover. In fact, a charming Shavuot tradition was the ritual of bringing the matza to the fish. No one in Pitigliano was sure of the origin and meaning of this custom. But I remember that no matza was supposed to be left in the house after Shavuot, yet no matza should be thrown away. Feeding it to the fish was a beautiful solution. After the Shavuot midday meal, we would go in groups of families to the banks of one of the clear water rivers that surround Pitigliano, with our paper bags full of broken pieces of our handmade *matzòt*. Sometimes we would stop at the center of a little bridge and drop the bits of food from there. The fish seemed to know that we would come because they were there by the hundreds as soon as the first few crumbs reached the water.

SHAVUOT MENU

Farina Gnocchi Roman Style
Gnocchi di Semolino alla Romana

Spinach Mold
Sformato di Spinaci

Creamed Fennel
Finocchi colla Besciamella

Matza Omelet
Matza Coperta

Sweet Shavuot Tortelli
Tortelli Dolci di Shavuot

Mascarpone Cheesecake
Torta al Mascarpone

Cherries
Ciliege